GIRL
BY
SEA

ALSO BY PENELOPE GREEN

When in Rome
See Naples and Die

GIRL
BY
SEA

Life, love and food on an Italian island

Penelope Green

hachette
AUSTRALIA

hachette
AUSTRALIA

Published in Australia and New Zealand in 2009
by Hachette Australia
(An imprint of Hachette Australia Pty Limited)
Level 17, 207 Kent Street, Sydney NSW 2000
www.hachette.com.au

National Library of Australia
Cataloguing-in-Publication data

Green, Penelope
Girl by sea/Penelope Green

978 0 7336 2333 2 (pbk.)

Green, Penelope–Travel.
Australians–Italy–Procida Island–Biography.
Procida Island (Italy)–Social life and customs.
Procida Island (Italy)–Description and travel.

914.573

Cover and text design by Christa Moffitt, Christabella Designs
Front cover photograph of Penelope Green by Carlo Hermann
Back cover photograph of Procida by Penelope Green
Map by Christa Moffitt, Christabella Designs
Typeset in 12.7/16.9 pt Adobe Garamond Pro by Bookhouse, Sydney
Printed in Australia by Griffin Press, Adelaide

Hachette Australia's policy is to use papers that are natural,
renewable and recyclable products and made from wood
grown in sustainable forests. The logging and manufacturing
processes are expected to conform to the environmental
regulations of the country of origin.

To Elisa and Michele, Enzo, Paola,
Maria Pia and your families,
che un giorno possiamo ricambiare la vostra generosita

CONTENTS

RECIPES

'*Quando mi voltai, e vidi che Procida si faceva lontana, mi prese una nostalgia cosi' amara, che non potei sopportarla. Rivoltai la prua, e tornammo indietro.*'

'When I turned, and saw that Procida was receding, I felt such bitter longing, that I couldn't bear it. I turned the prow, and we went back.'

L'isola di Arturo (*Arthur's Island*),
Elsa Morante

Procida

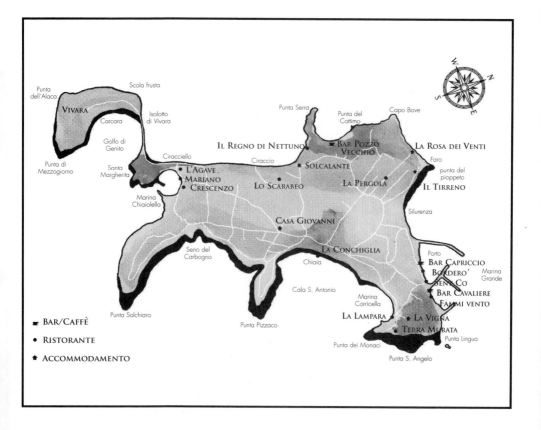

Punta
dell'Alaca

Scola frusta

VIVARA

Isolotto
di Vivara

Carcara

Punta Serra

Punta del
Cottimo

Capo Bove

Golfo di
Genito

Ciracciello

IL REGNO DI NETTUNO

BAR POZZO
VECCHIO

LA ROSA DEI VENTI

Punta di
Mezzogiorno

Santa
Margherita

Ciraccio

SOLCALANTE

Faro

punta del
pioppeto

L'AGAVE

MARIANO
CRESCENZO

LO SCARABEO

LA PERGOLA

IL TIRRENO

Marina
Chiaiolella

CASA GIOVANNI

Silurenza

LA CONCHIGLIA

Seno del
Carbogno

Chiaia

Porto

BAR CAPRICCIO

BORDERO'
SENT CO

Marina
Grande

Cala S. Antonio

Marina
Corricella

BAR CAVALIERE

FAMMI VENTO

Punta Solchiaro

Punta Pizzaco

LA LAMPARA

LA VIGNA

TERRA MURATA

Punta Lingua

BAR/CAFFÈ

RISTORANTE

ACCOMMODAMENTO

Punta dei Monaci

Punta S. Angelo

ARRIVEDERCI NAPOLI

Since I've tried and botched more than a few, I don't have a recipe for the perfect relationship. Smart girls know that Mr Right is an urban myth, and after a string of unsatisfying flirtations in my home base of Naples I remained unconvinced that even Mr Fair-to-middling existed.

Until I was wooed by a dreamy local musician who tempted me to think my luck had finally changed.

Alfonso has many winning qualities: his warmth, generosity and honesty, his flair as a raconteur and infectious passion for music and literature, and, of course, his sultry good looks. But really, he seduced me with his cooking.

While my accent will always brand me as *una straniera*, a foreigner, I have become a true Italian in at least one regard: I am obsessed with food. Italians spend most of their waking hours living and breathing their *cucina*, from the *mamma* who rises at dawn to prepare a killer *sugo* – the tomato-based sauce which features in so many Italian recipes – for the family's lunch, to the discussions you overhear on the street. It's not uncommon to come across a couple of businessmen on their way to an appointment, or a cluster of teens en route to school, talking animatedly about how good their last meal was, or what their next meal will be, or a new ingredient they have just discovered.

Fiercely proud of their culinary heritage, Italians like nothing better than to talk food – before soccer, politics and the scandal of the day. Not surprisingly, many adages centre on food, too, and the imagery is nothing short of delicious. *Come prezzemolo*, meaning 'like parsley', is used to express the idea that something is ubiquitous, just like parsley is in so many Italian dishes, while *come una cipolla*, 'like an onion', is most commonly used to describe a person who is dressed in layers to ward off the cold. *E' un pesce lesso* describes a boring person who is like 'boiled fish', and a person without a tan – which Italians can't live without – is *bianco come una mozzarella*, as white as the famous, milky cheese.

After five years in Italy, I haven't transformed into a master chef, but I can now distinguish between countless types of pasta – flat, thin, long, fat, twisted and stuffed – from the country's twenty regions, with their own very different cooking styles based on local products, and I can translate a detailed Italian restaurant menu in seconds.

When I moved to Naples in 2005, my passion for the Italian cuisine grew alongside my belly. In Italy's south, ingredients are more frequently fried, oil is used in abundance and the ricotta-rich sweets are beyond delectable.

I first met Alfonso when I interviewed 'A67, the Neapolitan rock band in which he plays bass guitar. 'A67 has won a string of national awards and international acclaim for both its unique sound and its commitment to speak out against the Camorra, the local mafia whose multiple clans are engaged in bloody turf wars for a slice of an annual turnover of 25-billion euro, built on deals in construction, toxic waste disposal, fashion and illicit drugs.

Alfonso, who also teaches computer courses intermittently to supplement his artist's income, immediately caught my eye. When he offered me a lift home after my interview with the band I had a hunch the feeling was mutual and I wasted no time inviting him over to my place a few days later.

Alfonso promised to cook dinner for me after I admitted that while I came top of my 3-Unit Home Science class in theory (covering handy topics like nutrient deficiency diseases, against which a nation such as Australia was well padded), I had never quite mastered a white sauce, and let's not even speak of my desperate attempts to peak egg whites for a classic lemon meringue pie.

When Alfonso arrived at my doorstep with a backpack I thought he might be being a little presumptuous, but I soon realised he had better intentions.

Like a magician pulling rabbits out of a hat, he rummaged in his backpack to produce a range of sumptuous ingredients, despite the fact I had asked him for a shopping list that I would have taken care of for him.

I watched as he carefully prepared *bruschetta* with smoked salmon, which we washed down with a chilly *prosecco*.

'Now I will make you a classic Neapolitan dish – *spaghetti alle vongole* (with clams),' said my knight with shining utensils, promising me his version of the dish would beat any other I had ever tasted.

His secret, Alfonso assured me, a sexy twinkle in his eye as he stood at ease by my oven, was that before boiling the spaghetti he dipped the ends of the pasta into the frying pan to let the tips soak up the juice of the clams and white wine. By now, I was well and truly under his spell, and though he didn't stay that night, we were soon inseparable.

Cibo (food) quickly become a central part of my relationship with Alfonso, who was shaping up to be far from a flash in the pan; he was, rather, extremely flash with my pans.

Almost every evening in the kitchen of my little apartment in the Quartieri Spagnoli, Naples' Spanish Quarter, I'd watch him create an array of delicious dishes, none of which, to his credit, were ever exactly the same.

After surviving on a staple rotation of roasted chicken drumsticks, oven-baked vegetables and tuna salads in my single days, every meal lovingly prepared and created by Chef Fonz was an *alle carte* affair. In fact, when we did venture out to dine in a local *trattoria*, Alfonso would taste his meal and lower his voice to triumphantly whisper, 'Admit it! I can make this better!'

Barely two months after we met I returned to Australia for a month's holiday. A few days before my departure I vacated my flat and left my belongings in the garage of Alfonso's parents' house, in the outer suburbs of Naples. Finding a place to share was our priority upon my return.

In Perth and Sydney and Orange, I relished the company of my family and closest friends and enjoyed the clean beaches I had so desperately missed, sending text messages daily to Alfonso, who was busy scanning the newspapers for places to rent.

Before long he sent me an email with some pictures of a gorgeous apartment on Procida, a little island about an hour from Naples by ferry.

Long favoured by my Neapolitan friends as a cheap holiday destination, Procida, I knew, was relatively isolated compared to the two other islands nearby: Capri, trampled year-round by tourists who think nothing of paying anything up to a thousand euro a night for a hotel room and twenty euro for a coffee in the main piazza, and Ischia, almost ten times as big as Procida and practically like being on the mainland.

Inspired by the photos, I did a quick internet search to learn some basic facts about the island. With a population of ten thousand and a surface area a fraction under four square kilometres, Procida was formed by the eruption of four volcanoes between fifteen and fifty-five thousand years ago. Settled in the eighth century by the Greeks, who believed the island was created after a fierce battle between Zeus and the giants, it became a holiday resort for the elite in Roman times. It has been attacked by Goths, Vandals, Saracens and even the Ottoman privateer, Barbarossa.

I was intrigued by the island's history, not to mention swayed by an apartment with sea views and spacious rooms, but we reluctantly decided that it made more sense to remain in Naples, where as editor of an English news website, I often had to start work early, and Alfonso had band practice three times a week and frequent gigs.

When I returned to Naples, the house hunt began in earnest, but it was a dispiriting exercise. After viewing yet another dimly lit apartment with hideous furniture and an excessive monthly rent, Alfonso and I cheered ourselves up over a long lunch at our favourite restaurant in Chiaia, in inner-city Naples, L'oca Verde, or The Green Duck. After home-made pasta *al sugo fresco, manzo tagliato* – sliced beef – on a bed of rocket with fresh juniper berries, washed down with *aglianico*, a local red wine, we somehow squeezed in the white chocolate soufflé with a hot, dark chocolate sauce. A round of grappa helped our digestion, but to further the cause we decided to take a walk along the Bay of Naples.

In the early afternoon, families and couples strolled along the curved path, the sun taking the bite out of the winter sea breeze. We stopped just near Castel Sant'Elmo and I glanced down at the boats bobbing in the small port. A gust of wind slapped my face and it occurred to me that one reason I felt so at home in Naples – the charming new local in my life notwithstanding – was because of its seaside setting. A bush kid, my happiest memories are of days spent by the sea, from childhood holidays on the New South Wales north coast to living near Sydney's Bondi Beach, where I swam regularly at the Icebergs ocean pool. I looked up at the beautiful, coloured buildings lining the port to see an old lady standing on her small balcony, smoking a cigarette, her scarved head tilted to the horizon.

'In a perfect world,' I told Alfonso, 'I would wake up to a view like hers.'

Alfonso smiled and turned to point out to sea.

'You can't see it from here, but Procida is so beautiful . . . I know we've decided on Naples, but it wouldn't hurt to go and have a look at that place I sent you photos of.'

'Let's go!' I said impulsively, keen to see something other than the dark, dank places we had viewed over the last few weeks.

Within twenty minutes we were at the ticket office of Naples' main port, Beverello, scanning the departures board.

To reach Procida, there is a slow *nave,* or ferry, which takes around an hour, or the *aliscafo,* the hydrofoil, which cuts at least fifteen minutes off the journey. The latter is almost twice as expensive, and we were in no particular hurry, so we opted for the *nave.*

Standing on the port I watched the huge white vessel approach. About twenty metres from the shore it did an impressive 360-degree turn before backing slowly into the port to offload its vehicles and passengers. The bone-rattling sound of the anchor dropping penetrated the air.

After the last truck had disembarked, we walked across the metal ramp and scaled two flights of stairs to the seating area. The cold wind made sitting outside impossible, but by the time we set off the boat had taken on the fun atmosphere of a floating RSL club, complete with a bar, gaming machines, adults chiding ants-in-their-pants kids, young couples cuddling and, most importantly, the television blaring. Glancing at the screen I did a double-take. The landscape looked so barren, so familiar. It was *McLeod's Daughters,* fresh from an Italian language school.

As the ferry approached Procida we rugged up and walked out onto the deck.

One theory about the origins of the island's name is that it came from the Greek verb *prokeitai,* meaning 'it lies forth'. The island's yellow and grey cliffs, formed from tufa, a hard volcanic rock, certainly seemed to jut out to meet us. So too did the *carcere,* or prison, looming majestically, high above a sheer cliff.

Alfonso, who had holidayed on Procida as a child, explained that the prison was a part of Terra Murata, the island's first settlement.

First glimpse of Procida from the ferry, which travels to the island from Naples

Procida's main port – a strip of shabby, multi-coloured buildings in a general state of jolly, crumbling decay – came into view as the ship finally entered the harbour. The port is widely known as Marina Grande, while further along it becomes the Marina di Sancio Cattolico; 'Sent' Co' in the dialect of the island.

Two big fishing trawlers motored in to the wharf, trailed by squawking seagulls and watched by a growing crowd. Further along, the bright yellow church of Santa Maria della Pieta and the neat rows of white masts of the yachts moored at the end of the port stood out against the charcoal sky, heavy with thunderclouds.

The ferry spun around in one powerful sweep, then with a grunt, the ramp dropped to let in a sliver of light and a view of the skyline. Within seconds it began to lower, to reveal the faded pink façade of an enormous building with Arabesque arches, its once pink coat of paint stripped away by age and mother nature.

When the rope barring our release was finally removed, we walked across the metal ramp and veered left. I stopped in my tracks. Not far ahead was a rather confronting statue of Jesus nailed to the cross.

'Cripes, not exactly welcoming,' I uttered aloud to no one in particular.

Alfonso had arranged to pick up the apartment's keys from the owner of Bar Capriccio, one of the handful of cafes along the wharf, since the small tourist agency handling the rental had closed early, being winter and all.

Behind the long, wooden-panelled bar a tanned streak of a man with a closely shaved head was slicing the skin of a lemon. He looked up and gave us a courteous smile.

'We're here to collect some house keys,' said Alfonso.

'*Che cos'e' la parola dell'ordine?*' the man said sternly, demanding the password. Then his face broke into a cheeky grin. 'This apartment is in a wonderful location, the cradle of civilisation, the very hub of Procida – it's in my street.'

Taking an instant liking to Enzo, as he asked us to call him, we decided to stop for an espresso.

'You know, young couples often come to Procida to live,' said Enzo, preparing a tray of cocktails for some other customers.

I had just started to smile when he concluded, 'But not many last.'

'The challenge has been issued,' I told Alfonso as Enzo disappeared outside with his order.

We leant on the bar and I scanned the bottles of alcohol stacked neatly along wooden shelves, illuminated by a row of tulip-shaped light bulbs hanging above. At the end of the bar, a narrow spiral staircase led to a mezzanine where some tourists were using the internet service. Behind us, a young couple smooched on one of the long, red couches in a small area with sketches of famous Italian cities in coloured frames decorating its walls. A video screen hung at the back of the room beside a television, but the only thing playing was rock music piped from some speakers.

A young man stood punching the buttons on the lone poker machine near the doorway, while to our right a pair of elderly men in windcheaters were enjoying an early *aperitivo,* perched on tall timber stools. Wooden panels carved in a wave pattern along the corridor entrance added to the cosy feeling of being in a ship's galley.

When we'd finished our coffees, Enzo took a piece of paper and scrawled us a rough map to our destination. Thanking him, we stepped outside, walked past a few tables of clients then hooked right along Marina Grande.

Some Vespas flew past us and we paused to watch two men in a dinghy unload a stack of white polystyrene crates brimming with fish, calamari and other *frutti di mare* – the fresh haul of *Ciro Padre,* a fishing trawler that bobbed in waters close to the port.

Further along the marina, past a cluster of restaurants whose lunchtime business had long finished, and a few fish shops doing a brisk afternoon trade, an old man sat on a plastic chair near a pile of orange and rust-red fishing nets. With his head lowered in concentration, he laboured to untangle and repair one of the nets that rested on his lap.

As I absorbed the atmosphere with rising excitement, I recalled reading that the tradition of shipbuilding on Procida dated back at least as far as the thirteenth century. From the seventeenth century, Procida's growing fleet transported coal, grain, wood and other raw materials to Sicily and around the Mediterranean. The following two centuries were the most splendid for Procida's maritime industry: shipbuilding flourished, the population peaked at sixteen thousand, and one third of the merchant ships of the Kingdom of Two Sicilies' fleet were built on the island.

The growth of motor-powered shipping and a local reluctance to abandon traditional sailing, alongside global competition brought the boom years to an end. Still, the majority of men from the island continue to work on merchant ships in Italy and abroad, while the old salt mending his nets is just one of an army of retirees whose lives are still entwined with the sea.

An impatient tug of my sleeve from Alfonso prompted me to press on.

We followed Enzo's map, passing the line of shops fronting the port, their façades rendered in various shades of pink, orange, yellow, blue and white. Above, sheets hung from windows and balconies.

The large, uneven cobblestones beneath our feet grew wet and slippery as we turned off Marina Grande and headed up *il Canale,* or the canal, a steep, narrow street which, Enzo had told us, was a natural drain for rainwater running off the island's hills.

We passed a hardware store, clothes boutiques, a butcher, pharmacy and drycleaners, before we caught sight of Piazza Posta, home not only to the post office, but also a string of specialty shops.

Just before the piazza we turned left and walked along a narrow lane inaccessible to cars, to arrive within minutes at our street, where we stopped briefly at the lookout with views down to the Corricella fishing port and up to Terra Murata, the highest point on the island.

We continued along the cobblestones to finally find the front door of our *palazzo*. Alfonso pushed open the heavy wooden door and we stepped into a brick-paved courtyard. Beyond it was a sprawling garden, which I suspected led right to the ocean, but the way was blocked by a wrought-iron fence with a padlocked gate.

I looked up to see the shield design of a loaf of bread and a sprig of rosemary painted on the main roof, a couple of steps from the entrance. Ah yes, food again.

We walked up three flights of stairs, puffing to open one of two doors on the top landing. It led to a room with an impossibly high, arched ceiling and a window offering views over a lemon orchard and the choppy sea. I opened the window to breathe in the fresh sea air and stared out to the horizon, dropped my gaze to the lemon trees below, marvelled at the gigantic magnolia in the backyard of a nearby apartment block, and then looked back to the sea . . .

I turned to Alfonso, trying hard not to go all emotional on him – without success. I shrieked and did a little leap in the air, then eagerly inspected the rest of the apartment: a small but functional kitchen, a lounge room with French doors and a narrow balcony facing the street below, a bathroom with a washing machine, a spacious bedroom with a window overlooking the street and the

Sea views from our roof terrace

primary school directly opposite, where I could glimpse some desks and the heads of a few children.

'But you haven't seen the best part!' said Alfonso, grabbing my arm and leading me through a door off the bedroom. We walked up another flight of stairs to a large, terracotta-tiled terrace. Dusk was falling and I drank in the spectacular panorama of the entire island, straining to make out church spires and houses and sea.

'Is that Ischia or Capri?' I asked, pointing at the fast-fading form of an island to my left.

'*Boh*, I think it's Capri,' Alfonso said with a shrug, apparently unmoved by one of Italy's most famous holiday spots.

We lingered for ten minutes before racing to get the *nave* back to Naples. On board, we tossed up the pros – gorgeous apartment, cheap rent, sea, views – and cons – daily travel for me, potential isolation and fewer entertainment prospects.

I didn't say it out loud, but I could tell that Alfonso was just as smitten with Procida as I was. Finally, we decided to look at a few more places in Naples; if nothing special came up, we'd reassess.

The following week, after seeing several more cramped, dark apartments, we found ourselves in my old neighbourhood, the bustling Quartieri Spagnoli, to look at another property.

The young real estate agent arrived and led us into a typically decrepit building and up four flights of dimly lit stairs. He buzzed the apartment door and we waited. He buzzed again. After a brief screaming match with a neighbour we learnt that the landlord had left town at short notice and forgotten to leave the keys.

Out on the street I turned to Alfonso, who is not only a fabulous chef, but also a mind-reader, and we agreed that this was a sign.

Within minutes we had called the Procida real estate agent, who said while we still had to sign the year-long lease, there was nothing to stop us moving in.

'*Va bene, andiamo!*' I agreed and suggested we act quickly.

We had lunch at the home of Alfonso's parents, who must have thought we were being rather rash. But they were quickly caught up in our enthusiasm and helped us pack Alfonso's little car, which we had decided to transport on the ferry so we could move as many of our belongings as possible straight away.

It was not until I was standing on the edge of the port in Naples, once again hearing the jarring rattle of the ferry's anchor, that I was seized by panic.

Was I, were we, barking mad? Alfonso and I had barely been together for three months, one of which I had spent in Australia. We were still in a blissful honeymoon phase – who knew if we were really compatible enough to live together, let alone start a new life on a speck in the Tyrrhenian Sea?

The words of Enzo, the owner of Bar Capriccio, echoed in my mind. Young couples might go to Procida, but not many stayed.

I glanced at Alfonso and inhaled deeply.

The desire to test our relationship, to know our destiny was strong, and the prospect of living on an idyllic island was simply too alluring to pass up.

I buried my fear as the ramp slowly began to lower.

MARZO

Easter mysteries

I wake for what seems like the umpteenth time to the howl of the wind. My heart pumps with fear. I can't remember where I am. As my eyes adjust to the dark I recall that, at one point in the night, Alfonso had played the clown to give me a fright, growling suddenly above the eerie whistle of the wind. Ah, that's right. I'm in our new apartment.

Not for the first time, I feel smug about my new set-up. Not only am I now living on a picturesque Italian island, I appear to have found a leading man. One, two, action. All I need is a luxury yacht and some combat scenes and I may as well have walked onto the set of the latest 007 flick. Come to think of it, Procida was one of the locations for *The Talented Mr Ripley* and the charming film *Il Postino*.

Still half asleep, I am trying to remember scenes from the latter film when I hear a wail far more powerful than the wind, rather

1

like a distorted horn. Three sharp drumbeats follow. Finally, there is the sound of scraping metal, like the sound of the chains on the ferry being released before the anchor drops.

I prod Alfonso, who wakes grumpily, and we haul ourselves out of bed and sleepwalk to the window. I glance at my watch, illuminated by the yellow glow of a streetlamp. It's four fifty-eight.

On the cobblestones below, in front of the church opposite our apartment building, a curious scene is unfolding. A rotund man swathed in a white, hooded smock with a blue satin sash draped over his shoulders stands with a large horn in his hand. Behind him is another man, dressed in the same costume, with a huge drum strapped around his girth. The first man blows his horn and takes a few small steps forward. The man behind him beats the drum three times with as much pomp as can be

The horn-player belts out a note during the *Processione dei Misteri*

mustered at such an ungodly hour. Behind them, another two men are dragging a huge metal chain along the cobblestones. A small cluster of people stand in the wild and windy conditions, silently watching the proceedings, unaware that we are also spying on them.

Then a small group of men wearing the white hooded smocks appear, carrying on their backs a prone figure mounted on a wooden slab. Squinting in the pre-dawn light, I realise the sculpture depicts Jesus Christ.

'Now I remember,' I tell Alfonso. 'It's the *Processione dei Misteri,* the Procession of the Mysteries.' Enzo had mentioned the upcoming Easter parade, apparently one of the most anticipated events on the island.

We watch until the procession is out of sight then hop back into bed. I stick in earplugs for good measure, to drown out the wind.

Two hours later we walk down to the port to buy the newspapers.

'*La Repubblica?*' I ask the short, bespectacled man at the counter.

'We don't get the papers until eight o'clock, when they come from Naples on the ferry,' he says, unapologetically.

I frown; that means I won't be able to buy the dailies when I catch the seven-fifteen ferry to work. Oh well, I'll use the time to catch up on other reading. As I turn to leave, one of the books for sale on a table nearby catches my eye. Sporting a cover photo of men dressed exactly like those we saw in the wee hours of the morning, it is a local guide to the *processione*. Keen to learn more, I buy it and we head to Bar Capriccio to wake up over a coffee.

There are at least six or seven other cafes along the port, but we have chosen Enzo's bar as our local, though he does the night shift so he's not there in the mornings.

Today we are greeted by a man with a cheery disposition who sings out hellos to the regulars while keeping one eye on the work at hand and the other on the *telegiornale,* the television news bulletin, on Channel 5, part of the monopoly of billionaire media magnate and the on-again, off-again prime minister, Silvio Berlusconi.

We sit outside to take in our new island home, surrounded by a few tables of weather-beaten old men, who I imagine are fishermen just returned from a night at sea. That, or they are pensioners doing a good job of looking weary from a lifetime of toil.

I bury my nose in my new book to read up on the procession that is set to add some colour to the island. I learn that we were woken because the Christ statue was being lugged up to Terra Murata, the neighbourhood nestled high on a cliff alongside the old prison. The statue will be the centrepiece of the parade which, at around midday, will wind down the hill and do a loop around the island before arriving at the church beside our home.

Staged on Good Friday, the *Processione dei Misteri* is said to be one of the oldest traditions on the island. The *misteri* are the floats decorated with papier-mâché figures and scenes from the Old and New Testaments – a kind of mardi gras, if you will.

For decades, the floats were built in the historic *portoni,* the main entrances of apartment buildings. But then a bunch of islanders disgruntled about the noise blocked access to their *palazzos.* To solve the problem, Procida's municipal council secured a grant to buy a fifty-square-metre space, only steps from the old prison. The area is now reserved exclusively for the construction of the *misteri.*

As the focus of the procession, the *Cristo morto* was traditionally subjected to a series of rituals before the parade. A gaggle of local devotees apparently polished it with cinnamon oil, imported from French mariners since the 1800s. This prompted talk of a special odour of the dead Christ.

'Ew, like you'd want to bottle it!' I exclaim to Alfonso, who laughs at my expression.

'They say that the Procidans find it hard to sleep on the eve of Good Friday, because they're afraid of missing the big event.'

Alfonso snorts.

'No chance that'll happen to us, living where we do,' he grumbles.

We walk back to our apartment, taking a wrong path at first, but eventually circling back to the right *portone*.

'*Buongiorno,*' a voice sings out as I push open the door.

An elderly pudding of a woman waddles out from a ground-floor apartment.

We introduce ourselves, and she tells us that her name is Rosa and she has lived in the *palazzo* for almost fifty years. Quickly establishing she is hearing-impaired, I try not to giggle as we shout our chitchat.

My stomach rumbling at the smell of *sugo* wafting from Rosa's apartment, I grab an apple as soon as we walk into our kitchen.

'*Vuoi un pezzo?*' I ask Alfonso if he wants a piece, already knowing the answer. In the short time we have been together, I have never seen my man eat a piece of fruit, a fact I blame on his mother; not that I'll be raising the matter with her anytime soon. I have a feeling that if Alfonso were faced with the choice of eating an apple or drinking milk two days past its use-by date, he'd pick the latter. The sense of disgust would be the same.

'*Su, Chunky Chunky, andiamo a vedere il processione,*' he says, urging me to hurry so we can watch the procession.

His new nickname for me – *Chunky Chunky* – occasionally grates; upon hearing me lament one day that I felt 'chunky', Alfonso stared at my hips with a frown of confusion, before explaining the Neapolitan meaning: *cianchi* – pronounced *chunky* – means hips. From then on I became *Chunky Chunky*. I guess it beats Fatso.

I grab my camera and we hurry down to the lookout over Corricella. As the minutes pass more and more people arrive, rugged up against the chill but practically all wearing sunglasses. Italians are obsessed with their *occhiali da sole*, as a fashion statement but also as part of the 'bronzed is best' mentality, which explains why men and women here go to solariums in winter and sunbake every day they can in summer. I, on the other hand, wear SPF15+ face cream and a hat in summer, the latter being something of a fashion and lifestyle crime in Italy. But I'll be damned if I'll be a raisin at forty like so many Italian women.

A cry goes out and we walk to the edge of the lookout to see the procession easing its way down from Terra Murata.

Another forty minutes or so pass before the action begins. The first thing we see is a woman wheeling a small boy in a pram. Dressed in a black smock with gold embroidery and nursing what appears to be a black hat with white and black feathers, the tot looks irritated by his costume. I read that new mothers use the procession as a chance to show off their offspring in a social baptism to a huge crowd. The newborns and toddlers who take part in the event for the first time are referred to as *angioletti*, little angels, and traditionally they wear the black and gold smock.

With the exception of the *angioletti*, all the participants are dressed in the hooded white smock, which I now notice has a series of elegant pleats layering the lower half, and a blue sash trimmed with gold.

An *angiolettio* works hard to keep up the *Processione* pace

Two men shuffle past with an air of importance, one carrying a large wooden cross. A few steps behind is a float with a primitive wooden boat. Carried by two rows of teenage boys, the sign on the front, handpainted in blue, identifies it as *L'arca di Noe*, Noah's Ark.

Before long another float appears, carried by slightly younger boys. Huge red papier-mâché lobsters sit beside a sign that reads, *Non di solo pane vive l'uomo, ma di ogni parola che viene da dio, Matteo 4.4*, Man lives not only from bread, but with every word that comes from God, Matthew 4.4.

It is followed by a small boy who walks with his father, carrying in his tiny hand a sign: *Le nozze di Cana.*

'What does that mean?' I ask Alfonso. While not a practising Catholic, like most Italians he has the religion stamped in his memory.

'The marriage of Cana – where Jesus goes to a wedding, but the family is so poor that Jesus takes some bread and some fish and performs a miracle by multiplying the food for all.'

As I listen I watch the little boy holding his sign with such nonchalance, most likely not knowing what all the hullabaloo of the event is about. It occurs to me that I haven't seen a single woman in the parade. The only feminine presence is a manhandled statue of the Madonna.

Behind her comes a float featuring Jesus in a white robe and ruby-red cape, standing beneath a sculpted arch.

A float stops nearby and I laugh as a boy I would guess to be around six or seven flashes a cheeky smile at a bunch of women beside us.

'*Angelo, ma quanto sei carino,*' one of the women says to the boy, complimenting him on his costume.

Alfonso and I swap smiles, looking from the cheeky boy to another little one beside him, younger and much more timid, his eyes lit up with excitement.

'He's so cute,' says Alfonso, who has already told me that our children will be beautiful if they resemble him.

Jokes aside, I think how rare it is for men in their early thirties, like Alfonso, to be so openly clucky. Funny, after years of dating blokes who guarded their emotions like a rugby football, I'd copped a guy who had absolutely no fear of being considered a wuss.

A float approaches, loaded with fishing nets and a sign reading: *Maestro, abbiamo faticato tutta la notte senza prendere neppure un pesce, ma su tua parola, gettero' le reti.* Master, we have toiled the whole night without catching even one fish, but on your word, I will cast the nets.

Alfonso explains that the float represents the biblical scene in which a group of fishermen, dismayed after catching not one

Many young hands make light work during the *Processione*

fish, are urged by Jesus to recast their nets. Soon their nets are so heavy with fish they can barely haul them in.

By two o'clock the floats are still coming and our bellies are rumbling. We head home and Alfonso whips up *penne all'arrabbiata*.

I watch as Chef Fonz drizzles some olive oil into a pan, tosses in some garlic with a dash of chilli along with a generous handful of cherry tomatoes.

When the mix turns to mush and the *penne* is judged *al dente*, I grab some leaves from the basil plant we keep on our balcony and tear them up roughly, ready to sprinkle on the pasta.

'Do you know that you should never cut basil with a knife, as it loses its aroma faster, but just do it with your hands?' I tell Alfonso with an air of authority.

'*Amore*, why do you always try to talk like you know anything about food? You come from Australia, a country with barely any history compared to Italy, whose cuisine is considered the best in the world,' he says, seizing the basil to drop it from a great height on the pasta with comic exaggeration.

'At least my country is not arrogant enough to think its cuisine is best. Australians have an amazing choice of food from all around the world,' I bite back, adding for good measure, 'In Naples there are only two Japanese restaurants, as for Procida . . . people here probably think pizza is exotic!'

Trying not to wolf down my pasta, I think how often I sabotaged pasta dishes before I came to Italy, throwing in too many ingredients to avoid a bland dish. In Italy, I was liberated by the common local knowledge that adding any more than three ingredients, garlic included, is a recipe for disaster. Also among the culinary crimes was marrying the wrong *sugo* with the wrong pasta.

As dusk falls, we decide to head to Bar Capriccio for an *aperitivo*.

'We didn't see the *Cristo morto* at the procession,' I say as we notice that the doors of the local church are wide open. 'Let's have a peek to see if they've done anything special to it for the parade.'

Inside, the church is lit by scores of candles, and we make our way to the statue where a small crowd has gathered. I wait my turn to move to the front then stand to examine the statue in silence. Freshly dragged off the cross, the suffering of the *Cristo morto* – his face ghostly white, his mouth agape to reveal a lolling tongue – sends a shiver down my spine.

Wanting to find out more about the *Cristo* and the procession, I spy a group of men standing near the entrance and ask if they can help us.

One man steps forward, obviously pleased that we are taking an interest in the day's events, and ushers us into a small room where we can talk.

Gabriele Scotto introduces himself as the director of the *Congrega dei Turchini,* the congregation, founded by Jesuits, which organises the *Processione dei Misteri.* For his whole life, he explains with pride, he has been a part of the event.

'I took part in every parade. At eighteen I was already a member of the *Congrega dei Turchini,* and at that age you are big enough to carry something heavier than the float. There is a custom of carrying the Madonna Adolerata for some years before you graduate to being able to carry the Dead Christ.'

'How old were you when you carried him for the first time?' I ask, wondering if listing the fact you've carried a Dead Christ on your CV takes you places in Italy, or at least on Procida.

'I was around twenty-one, and I still remember the emotion,' Scotto says, a slight tremor creeping into his soft voice. 'We young folk had to respect the older members of the congregation, because they were so passionate about it. You couldn't take their positions at the front of the statue or you'd be seen as cocky and put in your place!'

He explains that the *processione,* started in around 1600 by local Jesuits, was initially a type of penance in which participants dressed in hessian sacking would whip themselves with knotted ropes, drawing blood, in order to cleanse the entire population of their sins, atoning above all for the crucifixion of Christ.

The flagellation was later considered to be in bad taste, and in the seventeenth century, during the Counter-Reformation, the newly formed *Congrega dei Turchini* took it upon itself to organise things in a more civilised manner. At first, they introduced symbols of the Passion – nails, a thorned crown, and so on. But without the acts of whipping, the procession was lacking a sensational centrepiece, until one bright spark suggested carving a *Cristo morto*.

'Is it true that the statue was made by an inmate of the jail at Terra Murata?' I ask.

'Absolute myth,' responds Scotto, explaining that the statue was carved in 1728, well before the prison opened in 1800. 'We think it was made in Naples, by a local who lived in the historic centre, in the street where all the figurines for the nativity cribs are made.' I know he's referring to via San Gregorio Armeno, where trade in the *pastori*, or figurines, reaches manic proportions just before Christmas.

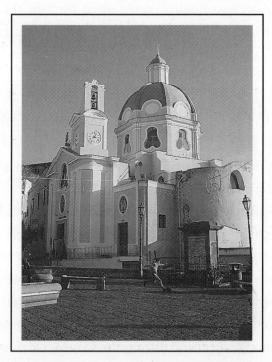

Soccer in the piazza in front of Santa Maria delle Grazie church

The procession continued in its simple format until the 1940s, when the first *misteri* began to appear depicting biblical images of the life, miracles and passion of Christ.

'In the 1950s the floats largely depicted episodes from the Passion.' Then a frown creases Scotto's forehead. 'But in 1968, with the war in Vietnam, there were problems. The floats began to reflect difficulties in society, a lot of anguish, which continued into the 1970s and 1980s. There were even floats about sex, the pill and drugs, a trend towards doing bigger things, making more of a spectacle.'

His displeasure is obvious.

'In the 1970s there was great change in Italy,' Alfonso tells me, 'with lots of student protests, terrorist acts by the Red Brigade and a growing support for the Communist Party against the ruling Christian Democrats.'

In the mid 1980s, Scotto concludes, the congregation managed to restore order and the procession returned to its spiritual roots, though its size and sophistication has continued to grow.

Remembering something I read in the book I'd bought, I ask Scotto about the miracle that apparently took place when the *Cristo morto* returned to Procida after being polished and restored in Naples.

'Yes, it happened in 1990. I was there in person,' he says.

To transport the restored statue to Procida, the church had commissioned a special ferry which was waiting at the port in Naples on what was a gloomy afternoon.

'We got on the boat and the weather was so bad that all the fishermen who had planned to welcome us into the port of Procida in their boats were forced to stay on land,' says Scotto. 'We were very worried during the crossing, but finally we made it to the port, with the rain pounding down.

'We were all saying to one another, "Well, we can't disembark, let's just stay here, we can't risk damaging the statue."'

'We were standing in the bowels of the boat, and the ramp was lowered. And in that instant . . .'

Suddenly he slices his hand through the air.

'*Boom!* The rain stopped. But I mean it stopped *instantaneously*, the moment the ramp touched land. And in that moment, the scores of Procidans who had been sheltering from the rain emerged in a flash. It was incredible, the whole piazza was suddenly teeming with people.'

Scotto pauses, his voice trembling with emotion.

'I remember the *sacredote* beside me saying, "How on earth did it happen? Did you see that rain?" It really was miraculous.'

According to Scotto, the Good Friday procession is still very important to Procidans.

'The whole island is involved, every family, and even though the women don't march they are busy helping their sons and husbands and brothers. The fishermen or husbands who can't make it home are very upset.'

Alfonso gives me a look that says he is keen to have an *aperitivo*.

We shake Scotto's hands and thank him for his time then wander down to the port. The night air bites and when we reach Marina Grande a gust of wind whips around us like a ghost.

At six o'clock on Good Friday, Bar Capriccio is almost empty, apart from Enzo behind the bar and a couple having an *aperitivo*.

Enzo introduces us to them: Gigi, a robust man with a closely shaved head, and his girlfriend Eliana, whose bright fashion sense extends to her bottle-red bob of ringlets.

Gigi had taken part in the morning's *processione*, having worked with a group of around twenty people to build one of the many *misteri*. A veteran of the parade, this year his group made a float loosely based on the Last Supper.

Between yawns, he attempts to explain the emotion of the day's events to us newcomers.

'You have to be Procidan to understand what the procession means,' he says matter-of-factly. 'It's not like barracking for a soccer team, it's something more, something you carry inside from the day you are born, a natural instinct. The moment Christmas ends, you start looking forward to the preparations for the procession. It lasts at least forty days, from when you meet your group and decide what float to build till the day you march.

'You invest a lot of energy, your time, money, your health, and sometimes you argue with your mates, but in the end you have fun,' Gigi continues as Enzo hands us a *spritz*, a refreshing blend of *prosecco* and Campari Bitter with a twist of orange rind.

Gigi explains that the use of the word *misteri* for the floats comes from the fact that there is great rivalry between the groups that build them.

Religion has little to do with why he takes part in the parade. Rather, his enthusiasm springs from a desire to meet and be part of a group with a purpose.

'When Good Friday arrives I almost wish it hadn't,' he says, 'because you get so used to the routine of meeting your group and mixing and discovering new things about them that when the big day finally dawns, for me it's like the end.' He stares into his beer glass sadly.

After the parade, he explains, the floats are destroyed, apart from any pieces that are valuable or can be recycled.

'Why aren't women allowed to participate?' I ask.

'The procession began at a time when women just weren't allowed,' Gigi explains. 'It wasn't even a consideration.'

'Macho man!' retorts Eliana, then shrugs. 'When I was younger, I would have liked to take part, but now I think the tradition is beautiful, and I don't just see it as a man's thing,' she says.

Gigi yawns again, and announces that he has to go home to rest. As he and Eliana leave, a tall, bulky man with a neat moustache and spectacles walks in.

'You should ask Michele what he thinks about the parade and the *congrega*,' says Enzo, introducing us to the newcomer.

Michele orders a beer, and I explain how Gabriele Scotto did not approve of some of the floats created during the 1960s and 1970s.

'At the time,' Michele remembers, 'Procida was growing and there was change in the wind. Those who direct the parade have always protected the vision of the event in the most closed manner imaginable. At one point, the congregation even tried to demand that we submit reports detailing what the concept of our float would be!' Unlike Gabriele Scotto, he remembers the seventies as the procession's golden era. 'Our group would meet, choose a theme from the Bible and think of how to make it relevant to the present,' he recalls. 'Like, if Jesus was here today and he met a prostitute who was about to get stoned to death, like Mary Magdalene, what would he do? Whatever we did, we caused a scandal!'

Michele laughs and describes the 1979 procession, when his group decided to reproduce *The Garden of Earthly Delights*, a painting by Hieronymus Bosch, who was notorious for his depictions of sin and human immorality.

'It was a painting rich in symbolism, very critical of the clergy, corruption and vice,' says Michele, who was only a teen at the time. 'We recreated a beautiful garden and the crowd loved it, but we were lambasted by the congregation. Even when we tried to explain our motives, no one wanted to listen.'

When I suggest that differences of opinion seem greater among a small island population, Michele nods.

'The problem here is that there is no culture of *listening*,' he says. 'If you try to explain why you behave in a certain way it falls on deaf ears. Today's youth are already resigned; they haven't had time to cultivate a critical spirit. I was a lucky man; for twenty years our procession group didn't do what we were told.'

'Did you ever fight with the congregation?' I ask.

'No, but about ten years ago I decided I didn't want to participate any more. There are too many factors now which make it harder – life, work . . .' he says, explaining that he is a marine expert and works on oil platforms abroad for months at a time.

Draining his beer glass, Michele gives us a friendly wave and sings out to Enzo, who is upstairs programming the music play list for the evening, then heads off.

Enzo gallops down the spiral staircase as one of my favourite Kings of Leon tunes kicks off his rock selection.

'He's a real personality,' Enzo says, explaining that Michele plays the drums in an island band called The Biggest, and in the past he organised many music events on Procida.

'He created the island's first radio station, Radio Procida Uno, which ran for about twenty years. It reported on all the council meetings and local issues and generally caused a bit of a stir,' recalls Enzo with a devilish grin.

We pay our bill and wander home, buoyed by our first encounters with the locals, but somewhat tired after the longest Good Friday I can remember.

Marzo

Penne all'arrabbiata
(Penne pasta with chilli tomato sauce)

Arrabbiata means 'angry', so this recipe takes its name from the fact there is chilli in the *sugo*, or sauce. This version is in its simplest form, but it changes in every Italian household, where it is not uncommon to find extra ingredients like pancetta, parmesan and *pecorino*.

Serves 4

> 500 grams dried penne pasta
> 2 tablespoons extra virgin olive oil
> 1 garlic clove, peeled
> about 30 cherry tomatoes, halved
> 1 red chilli, finely chopped
> handful rock salt (table salt will suffice, but rock salt, ideally an Italian brand, is preferable since it is the saltiest by far)
> handful basil leaves, torn

Method
1. Drizzle a generous amount of the olive oil into a frying pan and add the garlic clove. Cook for a few seconds to flavour the oil.

2. Toss in the cherry tomatoes, chilli and a pinch of salt. Simmer over a low heat. This is the tomato *sugo**.

3. Add a small handful of rock salt to a large pan of boiling water, before adding the pasta, cooking it for as long as the packet says until *al dente* (still slightly chewy).

4. If the tomato *sugo* reduces too much while the pasta is cooking, ladle a spoon of the salted pasta water into the sauce to make it go further, but not too much or it will be too salty.

5. When the pasta is cooked, drain it and toss it into the frying pan.

6. Stir the pasta quickly until it is coated with *sugo*.

7. Serve hot and sprinkle with basil to garnish.

* To test if the *sugo* is ready, draw a line on the bottom of the saucepan with a wooden spoon. If the *sugo* quickly re-covers the surface it's not ready, but when a streak remains, allowing you to see the bottom of the pan, it is done.

Don't forget to do the *scarpetta* at the end, which means using some bread to mop up the *sugo* at the bottom of your plate.

APRILE

Bar Capriccio

Procida is the most populated place per square metre in Europe, according to the local *tam-tam*, or grapevine. I'm still trying to confirm this claim, which puzzles me given that our new island home – at least on first impressions – seems deserted compared to where I lived in Naples' historic centre. There, in the thick of the grotty but vibrant Spanish Quarter, I was often kept awake well after midnight by random fireworks and cheeky youths on Vespas racing down the narrow cobblestoned street below my apartment.

On Procida, we are woken at odd hours by the peal of the bell tower of the church next door. On the good side, I no longer need to check my watch when we are at home; I just count how many times the bell tolls.

Thinking of Naples, where the incessant chaos often drove me batty, I can't help but pine for big-city life. I adored the chatter of the locals, who often left their front doors wide open onto the street. I used to love going for a stroll to peek into the houses, maybe glimpsing a family sitting around a table at lunch, or a granny dozing in front of the television in the afternoon.

Living on Procida, where most houses are hidden behind gates and walls, is proving somewhat of a culture shock.

Gabriele Scotto, the director of the *Congrega dei Turchini*, told me the islanders tend to have a closed character, which he believes is because most of the men are sailors. Accustomed to being at sea for months on end, with little contact with the outside world, they return home and just want to be left alone in their slice of paradise.

Scotto likened the Procidans to their properties: from the outside you see nothing, but inside there is a wealth of goodness to be discovered.

I hope he's right. It's not that the islanders are unfriendly, just somewhat aloof, unlike the Neapolitans, who generally open their hearts in an instant and are stickybeaks, but endearingly so.

A faint voice from outside interrupts my thoughts.

From our balcony we can see a small, battered car coming up the street. As it draws near we notice the loudspeaker, which has been crudely strapped to the roof with rope.

'*Stasera dalle sei a . . .*' A recorded announcement about parking restrictions booms out at three-second intervals.

I smile at the sight, remembering the strains of 'Greensleeves', the recording slightly warped from overuse, emanating from the pink Mr Whippy ice-cream van that circled the netball field where I played for my high school team every Saturday afternoon.

'*Hai fame?*' Alfonso asks if I am hungry, as if sensing the direction of my thoughts.

I nod and he disappears into the kitchen as I return to the box of books I am meant to be unpacking.

Weeks have passed since we moved in, but it's only at the weekend that I turn my attention to our nest. Today though, having woken with a killer headache, I took a rare day off work.

I frown at the furniture around me. When I first saw the apartment, its size and light and the mesmerising sea views obscured some of its less desirable features.

In Italy, when you rent a furnished apartment (free-standing houses are something of a luxury with a population of sixty million), you have to live with the interior decorating tastes of the landlord, usually a cardigan-clad pensioner who often dwells in the same block.

I have not yet set eyes on Doctor Ferrajoli, the owner of our building, as he lives in Naples and only appears on Procida for a month at most at the height of summer. All I know is that his *gusto,* his taste, is not to my liking. While I'm glad our apartment is not heaving with ugly antiques, as is often the case, I wouldn't mind something old to mix in with the cheap assortment of fake wooden furniture. We do what we can to spruce up our home without accumulating too much, since we are not sure how long we'll be here.

My two favourite objects are those we found during a stroll on the beach nearest home, at the end of via Dei Bagni. One is a piece of driftwood shaped like the torso of a woman, which we discovered wedged between some rocks, and the other is a white sea buoy – the type used as a fender between boats – with a royal blue top and a length of blue twine still attached. The size of a child's bouncing ball, it was being pummelled by little waves on the water's edge when we spied it. Of the few simple objects in our home, I cherish the sea buoy. It always makes me wonder how it came to be washed ashore here. A bit like us.

Bored with unpacking, I wander to the entrance room and stand beside the window. There is not a cloud in the sky and a few boats are bobbing in the sea. I turn and let the sunshine warm my back, marvelling again at our high, domed ceiling and the quaint antique chandelier hanging from an old chain.

Hearing the clatter of pans in the kitchen I go to investigate.

I find Alfonso staring into the fridge, an uninspired look on his face.

'Let's go to the shops,' he suggests.

While Italians have many staples in their fridges and pantries (parmesan, *prosciutto* and *salami* in the former, and enough pasta and tinned tomatoes to last two wars in the latter), they tend to shop each day, buying what is in season and, most importantly, what is freshest at their local fruit and veg market.

Without exception, Alfonso and I discuss daily what we feel like eating before we buy our produce. Actually, if I added up how many times we talk about food I would say we talk about it almost hourly. Because I am always hungry, and he always has his head in a cookbook looking for inspiration.

After sampling a few places on the island – condemning one shop owner who placed the *prosciutto* we had bought in the same bag as the washing detergent, appreciating the service of another who offered to deliver our groceries – we settle on Ortofrutticolo Silverio, a greengrocer around the corner.

The middle-aged couple and their son who own the shop have already begun to address us informally as residents, having cottoned on to the fact we do a fruit and veg shop practically every day.

I like the no-nonsense family and their fresh produce, and enjoy listening to their customers talking in the Procidan dialect, which is different in both words and inflection from the Neapolitan dialect and standard Italian.

The Silverio of the shop's title is a short, jovial man with a thin moustache, who often takes a pause to shell and eat some of the peanuts he sells.

His wife, who only comes up to my shoulders and wears a blue work apron, listens carefully to the customers' requests then scurries about the shop to fulfil their orders. Occasionally, usually while offering us cooking tips – from how best to infuse flavour into *spinaci*, to the easiest way to cook the thick strips of cod stacked one on top of the other and covered in thick salt in a plastic crate on the floor – she breaks into a pretty smile which transforms her small, angular face.

The couple's son, Giuseppe, at least half a metre taller than his parents but with his father's cheery nature, is also a mine of information about seasonal produce. Like his mother, he pays great attention to selecting the fruit I buy; greengrocers in Italy personally choose the produce for their clients, who are generally discouraged from helping themselves.

I have just asked the young son in the store for some apples when Alfonso notices a crate of fresh *fave*, or broad beans.

'These are in season now, right?' he asks Giuseppe.

He nods as he puts my bag of apples on the electronic scales.

'*Ragazzi*, I'll give you a superb recipe for those beans. Take a kilo of them, shell them then blend them with a big bunch of basil, some pine nuts, and about one hundred grams of pecorino. When your pasta is cooked, mix it through. I made it the other night, and my five friends couldn't get enough of it. We made a kilo and a half of pasta, and they were begging for more!'

Goodness, I never knew humble broad beans could invoke such excitement.

We thank Giuseppe and go next door to the cramped but well-stocked mini-market, complete with a delicatessen with fresh *mozzarella di bufala* and a wide range of local cheeses and cold meats. At the counter we greet the chirpy, bearded owner, Antonio, and buy some freshly grated pecorino.

Our final stop is the La Panetteria, a few metres down the street. Considered by all we know to be the finest bakery on the island, its slogan is 'Quality is not born by chance'. Behind the counter, two women with their hair covered by headscarves sell various types of bread, including soy and wholegrain buns, as well as home-made ravioli with a spinach and ricotta or meat filling, and scrumptious pizzas. Behind them, a few pot-bellied men in white aprons chatter as they bake.

We buy a loaf of bread and a few bags of *grissini*. The long, thin toasted bread sticks are not always available, so we stock up whenever we happen upon them. Buttery and crunchy, they are delicious on their own but even better – not to mention eye-catching – with a slice of *prosciutto crudo* wrapped around them.

Suddenly starving, we return home to snack on the *grissini* and *proscuitto* and a salad of fresh fennel drizzled with olive oil, lemon and salt.

'Let's make the *fava* pesto now, so later all we have to do is cook the pasta,' suggests Alfonso.

We soon realise our folly: we have no blender to make the pesto. On impulse, we walk up the street and buzz the home of Enzo and his wife Gilda.

Our friendship with Enzo, who is forty-one going on twenty and has a joyous, conspiratorial air of mischief, is growing as we frequent Bar Capriccio each day for a coffee or an *aperitivo*. I often wonder how our progressive integration on the island would have been possible without him. I see less of Gilda as she is a busy mum to the couple's five-year-old twins, Michele and Angelo, but I like her down-to-earth, sunny nature.

Gilda opens the first-floor window and we explain our predicament. She says she doesn't have a blender, but tells us we can use the one at Bar Capriccio, where Enzo is doing some odd jobs on the one day the bar closes.

We walk down to the port to find Enzo.

We accept his offer of a beer then Alfonso ducks behind the bar and blends the pesto ingredients until we have a huge container of light-green cream.

'Let's hope it tastes better than it looks,' he remarks.

As Enzo appears from the kitchen at the back of the bar I spontaneously invite his family to dinner.

'That'd be great. We'll feed the kids first and come around eight-thirty.'

At home we leaf through a recipe book and choose a *secondo,* or second-course dish: chicken drumsticks wrapped in *pancetta* and served with a cream of zucchini. We make a list and head back out to the shops. As we round the corner to our greengrocer I notice with a frown that it is shut, as is the deli next door.

I turn to Alfonso in sudden panic.

'It's Thursday, none of the shops are open in the afternoon! What the hell are we going to do for a second course?'

Alfonso rolls his eyes. 'You always get us into trouble!' he says.

'It's not my fault, neither of us realised what day it was!'

We split up in the hope of finding some shops open in different parts of the island. I head to Piazza Olmo, where our favourite butcher is, but alas, its roller door is shut. The bakery and another fruit shop are closed too, but I sigh with relief to see Il Dolce Peccato, or The Sweet Sin, pastry shop is open. I load up on profiteroles, trying to convince myself they could become a second course.

I arrive home just before Alfonso, who found one fruit shop open at the port.

We inspect the freezer and fridge again and revise our menu: pasta with *fava* pesto following Giuseppe's recipe, a second course of mixed *assaggini,* or sample tastes; a *ragu* made from a few rabbit sausages I quickly defrost, stir-fried strips of capsicum and diced zucchini with capers and white wine, and polenta with porcini mushrooms.

The minutes pass in a blur of chopping and stirring and cursing, but things are under control by the time the door buzzer sounds about an hour later.

With exaggerated enthusiasm for the benefit of his sons, Enzo suggests they play Nintendo Wii, which Alfonso's mother gave him for Christmas.

As I rustle up a cheese plate, Enzo and Alfonso set the twins up with the Wii hand controls and we watch as they begin a boxing match. Their small frames bounce and dodge without any coordination, and soon we are all in hysterics.

We leave Michele and Angelo to box their way to exhaustion and sit down to eat. As promised, the *fava* pesto is delicious, slightly bitter from the beans, but buttery in texture.

I throw Alfonso a look of relief. It's lovely to have friends over for dinner in our new home, and I take the opportunity to ask Enzo something that has been on my mind.

'Do you remember when we first arrived, the day we came to get the keys? You said that lots of people come here but they don't last, and I wondered why.'

I've been thinking a lot about Enzo's warning as we form new friendships with the locals.

'It's difficult for those who are not used to seeing the same people all the time. The island can seem too small,' he says, taking a breather from his pasta.

'What do you think is the typical attitude of Procidans to outsiders who come here?' I ask.

'It depends,' says Enzo. 'At the start it's not like they are open to you, but if you manage to get into their good books then maybe you will like it. But I do think that it's difficult for someone who was not born on the island to live here.'

'Yes, here it's not like Naples,' says Gilda, 'where you have a choice of theatres, cinema, swimming pools and so on. People who come to live here find it hard, where you see the same faces every day and live so cheek by jowl.'

'I guess it depends on what stage of life you're at,' I say as I begin to clear the plates, 'but I wonder how much the character of the Procidans influences the foreigners' decisions to stay or go?'

Enzo leans back in his chair.

'Here we say that Procidans are *amante dei forestieri,* lovers of outsiders. Because sometimes it's easier to socialise with a foreigner who doesn't know your family or your entire life story,' he explains.

As we tuck in to the second course the conversation chops and changes and we learn a little more about our guests. After finishing school, Enzo had only two options of further education on Procida: the Nautical Institute or the teaching college. He chose the former, but his career as a sailor didn't last long.

'Maybe it's different now, but back then the conditions were terrible,' he says with a shake of his head. 'You were forced to live with people you had nothing in common with, and the spaces were so confined. I did two long stints at sea of around seven months each, and I was earning good money; at eighteen with no experience I was paid fifteen hundred euro a month. But it just wasn't for me.'

In 1988 Enzo met Gilda back on Procida, where he had returned after injuring his hand during a long sea assignment. He was smitten when he spied Gilda, a slender and radiantly pretty brunette with her hair in long ringlets, in Piazza Posta. She was already *fidanzata*, or seeing someone else, but that didn't last long.

A year later, Enzo leapt at the chance to buy into Bar Capriccio with Stefano, the husband of his sister Maria Pia, when another brother-in-law suddenly decided he wanted out.

Enzo pours a digestive *grappa* for Alfonso at Bar Capriccio

'And now you work with yet another brother-in-law, Giuseppe, so it's always been a family business,' I say, suddenly noticing the resemblance between Gilda and Giuseppe, who works the morning shift at the cafe.

'I guess the twins keep you pretty busy,' Alfonso says with a grin as the squeals from the direction of the television reach fever pitch.

The couple nod with pleasure. Enzo has already told us that he and Gilda had great difficulty conceiving, finally becoming pregnant through an IVF program. Watching the couple with their children it's obvious how much joy they derive from parenthood.

'How do you see the future for them here?' I ask.

'I just want them to be happy, and to be happy you have to have a good social life, something that can be elusive here,' Enzo says. 'At the right time they have to decide for themselves. The family home will always be here, and I will work my hardest to give them a chance to study, but whether they stay on Procida or not, who knows?'

I pull the profiteroles from the fridge, Michele and Angelo appear on cue and we serve up the sticky sweet.

As the talk turns to which is the best *pasticceria* on the island, the boys start scrambling over Enzo's back. Sugar seems to dissolve in kids' bloodstreams in the time it takes to lick a gelato.

'It's late, we'd better get going,' says Gilda, calling her offspring to order. As they make their noisy way down the stairs, Alfonso and I close our door and turn to each other for a tired but happy hug.

As part of our deal – Alfonso cooks, I am the dish pig – I wash up before I join him in bed. My chef is snoring like a truck engine and doesn't even stir when I remove a book from his hands. I give him a slight kick to bring the engine down a gear or two, then pass out.

Procida is less than four square kilometres, and it seems to take me an average of only thirty minutes to walk at a brisk pace from our house to the farthest point on the island. But sometimes I still manage to get lost on my regular exploratory walks, though I usually carry a map. I study it before I leave home and pick a new place to walk to each time, but I am always sidetracked by an unmarked lane or track that inevitably leads me to a spectacular coastal view or orchards and crops largely hidden by fences and stone walls. The few times I have bumped into a local on private property, I have smiled and pleaded ignorance before making a quick exit. I have learnt how the different neighbourhoods have been settled by different populations. The port of Chiaiolella, for example, was settled by the Ischitani, from the nearby island of Ischia; the zone of Sant' Antonio by farmers; and the pretty port of Corricella by fishermen whose insular character was so unlike the Molfettese, from the southern region of Puglia, who settled Marina Grande.

One sunny afternoon, I open my map for inspiration for my stroll. With a little imagination, Procida looks a bit like a three-legged bull or a headless dog, with the islet of Vivara forming the tail. The remnants of the island's four extinct volcanoes form a series of crescent-shaped bays along the jagged coastline.

Pretty beaches with dark grainy sand, lazy fishing ports and isolated rocky points with phenomenal views over the island and across to the mainland or the nearby islands of Capri and Ischia are all on offer for my walk.

Scanning the map, my eyes rest on the point of *il faro,* the lighthouse, my favourite place on the island so far. I head off, turning left at our front door and following the road until I see the two huge arches that once led to one of Procida's ritziest hotels, closed for years and left to ruin. The fenced-off space between the arches is now used as a rubbish dump of sorts, with odd pieces of broken furniture and rusted prams creating a climbing frame for some of the mangy cats in our street. Directly opposite are the padlocked gates of Villa Angelina, a palatial two-storey property painted a light apricot. I've never seen any sign of life within the gates, though the garden seems to be reasonably well maintained. I like to entertain the idea that Brangelina are holed up inside, hiding their latest adopted child from the paparazzi.

When I reach San Giacomo, a little piazza, I take a sharp right and head towards the lighthouse.

I admire the varying colours of the *palazzi* that line this route. Most have their doors closed but occasionally I catch a glimpse inside of pretty courtyards and huge gardens. I am charmed by the

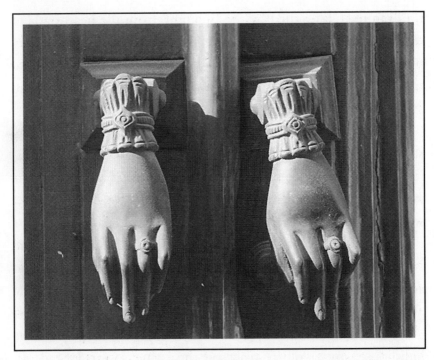

Door-knockers

doors, in particular. Many have knockers in the shape of sculpted hands, or colourful tiles with family names painted in sea blue. It's almost as if the Procidans make their entrances appealing as an apology for being so reserved.

The street is so narrow that occasionally I have to press up against the wall to allow cars to pass so it's a relief to turn in to via del Faro, where there's barely any traffic. I love the tranquillity of the long, flat street, where almost all homes are hidden behind concrete walls which range from white to grey and pink.

I have to stand on my tiptoes and peer through cracks in the gates to catch a glimpse of the local architecture, which is stunning in its simplicity: lots of arches and rustic cupolas, all in brilliant colours, most commonly shades of pink and yellow but with the odd flash of blue and green and even a red staircase.

Aprile

Built from lime and tufa, traditional Procidan homes comprise a pair of cubes. The one on top is the main dwelling, and the cube under it is a cistern to store rainwater drained from the dwelling's *cupola*. Occasionally another cube is added to create more space for expanding families.

The external staircases are divine. They are often quite long, some with arches mid-way and all with a thick, curved outer wall.

Procida is like a Greek island whose white buildings have been haphazardly bathed in colours which positively glow in the late afternoon sunshine.

The road starts to curve and offers a view of the lighthouse below. I take the public stairs leading to the new lighthouse – in reality just a power station – then another set of older, walled stairs to arrive at the original, now abandoned, lighthouse. From there I walk down a final set of steps to reach the platform of rocks that forms the neck of the bull I see on my map.

I stand about a metre from the edge, where waves are crashing, and inhale the sea air. A lone figure wanders the path along the rock sea-wall of the port, where a ferry has just lowered its ramp. Directly opposite me is Monte di Procida, a small *municipalità* on the mainland that was once a part of Procida's council administration.

I glance at my watch and decide I'd better make tracks. I catch my breath at the top of the three flights of stairs then set off along via del Faro to see where it ends.

I walk beside a white wall which gently veers until I reach a small dirt track that hugs a straight stretch of the coastline. To my left is a grey stone wall, while on the other side of the track a primitive wooden fence and long, thick grassland protects me from the sheer drop into the ocean. Looking out to sea and the headland beyond, I suddenly feel as if I'm the only living soul on earth.

Within twenty minutes I arrive at the Marina Grande, slightly sweaty but with a smile stretching from one ear to the other after my latest discovery.

I breeze past the pastel yellow Santa Maria della Pieta' church and various shops and restaurants then see the familiar green doors of Bar Capriccio, wedged between a fishmonger and a nautical equipment shop.

The bar attracts the full gamut of clientele on Procida, from crusty old fishermen to smartly dressed *carabinieri*. It also happens to be a magnet for many silent types who sit on impulse at tables outside without ordering anything. At heart, the name Bar Capriccio perfectly reflects its very random and often wayward customers.

From six-thirty in the morning until well past midnight, the bar is a welcome stop for all and sundry; the island's own version of *Cheers,* one of my favourite TV comedies of the 1980s.

Just like in the sitcom, Bar Capriccio has a cast of regulars and staff whose lives rotate around the marble counter, sharing their fortunes and woes and delighting in taking the mickey out of each other.

Thanks to Enzo, we now know a small group of locals who are fast becoming firm friends, provided we can catch them for a late afternoon ale or cocktail.

Before reaching the bar where Alfonso is waiting for me, I glance across to the port again, where a ferry is doing an enormous U-turn to dock. The thing I love most about Bar Capriccio is the spirit of evolving life, from the roundabout of clients to the boats arriving or leaving the port directly opposite. I sing out a hello to Enzo and order my eagerly awaited *spritz.*

Enzo places a glass in front of me, then a bowl of toasted bread drizzled with oil and spiced with garlic alongside a dish of peanuts, savoury biscuits and pretzels.

He turns to remove a beer glass from a small machine he uses to shake glasses of Guinness to produce the famous brew's froth. The Irish would have a fit if they saw it. He then goes to the cash register to accept a payment before returning to us where he glances around before a smile spreads across his face.

'Do you see that man?' he says, tilting his head discreetly to a table behind us. 'He comes in most afternoons and always orders the same thing, a pizza and a lemonade, and every single time he asks how much the bill is.'

'Well, I guess he wouldn't be the first strange type to walk in here,' I say.

'Oh, the nuts we get in here,' agrees Enzo. 'There was Salvatore, who went to school with me. He was always a bit odd, but then he spent three years working on an ocean liner. When he came back, he used to come in and he had it in his head that he had to write messages to the whole world.'

'What do you mean?' I ask.

'He began writing on banknotes,' Enzo explains. 'He'd ask me for a coffee and a banknote, usually the one-thousand-lira note. He'd write on it, then give it back to me. I wish I had kept them, some of them were so funny. Usually he wrote the nickname of a family, because we use nicknames a lot here, and other things that were difficult to understand. Soon he began to ask for larger sums, like ten- or twenty-thousand lira, all in thousand-lira notes, but we didn't have them all the time. One day I said to him, "Look, Salvatore, if you want fifty-thousand lira, then just write on the fifty-thousand-lira note." He looked me in the eye and said, "You're right, Enzo." From then on he'd ask for a fifty-thousand-lira note, write, drink up to eight coffees, then give the banknote back but usually leave without paying.

'Then there's Ciccio, lean as a pole, about fifty. He used to sweep out the front of Bar Cavaliere. He didn't have a job there, he just appeared and swept and they gave him a coffee in return.

'Anyway, the thing about Ciccio is that he blew magnificent *pernacchie,* raspberries,' says Enzo, making a strange noise somewhere between a fart and a pig squeal.

We bend over with laughter.

'You'd be in the street and you'd call out to him and he'd blow this amazing raspberry and then say your name.

'Then there's Giovanni,' says Enzo, continuing his rollcall of local eccentrics. 'He used to write tiny messages on cigarette packets. See how the tables over there have burn marks? Before the laws came in banning smoking in bars, he'd extinguish his cigarettes on the table.'

Enzo begins to giggle again.

'Giovanni was obsessed with sex and women. One day he came in and said to me, "Enzo, I can't take it any more, how can I meet a woman?" I said to him, "You're too stressed, you're highly strung and you frighten women. You need to whip the cobra . . . you know, masturbate!"'

Alfonso and I chuckle at the image of Enzo offering sex therapy to his clients.

'The next day I asked him if he'd followed my advice and he said, "But Enzo, how many times do I have to whip the thing?"'

Enzo moves on to Giacomo, a local man with a penchant for climbing fences to steal women's underwear. Apparently he had to take tranquillisers every few weeks, but one day he decided to skip his medical appointment.

'The police were searching the whole island for him and, of course, he was here, having a coffee,' says Enzo, as if it were only logical that a madman would seek refuge in his bar.

'Suddenly the police arrived and jumped Giacomo, who told them not to take him away, that he'd take his medication straightaway. So they gave him an injection in the bottom, right here in the bar.'

I look at Enzo with sudden admiration. He must have a hell of a lot of patience to turn up to work every day of the year, save for a few public holidays, and deal with the idiosyncrasies of a small community.

Spying the daily newspapers on the bench behind us, I ask Enzo if he saw a story on Procida in *La Repubblica*. A group of prominent Italian intellectuals and artists, including musician Enzo Morricone, launched an appeal to the state to save Procida from a spate of illegal building and rampant traffic problems that were turning the island paradise into a concrete jungle.

'Ah, it's a complex issue,' he says. 'I am as annoyed as anyone else about those people who come here on the weekends and spoil the place, because Procida is not like Ponza [the island off the coast of Rome], where only three thousand people live and their economy is based on tourism. Here we are independent, and it's always been like that.'

According to Enzo, the problem of illegal building came about because the council was so hell-bent on protecting the island with rigid laws that when there was a genuine need for apartments for new, smaller families people decided to take matters into their own hands.

'They built badly, and built eyesores, but if there had been an urban plan and the council had said, "Okay, you can build here only, with these characteristics," these problems could have been avoided. Now we are paying for the council's policies.'

As we consider his views, I notice the time, so we pay for our drinks and walk outside to a blue and pink sky. A flock of seagulls hovers over a small fishing trawler heading out to sea. We hear a shout behind us and Enzo emerges to greet an elderly couple at the bar's entrance.

'*Ragazzi*, meet my mum and dad,' Enzo says, taking a bag of lemons from his bespectacled mother, Elisa. I shake her hand and feel warm, grandmother-soft skin.

Enzo's father, Michele, then offers me his hand. He is an older, slightly pot-bellied and snow-haired version of his son: tall with ears that stick out and wide, ruddy cheeks.

I like to think I have a strong handshake, but my fingers are crushed by Michele's colossal hand. As he grins at me I yelp out loud, laughingly protesting that I am a friend of the family.

'Well, we're all having lunch together tomorrow, why don't you both join us?' Elisa says.

'We'd love to. I don't think we have any plans, do we?' I cast a glance at Alfonso. 'We enjoy eating out because it gives our cook a break,' I joke, tilting my head towards the Fonz, who with a roll of his eyes describes me as *un disastro* in the kitchen.

'Good, we'll see you tomorrow. Now we have to deliver this calamari to a friend who gave me a chicken yesterday,' Elisa says, opening her plastic shopping bag to show me the slimy sea creature. 'Michele caught it this morning.'

With a round of *ciaos*, the couple disappear and we bid farewell to Enzo before heading to Chiaiolella, a small fishing port on the other side of the island. Tonight a local community group is holding the *Festa del Carciofo*, or the festival of the artichoke, which apparently is rivalled only by lemons as the island's most famed agricultural export.

We arrive to see a hive of activity: women wearing bright yellow aprons fuss about makeshift tables bearing plate upon plate of artichoke dishes. Opposite the mushrooming stalls, staff at the handful of restaurants scurry to prepare for those who tire of the green-dominated smorgasbord.

Elegant yachts line two small jetties, and directly in front of the port is the lush green promontory called Santa Margherita Vecchia and, to the right, the small islet of Vivara. Along the port, the last rays of sun give the bright pink, yellow, apricot and blue buildings a mellow tone.

I pick up a brochure and read that the swampy plots where the artichokes are grown are known in local dialect as *parule*. The *mammarella* is the affectionate term given to the mother trunk of the plant, while the *figli*, or sons, are the small but equally tasty

Carciofi, or artichokes, star in many Procidan pasta and bread recipes

artichokes that hang from her. According to the brochure, both mother and sons are typically boiled and stuffed with garlic, parsley and chilli then sprinkled with salt. The *figli* are also battered or fried, or used to spice savoury pies and breads.

A woman standing nearby puts up a huge, handpainted sign which reveals that a total of two and a half thousand artichokes have been cooked for tonight's *festa*, all cultivated by local producers.

'Well, let's not muck around,' I say, as streams of people appear from every direction for the feast.

On the *antipasto* menu there is raw, roasted and marinated artichoke alongside savoury breads dotted with flecks of green artichoke.

I pay one euro for a ticket and stand in the fast-growing queue until I have a large, roasted globe on my plate. Oil drizzles onto my chin as I savour the vegetable, which has purplish outer leaves and is spiced with chilli.

'Round two,' I tell Alfonso, staring around me to check out the options for the *primi*, or starters. I dismiss the crepes with cream of artichokes and little dishes of polenta and artichokes in favour of the pasta with calamari and the star vegetable of the night.

I catch Alfonso's eye and touch my cheek with my right index finger then turn it slightly, an Italian gesture used to indicate goodness, but he is too busy eating pasta with artichoke and sausage to respond.

With little room left in my belly, I decide to skip the *secondi* in favour of the *dolci*. My eyes skim over various stalls offering sweets I have grown accustomed to in Naples, before I see a stall selling *frittelle dolci della nonna*, grandmother's fried biscuits.

I'm not a big fan of fried sweets, but these appear to be the only typical fare on offer. Listening to the chatter of those in the queue, I learn that potato is used in the dough. That's incentive enough for Alfonso to shell out some money and we buy a paper cone filled with biscuits, which are fried and dusted in sugar, a little like a doughnut.

'*Ciao* Penelope, *ciao* Alfonso!' I turn to see Gilda with her boys, each tugging her in a different direction. 'You have to try the artichokes roasted on the grill,' she says, motioning us to follow her through the crowd.

At the end of the port we find two industrial barbecues with rows and rows of green and purple artichokes being turned gently by a team of men wearing baseball caps.

Gilda passes us paper cones filled with the steaming artichokes.

I gingerly pick one up and take a huge bite, only to hear Gilda's high-pitched laugh.

'No, no, you have to tear off the outer leaves and then eat the softer ones in the centre,' she explains.

'Oh, I thought the barbecuing would make the outer leaves edible too,' I say, blushing at my ignorance.

Gilda sings out farewell as she spies another friend and Alfonso and I make our way along the marina towards home. The crowd is petering out and the faces of the women who volunteered to cook up all the delights are tired, but tinged with satisfaction.

As we hook left to climb up the slope I catch sight of a man with a grey ponytail sweeping on the other side of the intersection, and I grin. I remember Enzo's tales of eccentric islanders and don't think I will be able to look at a streetsweeper again without hearing the sound of a long, head-turning raspberry.

APRILE
Fava pesto
(Pasta with broad bean pesto)

Italians love their *fava* beans, also called broad beans, tossing them into everything from *zuppa* (soup) to pasta. This recipe is one of the most interesting I have come across using this humble bean, and one of the tastiest.

Serves 4

rock salt
pepper
200 grams fresh *fava* or broad beans, shelled
500 grams pasta of choice
2 handfuls basil, torn
3 tablespoons pine nuts
5 teaspoons extra virgin olive oil
100 grams *pecorino* (sheep's) cheese, grated

Note that the bigger *fava* beans have a thin, slightly bitter shell that you can remove if you prefer a less bitter pesto. Just break off the tiny 'tail' at one end of the bean, then press it between two fingers until the fava pops out ... or bite it to open then use your fingers to squeeze it out. If you can't source fresh *fava* or broad beans, just use frozen broad beans.

Method

1. Add a small handful of rock salt to a large pan of boiling water, before adding the pasta, cooking it for as long as the packet says until *al dente* (still slightly chewy).

2. Meanwhile, put the shelled, raw (or defrosted) beans, one handful of the basil, pine nuts, olive oil and *pecorino* into a blender and mix until creamy or crush using a mortar and pestle.

3. Drain the cooked pasta, reserving a tablespoon of the water.

4. Return the pasta to the pan on a low heat, and tip in the pesto mix. Add the tablespoon of water if needed. Mix well and serve with a garnish of the remaining basil leaves.

Depending on your palate, you can add more pine nuts or basil or cheese. If you can't cook this simple recipe, *non vali una fava* (you're not worth a bean).

MAGGIO

When Elisa met Michele

Think of a rugby ball. Now imagine a lemon that size. On Procida they exist, I can confirm, after spying six of the giant suckers drooping from a tree during one of my daily walks.

Lemons, and other citrus fruits, are as common on our new island home as blowflies and barbies in an Australian summer. Wherever you look, they sag from trees, or litter the roadside, squashed or soon to be juiced by passing traffic.

Which is why I have convinced myself I should feel absolutely no guilt about pilfering the lemons I can reach during my strolls around the island. Why should I pay for the fruit I squeeze on salads and into a cup of tea at night when it would otherwise just rot in backyards and orchards across Procida? I can't justify the expense, or deny the adrenalin rush I experience when I manage to swipe a lemon in a lonely lane a nanosecond before someone appears. It's daylight robbery, and it feels deliciously

44

naughty. Thankfully, there are no security cameras on our primitive island.

Soon the lemons overflow in our fruit bowl. I place a handful
in our bathroom to create a natural air freshener.

The Procidans use lemons in many other novel ways. For starters,
they feature in a traditional summer salad we sampled one day at a
restaurant in Chiaiolella. The lemons used, explained the patient
young waitress, are not your typical small numbers, but rather the
larger Procidan variety that has a thick white layer of pith. In times
of poverty and war, the pith was substituted for bread, hence that
part of the fruit is often referred to as *pane*. The salad is made of
lemon slices with plenty of pith, some mint, spring onions, a good
drizzle of olive oil and a touch of chilli. Even more refreshing is
the lemon *granita* on tap at every local bar in summer.

Medium-sized (but still big by Australian standards)
lemons on sale at the port

Lemon is also the star ingredient of two traditional sweets unique to Procida. The *lingua di bùe*, or ox's tongue, takes its name from its long, flat shape. The filo pastry sweet is filled with a lemon paste that is deliciously tart, or a lemon cream which is far sweeter.

Without question, though, the real standout is the *torta caprese al limone*.

Invented in Capri but typical throughout Italy's south, the standard *caprese* is a flat chocolate cake rendered moist and nutty thanks to almond meal used in place of flour. It's so good it doesn't need icing; it's just lightly sprinkled with icing sugar.

Procida has its own lemon version, which you might be lucky enough to find in Naples, but that won't taste as good. Until I bit into the *caprese al limone* I had never even entertained the idea this cake could compete with its darker sister. But in my view the lighter, tangier version wins hands down. I've sampled a few but I reckon the best version is served at Bar Cavaliere, where our new friends Gennaro and Maria Grazia work.

Skinny with wild curly hair and about the same age as Alfonso and me, Gennaro works at the bar and flits to Naples as often as he can to complete his language degree. Curvaceous and cheery, Maria Grazia, a language graduate, is often overshadowed by her husband, who is always quick with a joke and happiest playing the clown.

I'd like to invite Gennaro and Maria Grazia to our house for dinner, but the thing about planning a dinner on Procida, I think as I dress for a Saturday lunch at the home of Enzo's parents, is that it's hard to keep things small. While we don't know everyone intimately, if you invite one person you are usually obliged to invite another. If we invite Gennaro and Maria Grazia, I'd want to invite my friend Glorianna, which means we should invite Candida, her best friend. I'd then like to invite Graziella, who is a good friend of Eliana, whose boyfriend Gigi should also be included, along with Eliana's sister, Marina, who is always good for a laugh, and her boyfriend, Rosario. Then there's Maria Grazia's brother, Nicola, who we don't know that well because he stays in Naples during the week, but who we'd like to know better, and his partner, Maria Rosaria. Last but not least is Fabrizio, our boat-mechanic friend whose sunny nature makes him great company. And we are growing to love all the girls who work at Bar Capriccio, so those who weren't working that night would be more than welcome. Which brings us to at least fourteen dinner guests.

Still pondering this, we walk up the street to Enzo and Gilda's house and slide into the backseat of the family's car along with Angelo, who is absorbed in play with a plastic super-hero. As Gilda drives, Enzo nurses Michele and now and then sings a greeting to someone on the street.

'When I go jogging it's exhausting,' he says. 'I am puffing away but every few minutes I still have to say hello to someone!'

Gilda turns in to a lane and pulls up outside a set of two green wooden gates. Enzo unfolds his lanky frame from the car and we follow him into a small courtyard dominated by a lemon tree. Alongside is a huge vegetable patch. I spy the spindly leaves of a row of fennel and sigh. How nice it would be to have a vegie patch.

We walk down a side path alongside a house painted pink with bright red shutters and into the dining room. There we are greeted by Enzo's older sister Paola, her husband Michele and their two teenage kids, Camilla and Andrea. Enzo introduces us to his other sister, Maria Pia, her husband Stefano, and their two toddlers, Eleanora and Pier Paolo. Also at the table are Giulio, from central Italy, and his French wife Marie-Claude. The couple moved to Procida a few years earlier for a slice of the quiet life, and rent an apartment adjoining Michele and Elisa's sprawling home. Today there will be eighteen at the long table, set with a pretty linen cloth, silver cutlery, wine and glasses. I blush at earlier fretting about cooking for fourteen.

I walk into the kitchen to kiss Michele and Elisa. Warmth fills the room, emanating both from the pans that simmer on the stove and the colourful décor; from green cupboards to a yellow fridge.

Dressed casually in jeans and a jumper, Elisa breezes into the dining room and claps her hands.

'Al tavolo, tutti!' she says, ordering everyone to be seated.

I wedge myself beside Alfonso at the crowded table and attempt to pace myself between dishes. First up is a plate of *orechiette* pasta, which takes its name from the fact it is shaped like a little

Elisa is a master chef in *cucina casalinga* (home cooking)

ear, with a beef *ragu.* A second round of the same pasta is offered with sausage and broccoli fresh from the garden.

Then Paola, tall and lean like Enzo, brings in a huge dish of polenta. As she spoons it onto our plates Elisa follows with a cast-iron saucepan full of sausages in a thick tomato sauce. Michele carries in a large bowl of *friarielli,* a green leafy vegetable that is typically pan-fried with olive oil and chilli. I love the stuff.

As I finish my *secondo* I can't help but feel I have done rather well. I am full, but if I can avoid dessert I should be able to walk out of this place alive.

Michele is back again with a mountainous plate of creamy Russian salad, a mélange of mayonnaise, tuna, egg, carrot and kitchen scraps which, to me, has the appearance of a dog's breakfast. Thumping the dish onto the table, he ignores the faces of culinary defeat.

'I made it myself this morning, hand me your plates!' he bellows.

Alfonso resists with considerable force, but Michele won't have a bar of it. We pass him our plates and stomach the stuff in the name of courtesy.

I am just drawing breath when Michele reappears, this time carrying small plates of calamari and salad.

'Sorry, these were meant to be an appetiser, but we got distracted,' he says, his belly brushing the table as he leans over to distribute the plates.

I heave a sigh of relief when I learn there is no dessert, just fruit salad and Elisa's home-made almond toffee.

I lean back in my chair and listen to the soft voice of Marie-Claude. Fifty-something with long grey hair and piercing blue eyes, she speaks perfect Italian with a slight accent that reveals her origins.

She says she loves Italian food and cooks it so often that she has to refer to a recipe book when she wants to make something from her homeland.

'When I cook French food in Italy it always tastes better because generally the ingredients are fresher,' she says, 'but when I try to cook Italian in France it's never as good, though my friends still rave about it.'

This is music to the ears of Alfonso, who never tires of telling me that Italian cuisine cannot be beaten, and tends to have it in for the French.

'Last year our family had a friendly competition to see who could cook the tastiest *pastieria*,' says Maria Pia, referring to the traditional Neapolitan cake made from ricotta and candied fruit. 'We were so embarrassed; Marie-Claude's was the best by far.'

Michele hauls his large frame to his feet and invites Alfonso and me outside to play *bocce*, or bowls.

The late afternoon air is crisp and I follow Michele past the vegetable patch to a long strip of dirt at the far end of the garden. A primitive wooden cubbyhouse has been built in a nearby fig tree, with a child's seesaw beneath.

We start to play *bocce*, us versus Michele. As we heckle and chatter I look up to see Enzo – a few days ago he had subtly asked me to try to bring a little cheer to Michele, whose younger brother has cancer. Playing the clown is easy for me, and in any case Michele's amicable nature makes his company a pleasure.

As we play to the best of eleven games, I realise that in Michele and Elisa I see a surrogate version of my paternal grandparents. My grandmother passed away when I was eighteen, and my grandfather's health is spiralling. A lump builds in the back of my throat but I feign a whoop as Alfonso launches the last ball of the game and we wander back into the house.

The other guests disperse until Alfonso and I are alone at the table with our hosts, sipping coffee and Elisa's home-brewed *limoncello*. Behind us a log fire crackles, and I think of the fire at my parents' house in country New South Wales. When I mention the fireplace, Michele proudly reveals that he built it, along with the rest of the house.

Not wanting to be outdone, Elisa points out that she embroidered the pretty cream tablecloth.

She stands and beckons me to follow her to a small cloakroom adjoining the kitchen. She opens the door of a cupboard, which is crammed with white and cream fabric.

'I have some catching up to do; I'm making a *corredo*, a trousseau, for Eleanora,' she says, explaining the local tradition in which young women collect embroidered sheets, towels and dishcloths for their future married lives.

Back at the table, Elisa tells us she began embroidering around the age of fourteen.

'In our day, there was little possibility for young people to complete high school, because there was no public institution, so it was expensive. Besides, back then young girls were expected to stay at home,' she says, leaning forward to emphasise her point. 'I did three years of high school and then I worked at home, at Corricella, with my mother and two older sisters. In the morning we'd boil water on the hearth and use it for cooking and cleaning. In the evening we'd take a small boat across to Terra Murata to draw more water from the cistern. My mother taught me to cook a little and to sew.' In those days, women bought linen and flannel to make their sheets and cushion covers which were then embroidered.

I imagine a younger Elisa, sitting with her mother and sisters, sewing and dreaming of a future husband.

'How did you two meet?' I ask, always keen to hear a love story.

'Down on the beach one day,' begins Michele.

'He was a good-looking boy and I took a fancy to him,' interrupts Elisa. 'He came to say hello. I was nineteen, he was twenty-eight.'

Within two years, the pair were married, although Michele, a sailor, was rarely home.

'We didn't really see one another during our engagement,' says Elisa.

'That's why we got married,' ribs Michele.

Back then, letters were their only means of communication.

'Then my father finally got a telephone, because I had three brothers who were all at sea like me. I still remember the number: 336. No prefix, nothing.'

Michele would call his family home and a messenger would be sent to fetch Elisa.

'Once, I was living in a house on the other side of the island and a man who was selling gas cylinders turned up, saying there was a call for me. I used to get into such a tizz,' she says.

Elisa is frank when I ask her what it was like raising three children when their father was away from home so often.

'It wasn't great, but I was happy because I also grew, as if I were a child, too,' she says. 'When Enzo arrived I was happy, then Paola and Maria Pia, I was learning how to be a mother. It was a beautiful part of my life because they grew up strong and healthy. When Michele came home it was like one big party, so joyous, an extraordinary time of falling in love again.'

I have a flashback to the movie *When Harry Met Sally*, and old couples talking about how they met. It's the sort of stuff that makes your stomach turn gooey in a nice way.

'How long were you usually away at sea?' I ask Michele.

'I was lucky, the longest I was on board was eight months,' he replies, adding that he was at sea for the birth of his first two children, and had to leave the day before his third was born. He recalls how, when Elisa was pregnant with their second, Paola, he had to set sail for Russia. He had ignored a request from his superiors to update the photo on his identity card, which was at least ten years old, arguing he wouldn't be setting foot on dry land anyway.

'I had a feeling Paola was due to arrive so I asked the engineer to call Rome headquarters and check if there was a telegram with any news.'

When the boat finally docked there was a message about Paola's birth, and Michele wanted to call home. But since his identity card showed a younger man, port officials refused to let him off the boat.

'Our captain wrote a letter explaining the situation and ten minutes later a jeep with three military officials arrived at the port. They took me to an office where I phoned and got straight through. It was wonderful because usually you had to wait up to eight hours in the queue to phone home!'

Michele was eighteen when he began navigating, at first for a company that had boats chugging between Procida and Naples before signing on with a firm that did international cargo hauls, rising through the ranks to become a machinery director.

'Why did you become a sailor?' I ask.

'If you think there's nothing on Procida today, think how it was fifty years ago,' he says. 'Navigating wasn't an easy life – you were away from home and working hard – but it was another world, seeing new cities and having experiences that were otherwise impossible.'

'And of course,' says Elisa, 'he was earning good money.'

'How did you fill your days while Michele was at sea?' I ask her.

'I was raising the kids, and embroidering when I could,' she says quietly. 'Life was hard. Sometimes when Michele called I would burst into tears, thinking about everything I had to do.'

There was often conflict, Elisa tells us, between Michele and the children as they grew older and weren't willing to obey the rules of their absent father. The separation was hard on Michele, too.

'Have you ever been to Amsterdam?' Michele asked me. 'There is a boulevard there where all the houses are like shops, because they have windows at the front and you can look in. I was walking along that street one day and I peered in and saw an old man on a lounge reading, with his wife beside him, embroidering. I could have cried.' Tears spring into Michele's eyes at the memory.

'We're happier now than we were when we were young,' says Elisa.

'Yes, but now we're old!' retorts Michele.

Michele, who is seventy-three, stopped sailing when he was fifty.

'I was still young enough to keep going, but times had changed. Safety on board wasn't the best because firms were trying to save money. There were too many responsibilities lumped on you. So I called it a day and went on the pension.'

When I ask Michele about the advantages of life as a sailor he shakes his head.

'The only good thing is that you earn a lot. But you throw your family life away.'

He recalls the day he returned from sea with a thick beard. He caught a taxi home from the port and arrived to find his daughter Paola, then aged three, playing in the front yard with his father.

'I got out of the taxi and hugged my father, and Paola was watching me. It took her about ten minutes to realise who I was,' he says sadly.

'And every time Michele had to go,' Elisa remembers, 'it was a trauma. Whenever he picked up his leather jacket, Enzo thought he was leaving and became hysterical.'

Michele says he didn't want his only son to follow in his footsteps. He tried to make Enzo wait before getting the official documents, but he couldn't stop him in the end. When Michele took his son aboard to start as a cabin boy, he told the ship's superiors to keep an eye on him, otherwise there would be trouble.

'In any event, Enzo was happy to be woken at two, three, five in the morning. Pretty soon the captain was calling him in to work in the control room, putting him at the wheel!' says Michele with pride.

When Enzo called his dad to say he'd had enough of sailing and had heard about the offer to buy a half-share in Bar Capriccio, Michele was happy to have him back on dry land.

I joke about how Alfonso and I have been trying to persuade Enzo to come to Australia to set up a bar with us.

'It's too far away!' says Elisa, asking how long the plane ride is. When I tell her she gasps, but concedes that Australia must be a beautiful place to live and raise a family.

'Yes,' says Alfonso, 'but we have so many things here, it would be difficult to leave. I'm an only child. My mother would die if I were to go, she'd have a heart attack.' I glance at Alfonso with sympathy but quietly nurse dismay. I know his mother would miss him terribly if he moved abroad, but surely he must be free to lead his own life?

Michele nods. 'Italians are so family-oriented. It's no surprise that children stay at home until they're forty!'

Elisa leans forward in her chair. 'Penelope, don't you ever miss your homeland, your family?'

Words jumble in my head as I struggle to describe my feelings.

'I love Italy, but if I think about having children here with my own family so far away . . .' I stumble as I picture the faces of my nieces and nephews, and think of my parents and siblings. 'I really miss my sisters, because we're very close, I –'

To my horror tears begin to slide down my cheeks. I am so embarrassed, but after spending a day with a loving family that has practically adopted us, my emotions are begging to be released. Besides, I know Michele and Elisa understand very well the pain of separation.

'Don't cry!' says Elisa, her own voice shaking. 'It's a beautiful thing you just said, because it means you are a person who gives love!'

I excuse myself and go to the bathroom, where I splash cold water on my face and blush again at my outburst.

When I return, we chat a bit about work – Alfonso's band is due to start recording their second CD soon, while I have been toying with the idea of seeing if I can work part-time so I can pursue other freelance writing projects.

I glance at my watch; it is already six o'clock.

Alfonso and I stand up to leave, and I thank Michele and Elisa for inviting us to a wonderful family lunch. As we walk down the street, I think of my family and of Michele, alone in Amsterdam, missing his wife and children. My heart tightens with happiness for the time he can enjoy with them now.

Procida's ubiquitous walls can be off-putting for the curious. Determined not to be defeated by the concrete and the tall gates that block often breathtaking views along my morning walks, I search for ways to break through the barriers – personal as well as physical – and discover new parts of the island.

A chance to stickybeak arrives when I hear of Luigi Nappa, a Procidan-born former cruise ship captain, now an artist, who has a gallery at Marina Grande. Popping in there, I talk to Nappa's niece who tells me that Luigi divides his time between Sydney and Procida. I explain that I'm an Australian, and she gives me Luigi's number. When I call, he wastes no time in inviting me to his house for a coffee.

The next day I walk along the road leading to Ciraccio beach, staring with frustration at the clusters of enormous lemons that are just out of reach. I arrive at a cast-iron gate and press the button with Luigi's name on it. The gates part silently and I follow the path. To my left, an enormous piece of undeveloped land is partly hidden by trees, while to my right there is a garden and orchard.

Just ahead of me a door swings open on the top floor of a pretty pink building. I walk up the steps to be greeted by a man with a healthy tan and silver–grey hair parted neatly to one side.

The floor of the apartment is covered in beautiful, coloured antique tiles while the white walls of Luigi's spacious home are adorned with his watercolours, dominated by pastel hues. As he makes a pot of coffee I step out onto the terracotta-tiled terrace and admire the sweeping views across to the island of Ischia.

Luigi soon joins me, carrying espressos and a plate of pastries, including the lemony *lingua di bùe* I bought en route, as well as a jar of marmalade he tells me he made himself from the citrus fruits in his garden.

He laughs when I ask if he is a decent chef.

'Here I never cook, because everyone mistakenly thinks I can't. I eat lunch and dinner with my brother, who lives close by, or with the English lady who lives next door.'

In between delicious mouthfuls of pastry, I listen as Luigi explains how he came to create another life in my home country.

Despite showing a talent for painting in high school, he eventually chose a more practical occupation, completing his navigating diploma, like so many other Procidan men, at the Nautical Institute. He was eighteen when he began working on an oil tanker. Poverty had driven his decision to go to sea: when he was eleven his sailor father died of cancer, leaving his mother to raise the family on her own.

Aboard an ageing vessel, fighting nausea as he worked in abysmal conditions, Luigi docked in Saudia Arabia and saw a cruise ship arrive in the same port. He found out it was taking immigrants from England and Germany to Australia.

Tempted by better work conditions, not to mention a new adventure, he quit his job and returned to Italy where he contacted the Sitmar cruise ship company with whom he would chalk up a forty-five-year career.

In 1952, Sitmar, later bought by P&O, opened an office in Australia to promote its return voyages to Europe. It was in 1975, while captaining one of the *Fairstar*'s trips to the South Pacific that Luigi met his future wife, Felicity, who was the ship's cadet purser.

After a few years of globe-trotting the couple settled in Australia in 1978. Months after their arrival, Felicity gave birth to their son Giuseppe, Joe.

Luigi took up a post as general manager of operations and passenger programs, developing cruises as a marketable product.

'Instead of just going on the usual routes with main stopovers such as Noumea and Sydney, I wanted to add a bit of spice,' he says. 'I was convinced cruise ships could be like large yachts, so I investigated new ports and introduced new places, and set out to create a new product, providing entertainment on board such as new-release films, theatre, music, and cookery and dance lessons.'

Based in Sydney's Martin Place, Luigi grew to love Australia.

'Australia is beautiful because it is distant and so it's protected, but what really makes it special is the people,' he says with affection. 'They are fair dinkum; honest, sociable, easygoing – everything I wanted to be when I first arrived!'

When his marriage broke down, Luigi stayed in Australia, which he has called home for four decades. Now living on the pension, he enjoys the best of Sydney's warmth before heading to his homeland to paint and oversee his gallery during the northern summer.

'I return here,' he says, his eyes sweeping across the sea, 'for everything that is dear to me. I don't mean physically, but all my memories of childhood, in poor times straight after the war. We roamed through gardens, stealing food to bring home.'

I imagine how adept he must have been at pilfering lemons as a young boy, probably much better than me.

'But there is not the sense of community like before,' he laments.

'Yes, but that's surely a universal trend,' I say.

'Sure, Procida is a tiny part of the world, but with so many intelligent people living here we should be able to take care of the island better. When I was young, lying in my bed, I could tell who was walking by on the street, from their step, their heels, the squeaks. Now that's impossible because of the traffic. We live in a confusing noise; physical and mental. And no one meets on the streets any more. When I was young people were always talking to one another, stopping in the street, asking each other about a dish someone had made, what was on the table for lunch.'

I can't help but smile to myself. No matter the fast pace of globalisation, I don't think anything will ever stop the Italians talking about food at every opportunity.

When I ask Luigi if he misses Procida when he's in Australia and vice versa he shakes his head.

'When I am here I forget everything about Australia, and when I get to Sydney I can't remember Procida.'

I listen with amusement as Luigi lists the things he dislikes most. In Italy, it's the notoriously inefficient public service.

'Here you go to the bank and queue for half an hour and then, when you finally get to the teller and explain what you want, their telephone rings and you have to listen to them talking: "*Ciao* Concetta, how are you? What are you cooking? How are the kids?" In Australia personal telephone calls like that don't happen, and the queue moves quickly. Here you can lose a whole day if you need to go to the bank and then the post office!'

I burst out laughing, knowing how right he is.

Luigi's gripe with Australia is the drinking culture. Italians are introduced to wine from a young age and have a healthy respect for it, rather than indulging in binge drinking, he explains.

When Luigi asks if I intend to return to live in Australia I shrug, saying that while I have moments of homesickness, I adore Italy, and Procida is treating us well.

'It's very wise for you at your age and stage of life to move around. When you are like a fridge, full of knowledge, then you will decide where to go and live,' he says, offering the experience of his seventy years.

'The Procidan spirit is intrepid,' he reflects. 'Even if they are doing nothing, sitting in a room staring at the ceiling, they are always thinking and dreaming of getting away from everyone who knows them, their uneducated farmer parents, or fisherman parents. Once outside, away from everything, Procidans feel more at ease. That's how I feel in Australia.'

I nod, knowing that since arriving in Italy I have had experiences and challenged myself in ways I had never imagined, safe in the knowledge that no one I knew well would be able to judge me.

I thank Luigi for the coffee and he sees me to the gate. Instead of heading directly home, I look at my map and pick out a new place to visit: the beach known as Pozzo Vecchio, or Old Well.

I follow the lane, which is so narrow in some place that the walls feel particularly high, until I reach the simple entrance to Procida's cemetery, spread out on a small piece of land that slopes down to the sea. From where I stand I can see rows of tombstones and the water beyond, reminding me of the cemetery in Clovelly, in Sydney.

I pass the entrance and turn down a straight concrete footpath along the side of the cemetery that leads to Pozzo Vecchio.

Nestled in a bay, the deserted beach has fine dark sand and a pebbly shoreline. A little beach-side bar with a wooden verandah is closed, but I sit and rest on the railing for a moment. To my left, the sand peters out at a headland where a tiny dinghy has been pulled up on the rocks. In the other direction, the beach ends at a cluster of volcanic rocks, and I remember that beyond them lies La Spiaggetta degli Innamorati, or Lovers' Little Beach. From the look of it, romantics might have to be very fit to reach it.

I am about to leave when I notice a sign further up the beach, drawing attention to the fact that it features in scenes from the film *Il Postino.*

Inspired, on the way home I sign up as a member at the video store near our apartment and rent the film to watch later.

I find Alfonso in the kitchen, stooped over a Sicilian recipe book we bought recently, part of a collection of cookery books on every region in Italy. So far we've bought *Campania*, of which Naples is capital, *Toscana*, *Puglia*, *Veneto* and *Sicilia*, from where Alfonso has drawn what soon becomes dinner: *paccheri* pasta with eggplant, swordfish and mint.

'*Come e'?*' He asks for my opinion on his creation.

'*Buonissimo.*'

Early summer at Pozzo Vecchio beach

Alfonso sets up the DVD player so we can watch the film, while I wash the dishes and start to tidy the kitchen. I pick up the bottle of cold-pressed olive oil, a gift from Alfonso's mother during a trip to Puglia, to put it back in the cupboard, but my hand slips on the greasy glass and to my dismay the bottle crashes to the floor. A yellow–green river begins to run along the cracks between the tiles. Alfonso appears in the kitchen doorwary. His face freezes in horror.

'Sorry, but it's only oil,' I say, irritated at my tendency to break things. I frown at Alfonso, who touches the crotch of his jeans three times. I forget my anger and burst into laughter.

In Italy, the locals touch iron rather than wood to ward off bad luck. But if misfortune strikes, men often rub their nether regions three times to ward off any ills. It's a superstitious practice I find extremely amusing, despite Alfonso's somewhat indignant explanation that it has Latin origins, with an inscription at Pompeii sustaining the theory that the ancient city's inhabitants were fervent ball-rubbers.

'*Amore,* it's not funny! Breaking a bottle of oil in a house brings such bad luck, you have *no* idea,' says Alfonso, his voice rising in panic. He holds his head between his hands and paces the corridor outside the kitchen before returning to the doorway.

'*Cristo,* I don't know what the antidote is,' he mutters. I try to hide my smile as I clean up the mess.

'You know, we might have to move out,' says Alfonso, his face tense with worry.

I have grown to adore the Italians' superstitious nature, but sometimes the culture clash is so great I am tempted to buy a one-way ticket home.

I stare at the second bottle of the same olive oil, also given to us by Alfonso's mother, and resist an urge to shatter it in one final, clamorous encore.

I carefully bundle the glass and oily newspaper into a bag and walk downstairs to put it in the rubbish bin outside.

I turn to see Alfonso still staring at the floor.

'Just throw some salt over your left shoulder, that should fix things!' I snap as I leave. By the time I puff back up the stairs my temper has abated. Alfonso is also calmer, perhaps after convincing himself his immediate act of crotch-groping will ensure our house is not cursed.

I turn off the lights and slump beside him on the couch for some welcome light relief. A decade has passed since I last saw *Il Postino,* about the blossoming friendship between exiled Chilean writer and poet Pablo Neruda and the postman hired to deliver mail to his home on a tiny, unidentified Italian island.

Soon the unique colours and charm of our island home fill the room and I find myself falling in love with it all over again.

MAGGIO

INSALATA DI LIMONE
(LEMON SALAD)

I've never seen lemons as big as the ones that grow on Procida, which are ideal for this salad because of their thick pith. A standard Australian lemon won't suffice, but a bush lemon should fit the bill.

Serves 2

4 bush lemons
4 spring onions, finely sliced
I red chilli, finely chopped, or I teaspoon chilli oil
extra virgin olive oil
sprinkle of table salt
handful torn mint

Method

1. Cut off and discard the rind from the lemon and then cut off the white pith in thick slices. A little of the lemon fruit on the pith is fine.

2. Place the sliced lemon pith in a salad bowl and add the onion, chilli or chilli oil, a generous drizzle of olive oil and salt.

3. Mix well then toss in the washed mint at the last minute before serving. (If you add the mint too early the lemon will start to turn brown.)

On a hot day this is a refreshing dish because of the lemon and mint, while the chilli gives it an extra kick. Spread it out on a platter and if you have some spare lemon leaves use them to fringe the border of the plate. *Che insalata bella!* (That's a beautiful salad!)

GIUGNO

Tiffs and fish

The alarm goes off and the scramble to make it to the port in time to catch the seven-fifteen ferry begins. In the bathroom, I hurriedly search for the toothpaste, missing from the container where it keeps company with the toothbrushes. Eventually I find it on top of the washing machine, but the lid is nowhere to be found. I sigh. After years of living on my own or with girls who understand about things like putting the toothpaste in its right place, it's taking some adjustment to get used to cohabiting with a male. There have been a few early victories – toilet training to ensure the seat is left down, for example – but I am discovering that the smallest things can spark tiffs. Like the day I bought heaps of vegetables and fruit, only to have to suffer a lecture about the fridge being overloaded. I had to promise to eat an entire pineapple on the spot to keep the domestic peace.

If we get out of bed on the wrong side, we still do our best to turn on a smile at Bar Capriccio, lest we keep the islanders gossiping for a month. At times I feel claustrophobic, even paranoid, on our small patch of land hemmed by sea. After one squabble I went outside for a long walk at one-thirty in the afternoon, the time when the shops close and families gather around the table to eat and rest for three hours before doors reopen. At these times the island is one very small ghost town, which only made me feel more stir-crazy. I recently heard that a local girl left the island the day her former squeeze of fourteen years was due to marry. When the going gets tough, the practical evacuate.

When I arrived in Italy it seemed like everyone was always debating, arguing, shouting. I was – and still am – a non-confrontational person caught in the crossfire of an explosive population. At first I hated it, but now I appreciate the ease with which Italians get everything off their chests. Didn't I always want a man who was transparent and able to communicate his feelings?

I piously place the toothpaste back in its container and tell myself not to be anal, forcing myself to remember the best things about my *cretino*, and the fact that I am also far from perfect.

'*Amo'*, come here for a second,' Alfonso calls from the bedroom.

I poke my head in to find him straightening the cover on our bed, which I had hastily made minutes earlier.

He waits for me to give him my full attention before he throws back our doona. My pyjamas, T-shirt, socks and underwear are strewn across the bed.

'It's like Resina here!' he says, referring to the street market we go to near Naples to rifle through bundles of clothes at rock-bottom prices.

I might be fussy, but today I am no match for a finicky Virgo.

In the early light, we walk down towards the port.

Halfway along the street Alfonso, lately lamenting his growing *panza* – stomach in Neapolitan dialect – throws me a guilty look as he stops outside a bakery. I glance inside and see what has caught his eye: a fresh pizza with a tomato base, peppered with splotches of melted mozzarella and a basil leaf.

'*Aspetta un attimo.*' I wait a moment while he buys a slice to munch on as we go.

If we are what we eat, Alfonso is a gigantic *margherita*. Pizza was created in Naples, and it is not by chance my man eats at least one slice, sometimes two, most days. I often wonder if I will wake up one morning to find a steaming slab of dough lying beside me.

Along the Marina Grande I admire the crumbling old buildings in shades of pink, green, yellow and blue. Gilda once explained why the buildings in the main port are particularly bright: fishermen paint their homes in vibrant colours so they can see where to dock. 'And then,' Gilda told me with a smile, 'the Procidan sailors who pass the port when at sea like to be able to pick out their homes, to feel close to their loved ones.'

I hear voices and look up. On the top floor of two adjacent buildings two elderly women stand on their respective balconies and chatter as they hang out their washing.

At Bar Capriccio we order coffee from Giuseppe, who invites us to his place for – well, what do you know? – pizza that very evening.

'Hitch a ride with Enzo,' he suggests.

Seeing our ferry coming into the port we quickly pay and say our farewells.

On board I look around and return the nods of a few people who commute as often as we do. On Procida there is a string of people with whom I have exchanged words, usually at Bar Capriccio, but whose names I don't know.

My working day passes quickly and Alfonso meets me outside my office after his band practice. As we walk to the port he explains that in a few days he has to go to Milan to record his group, 'A67's second CD.

'That's great! Finally, after all this practice!' I say, not understanding why he appears so glum.

'Another thing,' he says, squeezing my hand. 'Our manager confirmed today that three-week tour in Brazil for the ethnic musical festival, and we leave pretty much straight after we finish recording. Then, as soon as we return, I'm teaching a computer course for a month, and the early starts mean I'll have to stay with my folks and only come back to Procida on weekends.'

I draw my breath.

'So, you'll be away for pretty much three months,' I calculate.

'*Sì,* if all goes well and we don't have to do any remixing on the CD after the course is over.'

I try to be positive. It's no big deal in the grand scheme of things. Sure, I'll miss my best friend and partner, but we'll be in contact. I think of Elise and Michele, who endured separations lasting three times as long. In a way, I like the idea of being a castaway for a few months, left to fend for myself on the island.

And then it hits me. Three months without my personal chef!

I think of my single days in Naples. I can't go back to omelettes and tinned tuna after eating like a queen for five months. Damn.

I stew on my predicament and by the time the ferry docks on Procida have cooked up a survival plan.

'Fancy an *aperitivo* at Capriccio for a change?' asks Alfonso, somewhat apologetic for being the bearer of bad news.

'Actually, I feel like going for a walk,' I say, telling him I'll see him at home a bit later.

I give him a kiss and stride off, my excitement growing as I walk past our home and another string of shops before turning in to a narrow street.

I stand outside the gate of Enzo's parents' house and look for the intercom buzzer common to every Italian home. I run my eyes over the walls on either side of the gates and find nothing. Puzzled, I look over the wall and see the kitchen light on.

'Elisa, Michele . . .' I sing out.

I hear a door slam and see Elisa approaching.

'Penelope! How are you?'

'I wanted to buzz, but I couldn't find the button,' I say apologetically.

'We don't have one. Michele always says whoever wants to find us should just enter.' She shows me how to squeeze my hand through a small hole to click open the door latch.

In the house, Michele has just returned from an afternoon fishing trip during which he caught six calamari.

'Pe! What are you doing here?' he says, giving me a friendly pat on the back.

'Well, I confess I have come for a reason,' I begin.

Elisa ushers us into the kitchen and brews some coffee as Michele disappears for a well-earned shower.

'Alfonso told me today that he has to go away for about three months,' I say, as she hands me a small cup, 'and it occurred to me that you two know a little about separation. I was wondering if I could pop by each week for a few cooking lessons? Apart from the fact that I need to learn, I reckon it would be fun!'

My desire to learn to cook is genuine, but mulling over things on the boat I decided that it would be great to spend more time with Elise and Michele. I wonder how easy it will be to maintain social contacts when Alfonso is away, and I like the idea of having a port of call, where I can always find friendly faces.

'Of course, pop in whenever you like,' says Elisa.

Grateful, I kiss her goodnight, sing out a farewell to Michele and head home. I expect to see Alfonso drooling in anticipation of pizza for dinner at Giuseppe's house, but instead I find him in bed.

'What's wrong?' He had seemed in robust health before he stopped in at Bar Capriccio.

La cucina (kitchen) is where all the action happens in Elisa's home

'I don't feel well, I think I have a fever.'

I place my hand on his forehead. We don't have a thermometer, but he does feel hot. In any case, when an Italian says they have *la febbre* there is no point questioning it. As widespread as the common cold in my homeland, *la febbre* is considered deadly serious, reason enough to stay in bed for two or three days.

I ask Alfonso if he wants me to stay, but he insists I go to the pizza night just as our intercom buzzes. I explain to Enzo, waiting on the street below, that Alfonso isn't coming but I will be down in a few minutes. I leave some aspirin on the bedside table and kiss Alfonso's forehead, feeling a little like an irresponsible mother.

A short time later, Enzo and I pull up in a small piazza and walk through a large gate into a huge backyard with a landscaped garden and swings.

I stare in amazement as I see Giuseppe standing in front of a brick wood-fired oven – and to think I'd been expecting takeaway! This is Italy's version of the Aussie barbecue.

'I finished it last weekend, do you like it?' says Giuseppe as he takes a small piece of dough and begins to flatten it on the bench beside the oven. Containers are set out on it filled with tomato paste, eggplant, sausage, ham and onion, all diced and ready to be sprinkled on the dough.

'Penny, how would you like your pizza?' asks the ever-genial Giuseppe.

'*Margherita*,' I say, explaining that I have to eat it in honour of Alfonso.

'What's wrong with him?' asks Giuseppe as he smears some tomato paste on the dough then sprinkles some mozzarella and a few basil leaves on top.

'He feels a bit sick, he might have *la febbre*.'

Giuseppe's eyes widen in sympathy.

'What a shame!'

He grabs a huge metal spatula and deftly slides it under the uncooked dough, then in one fluid movement turns and thrusts it into the roaring furnace.

'I'm planning to build another oven like this inside,' he says, pointing to the family home behind us, where a gaggle of elderly women are holding a hens' meeting.

Barely three minutes later he slides my pizza onto a disposable plate. Tonight plastic plates are convenient, but Italians seem to be obsessed with them for all occasions. I've been to formal dinners where elaborate meals have been unceremoniously served out on plastic plates. I put it down to the Italians' hedonistic trait. As much pleasure as possible while trying to avoid any serious effort. Nevermind the environment.

The cheese is still bubbling on my pizza as I carry it to the table beneath a pergola covered in grapevines. Gathered around me are most of the staff from Bar Capriccio. I have almost finished eating when Glorianna arrives. A local receptionist and former Bar Capriccio bar girl, she's one of my favourite *aperitivo* pals.

'You're late!' I say.

'Ah Pe, you know I have to watch *Un Posto Al Sole*,' she says. She rarely misses an episode of the famous Italian soap, filmed in Naples.

Giuseppe takes a break from cooking to play dad, bouncing four-month-old Marco on one knee. The bub drools to the delight of his enraptured audience, including Giuseppe's wife, Valentina, and their young daughter. I move over to sit with some of the women my age and listen to their chatter, every now and then chiming in, but struggling to follow threads of conversation that rotate as fast as the pizzas in the furnace nearby.

It's good fun watching the faces and expressions of those around me, but it's frustrating that I can't get all the jokes, told in Procidan dialect. I know the girls wouldn't mind speaking in

Italian for my benefit, indeed sometimes I ask them to do so, but they always slip back into their special island variation, and I am loath to interrupt them.

It's just before ten when Enzo taps me on the shoulder.

'Do you want to go home and check on Alfonso?' he asks.

I nod gratefully.

Our apartment is as quiet as a morgue and Alfonso sniffs in misery when I tell him I have come home early with a special treat. Giuseppe has made him a pizza.

'You sure know how to torture me,' he manages, before rolling over on his side.

He must be sick. I put the pizza in the kitchen and curl up beside him.

I stand at the port in a state of high excitement, watching the ferry ramp lower. Alfonso has recovered in time to join me in welcoming my dear friends Nic and Rob, from Sydney, and Penny, from London. The trio are staying on Procida for a few days before I travel south with them to Positano for the fiftieth birthday party of another Sydney friend, Trish. At the same time, Alfonso will head north to Milan to record.

Nic is first off the boat.

'Pen, it's amazing,' he raves, hugging me and looking around.

'Wait until you see the rest,' I tell him as I embrace Rob and Penny and introduce them to Alfonso.

We take a cab to their hotel and, in a particularly narrow stretch of road, pass one of the council's bright orange public mini-buses.

'Oh my gosh, it's like Noddyland,' says Penny, pointing at the bus.

At La Vigna, the hotel that takes its name from the sprawling vineyard at the back of the property, we are greeted by Vincenzo, whom Alfonso and I have met a few times at Bar Capriccio. When I ask about bus routes to some of the beaches, Vincenzo does not hesitate to offer us the use of his car. Being a local obviously has certain advantages.

'Thanks, we'll see how we go,' I say, touched.

As he leads us to my friends' rooms, Vincenzo is happy to answer Rob's questions about the history of the hotel. Once the property of an aristocratic Neapolitan family, its last owner was a vulcanologist who studied Vesuvius. As Alfonso and I step outside, where a pergola leads to the vineyard, I turn to look at the hotel's single turret behind us and imagine the vulcanologist, apparently considered rather nutty by some locals, pacing up and down and staring across at the hulking volcano that dominates the Bay of Naples.

Delighted with their spacious rooms oozing Mediterranean charm, Penny, Nic and Rob soon join us on the terrace. Its bright fuchsia hues contrast with the lush green grapevines like the flesh and skin of a watermelon.

We follow the narrow path leading past row upon row of grapevines until we reach the cliff edge, where a rustic wooden fence blocks the sheer drop to the sea below. As we point out Capri, Vesuvius and Naples, Nic, Rob and Penny sigh with holiday bliss.

The panoramas continue as we head out for a walk, arriving in Piazza dei Martiri, which offers a stunning view over the port of Corricella.

'It is just so *bella*!' says Nic, making me laugh.

I nod with pleasure. It is the first time we have had international guests and their timing is perfect. June is warm and sunny by day but cool in the evening, and the island is yet to be overrun by Neapolitan tourists who will fill the place in July and August. Right now, Procida really is a special place to be.

Our visitors' compliments continue when they walk through the front door of our apartment, which we have cleaned to within an inch of its life, and reach fever pitch when they step out onto our rooftop terrace. I point out Capri and then work my way around the 360-degree panorama to a chorus of *Oohs* and *Aahs*.

Alfonso and I leave our guests upstairs and head to the kitchen, where we – okay, let's be honest, where *he* – spent a good part of the morning making a *parmigiana di melanzane,* a baked dish with layers of fried eggplant, tomato *sugo* and *provola*.

Alfonso puts it in the oven to heat as I prepare an *antipasto* plate of *prosciutto crudo* wrapped around slices of rockmelon, which I carry up to the terrace with a bottle of white wine.

Lunchtime passes quickly as we catch up on gossip from London and Sydney.

In the evening we head to La Pergola, a restaurant on a narrow road leading to the lighthouse. Because it only opens in summer, this is our first visit. It was recommended to us by Pasquale, an American mechanic we have recently befriended at Bar Capriccio.

A tubby and very friendly foodie, Pasquale was born in New York but spent his childhood summers on Procida, where his grandparents and parents were born. Like many Procidan names, his is rather long – Pasquale Domenico Ambrosino di Brutto Pilo. Translated and abbreviated, it means 'Pasquale of the bad hair', which is ironic given our friend is bald.

Pasquale has the life I dream of, splitting his work neatly between two continents. In autumn and winter he works in his home country, at the port of Long Island, then in spring he heads to Procida, where he works at the island's ports until the end of summer. If I could work in two countries as Pasquale does, I'd flit between the northern and southern hemispheres so I'd never have to endure winter. We've invited him to join us for dinner.

Introductions are made outside the restaurant, then we walk down some large stepping stones and weave past rosebushes and lemon trees to reach the outdoor eating area, where about fifteen tables are set beneath the vine-covered pergola.

As we wait for the menus, Pasquale tells our Australian guests about himself.

'Our apartment dates back to 1759 and it was left to me by my great-uncle Franceso, who was an artist known as *Cecco di Procida*,' he says, adding that with his father's help he has turned one of the rooms into a small museum dedicated to his great-uncle's works of art.

Pretty pictured tiles decorate the entrances of many island homes

'If you want to come and have a look, you'd be more than welcome,' he says in his Brooklyn drawl.

'You sound like one of the Sopranos!' screeches Penny, making us all laugh.

There is no English menu, so Pasquale and I work our way through, translating for the benefit of our guests.

We order the house antipasto to share, then each choose a main course. Alfonso can't go past the artichoke and ricotta ravioli with rabbit *ragu*, while Penny and I order the fresh bream, crusted with salt and cooked on the outdoor grill. Rob, Nic and Pasquale order different pastas, all made by hand.

We clink wine glasses and Pasquale takes centre stage as our guests pepper him with questions about his family history and links to Procida.

His grandfather migrated to New York in the late 1940s, just one of many poor Italian immigrants to pass through Ellis Island. He became a tinsmith and eventually was granted citizenship, and spent much of his life travelling between New York and Procida.

Pasquale's father, Antonio, was born on Procida and was taught to paint by his uncle Cecco before he moved to New York at the age of thirteen. After studying art, he eventually became a product manager for a display company, creating store interiors and window-dressing. Each summer, he would return with his parents to Procida, and in his early twenties he met his future wife, Evalina. She soon followed him to America, where she gave birth to three children, Pasquale being her middle child.

Every summer the family would return to Procida, armed with supplies of milk chocolate, coffee and other treats which, at the time, were a luxury on the island.

'I had my first birthday on Procida, so naturally every time I come home there is someone, usually a friend of my parents or a relative, who stops me in the street and says "I remember when you took your first steps here",' says Pasquale with a huge smile.

'Did you speak Italian at home?' asks Nic, pouring some more wine into Pasquale's glass.

'Yes, I learnt Italian before English, but I was talking with my grandparents and parents, so I spoke dialect.'

The waitress arrives with a tray of goodies, including anchovies marinated in lemon and chilli, octopus salad, fried mozzarella balls and fish spiced with mint and vinegar.

'What was the island like when you were a kid?' asks Penny.

'Back then there were a lot less cars and buildings and it was more traditional. People lived off the island, off the fish they caught and the vegetables and fruit from their backyards,' Pasquale says, adding that his grandfather raised rabbits and chickens and had an enormous orchard.

'How do you find the Procidans?' Nic asks, explaining that Alfonso and I have spoken of the detached nature of the locals.

'I think maybe they are like that because, you know, they see one another so often that sometimes they want a bit of space. Maybe they also get a bit depressed at being on the island all the time.'

Pasquale's view on why Procidans can be so distant at times comes as a revelation.

'Now it makes more sense,' I say, almost with a sense of relief. 'Procidans have the attitude that, if they don't feel particularly chatty, they shouldn't feel obliged to talk to anyone because they know that person will understand how they feel. Also, if they give someone the cold shoulder it's no big deal as they're bound to run into the same person the next day. Is that what you are saying?'

'Yes, exactly,' says Pasquale with an emphatic nod. 'Procidans are generally really open. I think their reserve just comes from getting tired of the same old routine. It's not malicious.'

'Actually, it's kind of honest,' says Alfonso as the waitress clears our plates.

Pasquale takes a sip of wine and talks about his unique relationship with the island and his struggle to work out where home is.

'Once I wanted a full-time job in the States, but that would have meant I couldn't come here as I please, and it's very hard for me to forget Procida.

'I have so many friends and family here. You become a part of the whole cycle of the island and you adapt to these people and their culture. I am better off here than in New York, where it is just work, work, work and I don't have a chance to relax and cook like I do here. But when I tried to settle here on Procida full-time I found it more stressful – it was less work, but it was harder to get parts and people are less organised. In the States it's hectic, but business is far more efficient, which I like. There, I get paid immediately, whereas here on the island you have to pester people to settle their bills, and they always haggle.'

Our main courses arrive and they don't disappoint.

'This would have to be the best fish I have ever tasted,' I say, offering some of the delicate white flesh to Rob and Alfonso.

'The catch here is superb,' agrees Pasquale. 'The sea here is so clear and salty, and I've eaten fish and seafood prepared in so many different ways that would be unimaginable anywhere else. Like squid and zucchini flowers with *pappardelle* pasta, where sea and land are mixed, or pumpkin and clams with spaghetti.'

Nic tells us how flavoursome his meal is, particularly the tomatoes, and Pasquale nods.

'I feel healthier in Italy, because even if the fruit here is not that good-looking it's got so much more flavour. In America they want everything to look beautiful and so they pick it too early or produce genetically modified stuff that has no flavour. Here, you know what you eat and where it comes from.'

We eventually order desserts, including ricotta-filled *cannoli* and lemon sorbet, before sampling the restaurant's home-brewed digestive, a bitter orange version of *limoncello*.

The last table to leave, we thank the couple who own the restaurant.

'*Piacere, alla prossima,*' says the woman, with a smile. I return her smile and assure her there will definitely be a next time.

After a lazy day on the beach, we walk to Pasquale's house for a quick tour of the beautiful room he has renovated to display his uncle's oil paintings, then we all head down to Bar Capriccio to watch Italy's latest game in the European Union Football League competition.

Italy has had a shocking start in the series, being trounced by the hot favourites Holland, then drawing with Romania. Tonight, in a replay of the 2006 World Cup final, the team faces France.

We arrive right on kick-off to find our friends all standing behind the bar which is usually reserved for the staff only. Enzo has an unlit cigarette hanging from his lower lip, presumably to combat pre-match tension.

We manage to find space in the crowd and watch the game unfold. As Italy scores and the whole bar erupts Enzo flicks a switch to play a song I don't recognise, but it is clearly significant for the screaming, leaping Italians around me.

When the full-time whistle blows it signals Italy's victory, and the celebrations are loud and long.

Somewhat dusty after our late night at Bar Capriccio, the five of us catch the ferry to Naples together before parting company.

'*Fai la brava, Chunky*,' says Alfonso, telling me to behave myself in the next few months we will be apart.

'You have nothing to worry about, silly,' I reply, not letting my sadness show as we share a lingering embrace. 'After all, I'll be on an island, where gossip spreads in two seconds flat, while you'll be free as a bird in foreign cities!'

Nic, Rob and Penny give Alfonso a round of hugs, then it's my turn again before we board our boat to Positano, and Alfonso heads to his parents' home before travelling to Milan with the band the following day.

On the deck of the hydrofoil, we enjoy views of the spectacular coastline and more gossip. Sitting beside Nic, I savour his updates on Australian politics and his reviews of books I often have trouble finding in Naples.

'Pen, we love Alfonso,' he says, squeezing my hand.

'You sound like my mother,' I say with a smile. I feel my face flushing, but his opinion means a lot to me. The fact Nic and Rob and Penny have bonded so quickly with Al has been heartening. While I trust my own instincts about the relationship, I often miss the sounding board of my Australian friends.

The hydrofoil slows to a halt at Sorrento, where we are told we must alight because heavy seas mean the boat can't dock in Positano. I negotiate a fixed fee with a taxi driver to take us there instead and we are soon hugging the narrow road high above the Amalfi coast.

'Argh, I can't look,' says Nic, who is sitting by the window closest to the edge.

My friends have booked rooms in a modern hotel but I have managed to book two nights in a small, family-run *pensione* or

B&B. While simple, it is spotless and offers a glimpse of true Italian life I know my visitors won't see.

The moment I walk in, the elderly woman who runs the place invites me into her kitchen, where she puts a small coffee pot on the stove. After a chat and a caffeine hit, I leave the kitchen and practically trip over her husband, who sits pitting *amarene,* or sour cherries. They are in season now and perfect for the jam his wife makes to serve to guests at breakfast.

I walk down the steep hill into the village of Positano, which is crawling with tourists. Bypassing all the shops, I sit on a bench at the main beach, where bronzed bodies are draped over the neat rows of orange deck-chairs and boats arrive and depart on the hour. Behind me, pastel-painted homes rise up the hill to create the panorama that makes Positano so picture-perfect.

For the next two days I soak up the sun and the fantastic company of Trish, the birthday girl, and her friends, mainly Australians, at Fornillo Beach, where one of the bars is run by the son of the woman who owns my *pensione.*

On our last day together, as the heat intensifies, I have a cool outdoor shower rather than a dip in the ocean.

'I just heard someone say there is a sanitary napkin in there somewhere,' says Nic, looking at the rubbish floating along the beachfront. The litter on Procida's sandy beaches might enrage me, but at least the water is almost always clean.

The next morning I find myself back on the same bench as I wait for Nic, Rob and Penny, who will see me onto the boat back to Naples.

As I listen to the noisy travellers around me and hear the PA announcements for boats departing, I am grateful that Procida is relatively untamed, with barely a tourist menu in sight.

I hug my friends goodbye and step quickly into the air-conditioned boat, where I manage to keep my tears at bay. Spending time with my close friends has made me feel even more of an outsider on Procida. I've missed my culture and language more than I realised. In Naples, I just manage to catch an afternoon hydrofoil packed not only with locals going to Procida or Ischia, but tourists as well. As July approaches the ferry and hydrofoil companies run more services from Naples, but so far Procida seems unlikely to suffer the same fate as Capri, which is inundated from the early hours by boatloads of Japanese and Russian tourists.

As I step off the boat at Marina Grande I walk past Bar Capriccio without stopping in, desperate to get to the most remote place I can find.

At home I dump my bags, put on my swimmers and head for the lighthouse.

I walk down the steps and, to my delight, find that I am the only person on the rocky outcrop.

As I stare out across to the mainland and back at the port, I remember when Alfonso and I fought last week after I went for a long swim off the lighthouse rock.

'I'm going to swim to that beach over there,' I'd told him, pointing at the sandy bay along the coast.

'*Amo*, don't go all the way, it's dangerous,' he pleaded before I dug my heels in, telling him the water was calm and that I would stick to the coastline.

Diving in, the water was so beautiful that I swam for forty minutes, arriving at the port beach then swimming the length of it before returning.

When I got back, Alfonso was as dark as a thunder cloud, telling me he had climbed up the stairs to try to see where I was from the cliff above.

'I thought you had drowned!' he said.

Tempted to laugh, I resisted when I realised he was seriously angry.

'Sweetie, in Australia I swam ocean races. You never have to worry about me in the water!'

'Promise me that when I am here you will never go beyond that outcrop there,' he said, pointing at a far cliff.

'No!' I said indignantly. 'I know my limits.'

'Fine, I won't come here with you again,' he said sulkily.

Eventually I gave in, to keep the peace. I wonder what's worse: a non-committal boyfriend who often makes you feel worthless, or a loving but sometimes over-protective partner.

Today the sea is calm and I grab my goggles and edge out onto the rock. My body hits the water and my spirits soar as I swim for my life, my fingers pushing out to startle the odd school of fish as I follow the jagged coastline to reach the beach near the port. I swim the entire length twice before doubling back to the lighthouse, where I scramble up the mossy rocks to my towel. Intoxicating freedom pumps like adrenalin through my veins as I stand gazing out to sea, listening to the sound of the waves crashing onto the rocks at my feet. It's only a nip in the evening air that reminds me it's time to go home.

'Mozzarella bellllaaaaaa,' a voice sings out as I turn in to a small lane on my way home from my daily walk. A man hops out of his van and takes a crate from the back. I peer into it to see bags of fresh *mozzarella,* the cheese produced mainly in the Campania region of which Naples is the capital. On Procida, scores of little three-wheeled *ape* utes drive around selling fruit, vegetables and seafood, but I've never come across a *mozzarella* vendor before. Inspired, I buy a bag for three euro and decide to do *la spesa,* the food shopping, since Alfonso's absence means I can load up the fridge to my belly's content.

I have just lugged my grocery bags home when a text message arrives from Glorianna. She tells me there is a bread festival on tonight just up the road from us. In summer, Italy's twenty regions host scores of *sagre* celebrating local saints, the Madonna or local produce, typically cheese, mushrooms or meats. All in all they are just another good excuse for the locals to get together and eat.

I can barely wait until lunchtime to make my first solo meal: *caprese* salad. I open the bag of fresh *mozzarella* and carefully pick up the pure white ball of cheese without spilling the juice in the bag. I cut half of it into thick slices and put the remainder back in the bag and leave it in a bowl on the bench. Fresh *mozzarella* is never kept in the fridge because it dries out and hardens. Next I slice a tomato and then with what I like to think is culinary flair, I place slices of cheese, tomato and basil leaves across the middle of the plate until I have formed a line coloured like the Italian flag. I drizzle some olive oil over the arrangement and sprinkle a little salt on top. I sit at the table in the midday sunshine and hoe in, using bread to mop up the delicious milky juice of the *mozzarella.* You can buy it in Australia, but trust me, you have not tasted the real *mozzarella di bufala* unless you've been to Naples, or the Campania region. I'm not a die-hard cheese-eater, but even I get emotional when I happen upon a super-fresh *mozzarella.*

One of the best things about living in Italy is taking an afternoon nap, considered a national right. Usually I can't nod off unless my belly is full of pasta, but to my surprise I fall into a slumber for almost two hours. It must be the sleep I was deprived of in Positano.

In the evening, I walk up to the *sagra* where I find Glorianna, Candida, and Maria Grazia, the wife of Bar Capricco's Gennaro. We each buy a ticket for ten euro, which entitles us to a main meal, wine and dessert. The street is lined with makeshift stalls covered in pretty cloths and produce, with plump women in white aprons and chef hats preparing the food.

'What is the name of that savoury cake again?' I ask Glorianna, pointing at the pastry I know is buttery on the inside and filled with chunks of bacon, capsicum and various spices. It can only be found in the south of Italy.

'The *casatiello*,' she replies as we walk towards a plume of smoke rising from the stand selling fresh bread rolls with *salsiccia*, sausage. We patiently wait our turn and I take the opportunity to refill my glass with some red wine.

'All the wine here is made locally,' says Glorianna, eyeing the fat fingers of meat on the grill.

'It's not bad,' I comment, noticing that it's much lighter than the commercial varieties.

With our sausages in hand, we continue to walk along the road, by now teeming with what seems to be the entire island population, half of which are children.

I spy a stall selling rolls smeared with Nutella, a spread found in every Italian household. Nearby, sugar-charged kids race around and jump on an inflatable castle. Suddenly I see Elisa at the stand offering *pesce fijuto*. Loosely translated as 'runaway fish', the broth of tomatoes, garlic, chilli, parsley and chunks of bread was served in hard times when there were no fish in the nets. I wave to her and join the queue; one of her sisters, Antonietta, serves me a generous dish.

We roam the stalls selling sweets and I settle on a slice of dense chocolate *caprese* cake, a piece of pear and ricotta slice and a small *baba'*, the rum-soaked sponge cake typical to Naples. Around midnight the girls decide to head to Bar Capriccio. Full and groggy, I opt out, tired despite my post-lunch kip.

The wind has picked up when I arrive home and I lie in bed remembering our first night on the island, when we were kept awake by the howling of the rain and wind, then woken again before daybreak by the horns and dragging chains of the *Processione dei Misteri* beneath our window. I suddenly pine for Alfonso, and I send a text message before nodding off.

Sunday dawns and I wake feeling a little at a loose end without Alfonso, and still missing the company of Nic, Rob and Penny. This is traditionally a big family lunch day in Italy, but I know that Elisa and Michele have their gatherings on a Saturday due to their children's work commitments.

Before long I find myself pushing open their gate, to come across Elisa in the kitchen, where the sun streams in the window, reflecting off the yellow fridge. On every shelf of the green kitchen cabinet there are jars of ingredients and bottles of everything from fresh tomato paste to marinated figs.

'Pe, how are you?' she says, kissing my cheeks. 'Michele is out cleaning his boat, and I'm just about to make *pizza di pasta*, so you can watch how it's done.'

Elisa tells me that when her children were young, she would cook the dish, a type of pasta omelette, in the morning before taking her clan to the beach, then return to a ready-made lunch.

As she puts about half a packet of *capellini* – angel hair pasta – on to boil, I imagine her as a young woman, raising three small kids on her own.

It makes me think of something Gilda mentioned in passing: that once upon a time in Procida, left alone without their sailor husbands, local women sometimes took lovers. When they accidentally fell pregnant, the illegitimate children were usually adopted out, but I heard that some unwanted babies were thrown off the island's rocky cliffs.

I ask Elisa if it's true. She nods and sits down opposite me at the small, marble-topped kitchen table.

'Lots of people told me this tale when I was a young girl; everyone knew about it, being a small island,' she begins, lowering her voice suddenly despite the fact we are alone.

I lean forward in anticipation.

'There was a young woman; she was related to influential priests here,' Elisa continues. 'Her husband was a sailor and maybe she thought he was being unfaithful, but in any case she fell pregnant to someone else.

'One day a fisherman and his son were walking down to the rocks near Punta Pizzaco to catch some octopus when the son thought he heard a voice, or a cat wailing. Following the sound they found a baby girl wrapped up in a sack. She had obviously been thrown from the hill above, but hadn't quite rolled into the sea; saved by the branch of a tree.

'The father and son raced to the police who, thanks to rumours and anonymous reports, soon worked out whose baby it was.'

Eventually, the baby girl was adopted by the fisherman who found her. Later she married one of his sons, and they had three girls.

'The woman who was abandoned as a child always felt rejected, and it seems her daughters, one of whom my own daughter knows, have always been unlucky in love, searching for the perfect man to no avail.' Elisa stands and excuses herself for a moment to check the pasta.

I watch as she drains it and leaves it in its saucepan. She whisks four eggs and pours them into the pasta, then adds a glass of milk and a little grated parmesan. She dices some bacon and smoked cheese then adds about half of it to the mix and drizzles some oil into a deep frying pan. When it has heated, she tips half the pasta mix in, sprinkles the leftover cheese and bacon on top then adds the rest of the creamy mixture.

Elisa sits down again and I draw her attention back to the abandoned baby.

'Is she still alive?'

Elisa nods, saying the woman who had been abandoned is in her mid seventies.

'Has she ever spoken about what happened?'

Elisa shakes her head, and explains that many Procidan women fell pregnant when their husbands were at sea. To hide their condition they wore flowing dresses and generally stayed at home, sitting and embroidering sheets thrown over their growing bellies. Some of them, however, resorted to crude abortions and even tried witchcraft to terminate their pregnancies.

'There were various *mammane,* or midwives who knew what to do. I heard they even used the stem of parsley, for example, to clean out the womb . . . I don't know if that's true.'

The kitchen has filled with the delicious smell of egg and bacon, making my stomach rumble.

Elisa announces that it's time to flip what has now become a type of spaghetti frittata. She takes a plate and places it on top of the pan, flips it over and slides the frittata back onto the flame to cook on the other side.

Ten minutes later she turns the frittata onto a plate as Michele walks in. The antique wooden clock on the wall reveals it is almost twelve o'clock, and I remember that the couple eat lunch punctually at midday, and dinner at seven. By nine o'clock it's lights out in this household.

Elisa opens the oven to pull out a large baking dish filled with *parmigiana di melanzane,* which looks even tastier than Alfonso's version.

'I had some extra eggplant and I thought I might give some of this to Maria Pia or Paola,' she says. Elisa's daughters pop in regularly to collect a tasty dish from their mother to divide up between their own families, and they return the favour just as frequently.

With a lot of protesting, I manage to graciously decline an invitation to lunch, though as I move to leave, Elisa insists on cutting me a huge wedge of the *pizza di pasta*.

'Summer's on its way, I'm trying not to eat so much pasta,' I protest.

'Bah! It's not like I'm giving you the whole thing!' she says dismissively.

She puts it in a bag alongside some garden-fresh broccoli and a jar of mandarin jam.

I kiss her goodbye and walk out past the enormous lemon tree to the front gate. As I walk home I think of the plight of the baby abandoned by her mother and the Procidan women like Elisa who faced child-raising on their own.

My thoughts turn to Alfonso, who sent me a message earlier in the day, but has been otherwise out of contact in the recording studio. I wish I could talk to him about Elisa's comments. A few Italian friends have told me that it is almost taken for granted in Italy that a partner will cheat on the other before or during marriage.

My mobile phone rings as I open our apartment door. When I hear Alfonso's voice, weary but affectionate after finishing his second day in the studio, my feeling of insecurity vanishes almost as quickly as the *pizza di pasta* I devour half an hour later.

Then, to digest the rock of pasta in my belly, I grab my map and head to Punta Pizzaco, the place where Elisa said the fisherman and his son found the baby girl.

I follow the main road before taking a street I haven't walked down before. It quickly becomes a dirt track with the odd house hidden behind a large gate or wall. The track ends and drops down into bushland. I follow a narrow path, scratching my legs on bushes and countless Indian fig plants, to arrive at a rocky outcrop overlooking the sea. I glimpse another path to the left and duck under hanging branches until I emerge into the open on a sloping cliff, where I stop to catch my breath. Across the bay is the majestic but forbidding prison perched on the cliff of Terra Murata. My eyes flit to the left and I can just make out our rooftop among the buildings high above Chiaia beach. To the right, Corricella basks in the afternoon sun, a colourful patchwork of houses with curved walls and staircases built on top of one another, rising up the cliff and petering out at the foot of the old prison.

Using my hands and feet, I ease my way down the cliff and over the rocks until I reach the sea.

I turn to gaze up at the cliff and shudder as I imagine the fate of anyone – infant or adult – who happened to lose their grip.

Procida's untamed beauty soon sweeps away the last remnants of my conversation with Elisa. Happy to have found a new hideout I begin the upward climb only when the sunlight dips and the sparkling sea turns steel grey.

GIUGNO

PARMIGIANA DI MELANZANE
(EGGPLANT BAKE)

Every Italian vows their recipe for this eggplant dish is the best, but I reckon Alfonso's version is pretty hard to top. This dish is so rich you only need a small serving so it's likely you'll have some left over, which is lucky, since, like many classic recipes, it tastes even better when reheated on day two. The Italians often use the leftovers as a filling for a *panini* (bread roll). Delicious.

Serves 6

3 large eggplants, sliced lengthways into ½
    centimetre slices
1 tablespoon table salt (for eggplant)
½ cup extra virgin olive oil
2 garlic cloves, finely diced
700 grams *passata*, plain tomato pasta sauce or 20
    small tomatoes
handful basil leaves, torn
1 large *mozzarella* ball (about 250 grams), diced into
    ½ centimetre cubes
6 tablespoons parmesan cheese, grated
salt and pepper to taste

Method

1. Place the eggplant slices in a colander and sprinkle well with the table salt. Cover with a tea towel or put a weight on top and leave for 30 minutes to an hour (the salt draws out the bitter juices).

2. Drizzle some of the olive oil in a frying pan and toss in the garlic. Cook for a few seconds (don't allow to turn golden) then add the tomato pasta sauce. (Note that you can also use fresh tomatoes to make the sauce: boil the small tomatoes in water, push them through a sieve and use their juice. This will be your *sugo*.)

3. After about 10 minutes, when the sauce has become a little thicker, remove from the heat and add most of the basil.

4. Place the *mozzarella* cubes on a paper towel to dry.

5. Rinse the eggplant slices and squeeze the water from them really well. Pat them dry with a paper towel or between two tea towels. Drizzle some extra virgin olive oil in a frying pan and cook the eggplant slices (in batches) until golden on both sides.

6. Preheat oven to 200 degrees Celsius. In a baking tray (or ovenproof dish without a lid), drizzle a little extra

virgin olive oil then cover the bottom with a neat layer of eggplant slices, placed alongside one another. Spread several spoonfuls of tomato *sugo* on top of the eggplant layer, then place a few basil leaves and finally a layer of *mozzarella*.

7. Repeat until you have used all the ingredients, but make sure your last layer is tomato *sugo*. Sprinkle with the parmesan and bake for 30–45 minutes or until the top is golden and bubbling.

You can grill the eggplant for a healthier dish – it will still be tasty, just less oily. However, there's not a lot of oil in the dish, and Italians would scoff at any lightweight version. If you would like an even richer version, you can do what my mentor, Elisa, does: batter the eggplant in flour, egg and parmesan before frying it. You can also follow Alfonso's lead and substitute the *mozzarella* with *provola*, a soft cheese made from cow's milk with a delicious smoky flavour.

Serve the dish hot, but it's even yummier when it cools a little. Garnish it with basil and your mates will be dishing out the *complimenti*.

LUGLIO

Peril at sea

Michele Cardito must be one very busy man. From Monday to Friday, not a day passes when I do not count at least three people standing outside the light-blue door of his surgery, which I march past on my way to catch the ferry. This would be understandable if it wasn't six-thirty in the morning.

My friend Glorianna is Doctor Cardito's receptionist, so I ask her about this as we lie on the beach below our house one Saturday afternoon. At the primitive wooden hut which serves as a cafe behind us, a mother stands sipping an espresso as her toddler son slurps an ice cream. The wintery months of our arrival have vanished to make way for endless days of sun. On those days when I don't start work until midday, Chiaia is my preferred place to have a long swim before I race to catch the hydrofoil.

'Why on earth do these people feel the need to stand in the dark three hours before the surgery opens?' I ask, knowing how hard it is sometimes to drag my own body out of bed in the morning.

'They are generally old or pensioners,' Glorianna explains. 'They see the surgery as a place to meet people, to have a chat and to feel useful. In fact, most of them come to see the doctor on behalf of other people, to get prescriptions for their children or other relatives who work and don't have the time to wait themselves. There is a woman by the name of Annamaria who comes to us every single day, without exception, to get prescriptions for her entire family. She is so regular that if she fails to turn up I call to make sure she is okay.'

I burst into laughter and Glorianna joins me.

'In the early days of working for Michele – soon it will be ten years – there was a man named Salvatore who came every day to see me to get prescriptions for himself and his family. And at the end of the month he'd collect the pension books for his old friends and go to the post office at 4 am to be in pole position to collect his own pension and help his mates slot in after him. One day he didn't turn up for his usual visit and that night I heard he had died.'

Enlightened, I reflect on the sense of community on Procida, which is fast growing on me. While it's true that the locals are reserved, when they decide you are one of them, and when it suits their mood, they are happy to let their guard down and even welcome you into their homes. Whether I am on the ferry, taking a stroll, having an *aperitivo* or doing the shopping, there is usually someone – a friend or an acquaintance – who says hello or toots their horn and waves. Locals like Glorianna might take it for granted, but gestures such as these give me an exquisite sense of belonging.

The next morning I look out our lounge-room window with a sense of nervous anticipation. I suspect that my commute to Naples on the hydrofoil might be a little hairy.

In the blue–grey light, the panorama seems like a half-finished Van Gogh. At the bottom of the frame, the lemon trees in the orchard are being whipped by violent winds. In mid frame, the ocean appears as a lumpy blue blanket hiding a writhing, distant cousin of the Loch Ness monster. The only point of stillness is the sky, brooding with charcoal clouds.

I shower and dress more elegantly than usual as I have to look my professional best. Today the contract for my job editing the English website of ANSA*med* – a Mediterranean news service founded by ANSA, Italy's oldest and biggest news agency – officially expires and, should it be renewed, I have requested to work a four-day week, from home, allowing me to do some extra freelance work.

My boss, Antonella, has accepted my request, but the director of the news agency is not convinced. At a time when jobs are being cut left, right and centre, my timing is hardly ideal. But I am craving a change. I have suddenly realised how much I loathe office politics, and there is no technical reason why I can't work from home.

Unsure of whether my request will be accommodated, I have personally filed an application to the government to renew my stay permit, which also expires today. My employer helped me obtain my last one, but by the end of the day I may have lost my job. If so, I will have to pray my application for a new permit is approved. Otherwise I will, once again, be an illegal resident in Italy.

Alfonso has told me he'll marry me if push comes to shove and I need a permit, but it hardly seems romantic. Besides, the idea of marriage frightens the bejesus out of me. I am not sure

I can say my vows with someone who doesn't know where the toothpaste belongs. I smile to myself and my heart tightens. I miss Alfonso, not to mention his cooking. I reckon I've lost a kilo in his absence, and he's only been gone two weeks. Before long he won't be able to call me *Chunky.*

I grab my umbrella and slam our apartment door behind me.

Outside I am greeted by drizzle and a wind so strong I am forced back inside to open my umbrella. I stick close to the walls as I negotiate the road to the port, dodging puddles and cursing the odd car that passes too close.

Even in this weather, I see two old men with umbrellas standing outside Dr Cardito's surgery. Just waiting in the queue today will probably give them bronchitis.

The wind gushes up the hill against me as I try to work my way down to the port. I tilt my umbrella to avoid a Mary Poppins scenario and heave a sigh of relief as I reach the ticket office. As I stand in the short queue I look down and see that rain has saturated my pants from the shin down and my feet are making farting noises as I pace in my soggy sandals. Charming.

I buy my *biglietto* before sheltering under the awning of the ticket office.

It's the first time I have seen the waters within the port's sea walls almost as rough as the open sea beyond. I relax a little when I see that today's hydrofoil is the *Pacinotti*, a luxury craft compared to my least favourite, *San Pietro*, which sends up an enormous plume of thick smoke that covers the upper seating area. I join the throng that races towards the ramp to board and choose my favourite seat on the top deck.

A friend once told me that in the event of a bus crash, the seat three from the back on the opposite side to the driver is the safest place to sit. On a hydrofoil I have no idea which spot is the safest, but in my view those who choose the lower deck have a death wish. As I wait for the rest of the crowd to board I do my best to ignore the wild rocking of the boat. I look away from the water and take note of the faces of those around me. Some, mostly the men, appear underwhelmed by the tempest, but a few women stare nervously out to sea.

It is not until the *Pacinotti* edges out of the port walls that I rue my decision to take the fast option rather than wait for the seven-fifteen ferry. Though slower than the hydrofoils, the ferries are reassuring in their bulk, and even in the heaviest of seas the rocking is kept to a minimum.

I bury my head in my book to distract myself from the voyage ahead.

Barely a minute has passed before I feel the boat begin to tilt. I raise my head and look out the window to see a huge wave. The boat continues to tilt. As I struggle not to scream, a woman two rows in front clings to the man beside her and I hear her faint shrieks, muffled by the roar of the ocean and the steady thud of waves hitting the boat. As two crew members with grim faces walk along the corridors handing out white plastic bags, my stomach lurches, not from nausea but from pure fear. I look around, searching for comfort in the expressions of the other passengers, needing to know they too are entertaining the idea that they will perish at sea. But apart from the shrieking woman, no face registers the panic that is pressing my stomach. I have no choice but to maintain the charade. I put my head down and pretend to read, but suddenly feel the need to send a mayday text message to Alfonso.

'*Non chiamami, ti vorrei solo dire che ho appena visto un'onda che pensavo avrebbe spezzato la barca in due. Mare molto mosso. La tempesta perfetta.*' Don't call me, I just wanted to say I saw a wave that I thought would split the boat in two. Very agitated sea. The Perfect Storm.

Alfonso's reply is immediate. He tells me he is worried, and to call him when I arrive in Naples.

God willing. To avoid looking out the window for fear of seeing another tsunami, I decide to focus on my own survival plan should the *Pacinotti* capsize. Because who knows if the crew will have time to save us all? In the worst-case scenario, I will pull off my shoes and short leather jacket and prepare to abandon ship. Depending on the distance to land, I will either keep afloat using my water polo skills – egg-beater kick – and try to help the children/elderly/panicked, or I will swim to shore and raise the alarm.

The boat suddenly seems to take stock and I see the sea wall of the port. As the *Pacinotti* limps in to the dock the muscles in my body finally relax. I step onto the back deck to disembark and look at the crew, who give no indication they found the crossing traumatic. As I walk across the ramp to the shore, I feel like I merit a medal for sea bravery.

In the bathroom at work, I notice with amusement that my mascara has been smeared by the morning drizzle to render me a vampire. I clean my face and kick off my drenched shoes and air them on the balcony.

By the end of the day there has been no official word about my contract. I have little choice but to clean out my desk drawer and say farewell. It feels strange to be leaving on such uncertain terms, though the company is notorious for its disorganisation, not uncommon in Italian businesses. In any case, I'm happy to escape the monotony of the office.

As I walk down to the port my mind races with concerns about what my future holds. When I first arrived in Rome I worked myself ragged as a waitress for a few years as I learnt the language then attempted to drum up freelance work as a journalist for magazines in Australia. I was relieved when I was offered my first serious job in Italy, to work for the news agency in Naples. Now I face the uncertainty of not knowing where my next penny will come from. Procida hardly offers many job opportunities. Bloody hell. I'm less than ten minutes out of the office and I am already stressing. *Basta!*

The five-thirty ferry is the only one leaving due to the huge swell. The ferry rocks, but it's a breeze compared to the hellish morning conditions.

As the ramp lowers on Procida my stress has already diminished, and when I see the glow of Bar Capriccio I quicken my step.

'Hey! I'm unemployed and *clandestina*!' I sing out to Enzo as I walk into the bar.

I order a glass of wine and explain my predicament before the chatter turns to more interesting fodder. A few hours earlier two ferries clipped each other as they were turning in the port. Thankfully, no one was hurt, but the spectacle has caused a stir. As I listen to my friends recount the drama that unfolded, my own hair-raising boat ride seems tame in comparison.

I wake on the fifth day of unemployment with a sense of restlessness. I thought my chances of being offered my old job were fair, but feedback from my former boss is not promising. There are rumours the office will be moved to Rome.

I take deep breaths and remind myself what I am not missing. I remember racing to catch the ferry to work in Naples and how I would look back at the tiny port of Procida with a sense of regret. As I stepped off the boat my ears would be assaulted by the chaos and the noisy Neapolitans, and as I dodged the traffic

Procidan garages store everything from cars to boats and Vespas

in the morning rush I bristled at the aggressive attitudes in the big city. I couldn't wait until the working day ended to leap onto a boat to carry me home. I'd often sit outside on the top deck so I could watch Procida edge closer.

Now that I don't have to commute I can pitch freelance ideas and I will have more time to explore the island. But for as much as I am making the most of my time, when I see my Procidan friends at work or study or playing mum like Gilda, I suddenly feel at a loss. It's amazing how much of our self-worth is tied up in gainful employment, not to mention our financial security. As I look out our lounge-room window I imagine banknotes, not lemons and oranges, growing from the trees.

'*Amore,* don't stress, you've worked hard since you arrived in Italy. Just try to enjoy the moment,' Alfonso tells me when he calls early in the morning. 'Until you get the final word from ANSA or from the immigration office about your permit, there's no point in dwelling on things.'

I resolve to stop navel-gazing and fill my time productively.

As I begin to do a bit of cleaning I feel a strange lump on my finger. Puzzled, I call Glorianna to get a telephone number for my doctor Michele Cardito, who on a sunny Saturday is off duty but on call. He tells me he is with friends at Bar Cavaliere and invites me down for an informal medical check.

I wander down to Marina Grande and see Michele through the window of the bar, sitting at a table of male friends who are all enjoying a martini.

'Would you like to join us?' he asks.

'As much as I'm tempted to have a cocktail at eleven in the morning, I'll have an espresso, instead.' I laugh.

Michele feels the lump on my finger and quickly diagnoses it as a cyst which should eventually disappear.

I thank him as I finish my coffee and stand to leave.

'Why don't you join us for lunch at home tomorrow?' says Michele.

'Thank you. I would love to, especially as my personal chef is still away,' I say, wishing him a *buona giornata* before I head home.

During my ramblings on the island I have passed my doctor's home a few times, but the next day I get confused and end up taking the long route, heading around the curved, coastal road known as the Panorama, where a hidden track leads to a pretty little bay known as Seno del Carbogno.

I am minutes from my destination when I hear a horn toot and turn to see Glorianna's car. As she pulls over I notice her dark sunglasses on what is an overcast day.

'Last night after you left Bar Capriccio we went dancing until 5 am,' she admits, telling me to jump in.

Like most Procidan properties, the Cardito home is almost completely hidden from view by a sombre grey wall. The only thing visible is the top storey, painted a deep yellow. The House of the Rising Sun, indeed.

We buzz and the door clicks open. In the pretty landscaped courtyard, Michele's daughter, Candida, greets us and offers to show me her apartment, attached to the main house. We step inside to a colourful wonderland, featuring orange, yellow and lime-green walls covered in art. With evident pride, Candida shows me the wooden sculpture she is working on, as well as a long, rectangular canvas she has sprayed with colours.

'Very Pollack,' I comment.

'*Brava!*' says Candida.

She takes a dish from the oven in her kitchen and leads us back across the courtyard.

We step into the main family home where Doctor Cardito is bidding farewell to a visiting friend. I am suddenly acutely aware of being in the private domain of my doctor, who is dressed casually in jeans, a blue jumper and sandshoes. In Australia, my contact with my white-coated GP never went beyond the confines of her surgery. Since arriving in Italy I have become accustomed to being on friendly, *aperitivo* terms with my landlords, even socialising with them at parties. On Procida, my rapport with random professionals has taken on even closer dimensions. I am no longer surprised to see my doctor at *aperitivo* hour, and my greengrocer, Giuseppe, at Bar Capriccio well after midnight.

I peck Michele hello on the cheeks and think how much he resembles Roberto Donadoni, the former coach of Italy's football team. Both men are lean, of athletic build and in robust health, with tanned complexions, curly steel-grey hair and neat beards. I suspect Doctor Cardito brings on heart flutters for more than a few of the island's middle-aged female population. He lives alone now after separating from his wife. His son Nicola, himself a young father, returns to the family nest when not sailing around the world for months on end.

As Candida moves plates around the kitchen hearth that is decorated with pretty white and blue tiles, I gaze at the colourful interiors of her father's home. Paintings of fruit and flowers adorn the yellow walls of the kitchen, which has a big blue fridge in one corner.

Michele joins me in front of the hearth.

'I built this so we could cook here in the kitchen,' he says, explaining that he loves roasting fish on the iron grill.

Candy puts a plate of cheese and *prosciutto* on the table and I notice on the bench nearby a meat slicer of the type used in all delicatessens in Italy.

'Wow, I've never seen one of these in a private home before.'

She explains that it comes in handy because so many of her dad's patients shower him with gifts during public holidays, like Christmas and Easter. Along with the gigantic legs of *prosciutto*, he receives crates of fresh fish and calamari and, adds Michele, countless chickens.

'Once I found a chook outside the gate here,' he says. 'I carried it inside and as I was shoving it in the fridge I heard this *cawwwww* . . . I hadn't realised that it was still alive!'

We sit around the table and Candida places a steaming plate of penne with a rich *ragu* in the centre.

'Is your family originally from Procida?' I ask Michele, passing him the parmesan.

'My grandfather was born in Piazza Mercato in Naples; he was a sailor. He came here and married a woman by the surname of Meglio, an old Procidan family.'

I giggle at the surname, which means 'better'.

'Beh, non c'e meglio di un Meglio!' I suggest there could be no better choice than a Better, sparking laughter around the table.

My grin is wider than everyone else's. Given that half of my jokes get lost in translation, moments like these can only be described as golden.

Michele's father was a primary school teacher, while his mother came from a local farming family dating back to the 1700s with the surname of Ambrosino, a name which I seem to read on every second mailbox. The most common surname, however, is Scotto, which is usually followed by *di* and another name. There are two theories about this name. The first is that it is thought a Scottish fleet arrived on the island centuries ago, though I have been unable to confirm such a claim. The second, and more plausible, is that it comes from the *scotto* or fee that farmers once paid landowners to cultivate their soils. When the farmers paid they were given a receipt saying simply *Scotto di* followed by their surname.

I think of Michele's family tree, of farming and sailing origins. Candida once told me it was hard not to find a wealthy Procidan, with most residents deriving their income from the sea.

When I raise this with Michele he nods.

'Once upon a time Procidans saved their money,' he says. 'Sailors would come home with cash which their wives would guard carefully. Until thirty years ago, Procida was one of the richest places in the country as far as bank savings. But then my generation arrived, and we spent all our parents' savings.' He laughs.

'Procidans generally live well,' he says, 'without doing all that much work.'

I finish the pasta and within seconds Candida has gently ladled the next dish onto my plate: *involtini* – rolls of meat, stewed in a tomato sauce until tender, held together by a toothpick – and sausage, also in a thick tomato *sugo*. I lean across to inhale the aroma and hear another telling clunk on the wooden table – a dish of potatoes, roasted golden and sprinkled with salt and rosemary.

'So the fishermen here earn as much as the sailors, then?' I ask.

'*Assolutamente!*' exclaims Glorianna.

'The owners of the fishing trawlers can earn a great deal,' says Michele, 'because usually half the earnings from their daily haul is theirs. The rest is divvied up among the captain and crew. But they are all well paid.'

One of the many fishing trawlers moored at Marina Grande

'How many Procidans earn their keep from fishing?' I want to know, picturing the trawlers I see some afternoons returning to the main port, seagulls hovering and squawking over their fresh catches.

'There are about twelve or so trawlers, each with a crew of about ten, so I guess you have at least one hundred families involved, with up to five members, so that brings us to at least five hundred people – no small amount considering the island's population of ten thousand,' Michele says, adding that there is also a fleet of independent fishermen.

According to Michele, the island's maritime industry is witnessing a new boom.

'Once upon a time, young people waited for a job promised to them by family or friends, but now they want new cars and material things, and fishing brings good money.'

'Did you ever sail when you were young?' I ask, trying to imagine my doctor at sea. 'No, my father did everything he could to stop me, which was very rare in those days.' Instead, most men enrolled in its nautical institute. Michele's father insisted on sending him to Naples to complete high school then gave him a choice of enrolling at university in architecture or medicine. Michele opted for the latter.

'My father didn't have that sailing culture deeply rooted in his family, so he sent me to high school in Naples.'

When his father gave him the choice of studying architecture or medicine, Michele chose the latter.

In 1974, when he was still studying, his girlfriend Gloria fell pregnant and the young lovers married.

In between his studies in Naples, Michele worked part-time at the outpatients clinic at the hospital on Ischia and as a medic at a local hotel.

'I never had a coin in my pocket,' he remembers. 'I went to do the grocery shopping and shopkeepers would give me scraps for free. The butcher in my street in Naples used to tell me how to cook the very cheapest cuts. He once gave me bull's testicles!'

'Gross!' I exclaim before curiosity gets the better of me and I ask him how one cooks bull's balls.

'You boil them until they pop out of their sacs, then slice them and cook them in a *ragu*,' he says, with a cheeky smile. 'Delicious!'

'How big are they?' Glorianna can't help herself.

Michele points at the profiteroles that she has just placed on the table.

'Bigger,' he chuckles, 'and more tender.'

In 1978 Michele and Gloria returned to Procida, where Michele began working as the doctor on call at the island's small hospital, still standing today, as well as doing house visits. Eventually he left the hospital to become a visiting medic, but soon he was so overworked that he decided to open a surgery.

As Michele spoons some profiteroles onto my plate, I try not to visualise bull's testicles and ask him about the hairiest medical emergencies he has faced on the island.

Michele pauses before remembering an incident with his own son, Nicola, when he was barely a week old.

'All of a sudden Nicola was practically choking and he lost consciousness; it was just horrible,' recalls Michele, who said he tried to administer a few things before resorting to mouth-to-mouth resuscitation and calling the captain's office at the port to organise a boat for an emergency trip to the mainland. 'He didn't regain consciousness until we got to the hospital there. I honestly thought he would die.'

Michele's story reminds me of a conversation I overheard about an accident involving a hydrofoil in the port at Procida. When

I mention it, Michele confirms it was in 1996 and tells me that two of his aunts were on board.

'They were among the four who died,' he adds solemnly.

I offer my clumsy condolences as Candida disappears into another room to gather newspaper and magazine clippings the family collected following the accident.

Michele describes the events of 26 June, a tepid summer day with a fog so thick you could practically slice it. A few captains had refused to leave, but the skipper of the *Procida* claimed to know the port like the back of his hand.

At six-fifty in the morning the hydrofoil, which had arrived from Ischia, set out for Naples with one hundred and sixty-two people on board.

Within minutes, it clipped the sea wall and began to sink.

'Many of my relatives were on board,' remembers Michele, who was in his surgery when he got the emergency call. 'My cousin Amelia, who can't swim, was the only one who didn't get wet. She scrambled to the top of the boat and called her boyfriend on her mobile phone. He was sleeping and she left a message saying, "If I die, you should know that I loved you!"'

Michele laughs despite himself, then continues. 'I raced to the hospital but there was no one there and so I rushed to the port. It was a peculiar situation: the fog was so thick that you couldn't see a thing, but the sea was calm, and a stream of passengers were swimming to shore.' As they scrambled to dry land, he tells us, Candida and Glorianna were among the growing crowd of locals who had raced to the port.

Michele helped transport the survivors up to the hospital. Some had light wounds, others were simply in shock. At one point a colleague called out to him.

'He said, "There's something strange going on – there's a woman here on a trolley who seems dead, yet she looks half alive,"' recalls Michele.

Moving over to the trolley, Michele saw the woman had one eye open, and the other shut.

'I knew it was my aunt Letizia, because she always had this funny problem with her eye,' says Michele, who then saw his other aunt, Rosina, lifeless on a trolley nearby.

Michele sighs. 'The irony is that my aunts were going to Naples that day because Rosina had a problem with her liver and she said she had found a "miracle" doctor. She wanted to have some checks done, convinced he would work wonders, but there was nothing to do for her.'

I groan and my dismay only worsens when Candida tells me that Letizia was a strong swimmer who could have saved herself, but she didn't want to leave her sister. The pair managed to put on life jackets, but were trapped when the boat sank so quickly. Their bodies were found in an embrace.

I shake my head in dismay.

'What happened to the captain?' I ask.

'He was charged, but he didn't go to jail,' says Candida.

'He stopped working,' says Glorianna, who along with Candida and most of the island population had rushed down to the port to witness the drama.

Michele tops up my small glass of *amaro* and, to my relief, changes the subject in his laid-back manner.

'So, are you enjoying Procida, then?'

'Very much,' I say, mentioning how Enzo had warned us that newcomers to the island don't last long.

Michele nods.

'You have to be Procidan to live here, because you have to justify so many things: the rubbish, the traffic. If you don't have roots here it's easier to leave. I have my family and friends from childhood, so it's more difficult.'

Procida needs a sports centre, my doctor says, and more opportunities for the island's young people, such as a theatre. 'Here, there are only four nightclubs, and what else?' He shrugs. 'You find yourself isolated, but I don't think the current council is capable of improving things. But it's not just a matter of having ideas. We have to work first at the most simple things: cleaning up the island and stopping the illegal construction of houses.'

Michele goes on to talk about other problems on the island such as all the buildings that go up with council permission. When he raises the issue of the council's inability to find a resolution to the heavy traffic, I am all ears.

During my first weeks on Procida I would set out on my walks to explore the beauties around me, only to find myself dodging traffic and breathing exhaust fumes. Undeterred, I decided to stroll at off-peak times – in the early morning and during the long lunch hour – when there was less traffic.

'The thing is,' says Michele, 'I don't think it would take much to resolve problems like the traffic. They should organise some parking space and convince people to park in their garages instead of renting them out. Fine, it's impossible to ban traffic from the entire island, but if cars weren't parked along the streets, the traffic flow wouldn't be so bad.'

Procidans, I protest, are bone lazy. They should be encouraged to walk, or the council should offer a bus service, to run around the island every twenty minutes.

'Bah! Where do you have to go on Procida every twenty minutes?' laughs Michele, standing to stretch his legs after a lunch that has lasted for more than two hours. 'The point is you can do many things without spending money or very little; you just have to involve people. You know, tell them to paint their house because it's dirty, or clean a beach, and so forth.'

I think about this; I coped for two years in Naples, the crime capital of Italy, famous for its murderous local Camorra and its never-ending rubbish crisis, to come to an island that suddenly seems far from idyllic.

'*Cristo*, can you tell me something good about this rock?' I joke feebly.

'In Naples you can get robbed at any time of the day; here, even in the dead of the night, nothing will happen to you,' says Michele, quick to defend his homeland. 'The island is beautiful,' he says, 'we're just doing all we can to destroy it.'

Glorianna stands to leave and offers me a lift home, an invitation I decline as it would be good to walk. I farewell Michele and Candida and thank them for their hospitality.

It's just past three, a time when Procida is particularly delightful, and when most residents are either still at the table or sleeping off their Sunday lunch. I close the Carditos' gate behind me and tackle the steep hill that leads to Punta Solchiaro. Second only to the lighthouse as my favourite place on Procida, it is a finger of land that's mostly inaccessible to cars. I walk along the sealed road which peters into a dirt track, taking in the views over Terra Murata and into gorgeous private gardens. At the end of the path I loop back the other side, this time looking out over the sea, the islet of Vivara, the Santa Margherita Vecchia promontory and the island of Ischia. I bask for a moment in the absolute peace before heading home.

I hesitate outside Michele and Elisa's house. They have always told me to come in whenever I please, but today I feel intimidated by the white walls that surround their home. I push the gate open, telling myself if my timing is bad the couple will soon let me know.

Elisa is in the kitchen, cutting up rabbit.

'We didn't have our usual big lunch today, because when Michele saw how nice the weather was he took the boat out,' she says.

I tell her how much I love *coniglio alla Procidana* – rabbit cooked Procidan-style, with herbs and tomatoes – so she invites me to stay and watch her prepare the dish.

'With pleasure,' I say, feeling silly for my earlier concerns.

Elisa pours oil into a frying pan and throws in a clove of garlic before she tosses in the rabbit pieces, browning them to seal in their juices.

'The rabbits on Procida are fed better than those that are bred by the hundreds in factories, and they taste better!' she says as she stirs the meat. She tells me it was a gift from Michele's relatives who breed bunnies for their own culinary enjoyment.

She takes a larger frying pan and pours another small pool of oil into it, then tosses the rabbit in and turns to take a jar of white paste from the fridge.

'Pig's lard,' she says, dolloping some into the pan, 'but you can also use bacon or *proscuitto crudo* . . . it's just to add flavour.'

She disappears to return with a bottle of local white wine and pours some into the pan. The wine, she explains, adds flavour and tenderises the meat.

We chatter as the wine simmers until it has all but evaporated.

'Now we can throw in these,' Elisa says, brandishing a big handful of cherry tomatoes. 'You have to wait until the wine has reduced, otherwise the acid in the wine and tomatoes will mix and ruin the flavour.'

She pours in a glass or so of water then takes a head of garlic and cuts it in half before tossing it into the bubbling brew.

'The garlic is from our garden; we plant it around September and pick it in June. Ah, I need some parsley, come with me!'

I follow Elisa outside to the vegetable patch, where she fossicks among the plants, pointing out lettuce, fennel, artichokes, onions, peas and broccoli. She picks some *prezzemolo*, parsley, and strides back into the kitchen, where she washes it and tears it with her hands before throwing it into the pan. She tells me not to cut it with a knife as the flavour would be tainted. With a satisfied nod she covers the pan.

On the kitchen wall I notice a framed black-and-white photo of an old man, dressed elegantly, wearing a beret and with a pipe hanging from the corner of his mouth.

'Is that your father?'

'No, my grandfather,' Elisa says. 'See behind him? Those ropes are fishing nets. He was a fisherman, and my grandma said he used to sail as far as Marseilles.'

She brings out some more photos from the cupboard, and I flick through shots of her children in various costumes and poses, before my eye rests on an old image of some young boys carrying a statue of the Madonna in the *Processione dei Misteri*. I pick out Elisa's husband in the front row, dressed in a military uniform.

'He was pretty handsome in his day!' I say.

'Speaking of men, how are you managing without Alfonso?' asks Elisa, adding that I appear slimmer.

'It's nice to have some time to myself, but I guess I'm not eating as well as I normally do.'

The fact I am not staying overnight in Naples once or twice a week at Alfonso's parents' house, as I used to do when I finished work too late to catch the ferry home, has probably contributed to my slight weight loss, I tell her.

'What does Alfonso's mother cook?' asks Elisa.

I list a range of dishes I normally find on Maria Rosaria's table: lasagne or spaghetti with clams, calamari stuffed with ricotta and spinach and pine nuts, fresh fish cooked in a tomato broth, sausages and baked potatoes . . .

I suddenly realise I miss not just Alfonso but his mother, too.

Almost two hours have flown by when Elisa finally deems the rabbit to be ready. She turns off the flame and pulls me over to the oven to smell the rich aromas of meat, wine and tomatoes.

'Stay for dinner; Michele should be home soon.'

'I'd love to, but I have some errands to run,' I say, having no appetite at their early dinner hour.

Back home I fill the silence with my favourite Joni Mitchell CD, but when she starts wailing that her bed's too big and her frying pan too wide without her lover, I turn off the stereo and plonk myself down on the couch with the news clippings Candida lent me about the 1996 hydrofoil accident. I stare at the grim images of the half-sunken *Procida,* and spot her face among the funeral mourners.

The silence begins to suffocate me. Before I can change my mind I send a message to Glorianna and two of my waitress friends from Bar Capriccio – Rosalba and Nicoletta – inviting them to dinner the following evening. If I don't practise what Elisa teaches me, I'll never be able to recreate her dishes.

The next morning I walk to my favourite butcher up the street to buy half a rabbit. As the cheery fellow starts to chop it into pieces I remember Enzo telling me a few days earlier that the butcher had somehow managed to slice his stomach during a particularly tricky filleting move. He had to go to Naples for treatment. I don't have the nerve to ask him how his wound is healing.

At the greengrocer I chat to Silverio's wife and confess I am nervous about cooking the rabbit. She runs through the recipe with me, stressing that the key to a tasty dish is to monitor the rabbit carefully and never leave the kitchen. I smile nervously and promise to update her tomorrow.

My guests are due at eight and by six-thirty I start to follow the notes I wrote when I watched Elise cook *coniglio alla Procidana*. I am doing well until I realise I left Elisa's home before she cooked the pasta, and I'm not sure if I will have enough sauce. Fortunately, Rosalba, who has worked as a cook in some of the local restaurants, arrives a little early.

'*Bravaaa!*' she says as she walks through the door, adding that a delicious aroma of rabbit fills our apartment stairwell.

When I ask her about the sauce, she says, 'Add about six or seven more tomatoes and a dash of water, and it will be perfect.'

I follow her instructions, then throw some salt into a boiling pot of water and tip in some spaghetti.

Glorianna and Nicoletta arrive, each brandishing a bottle of wine. Soon we are all seated around the table I have set with care and I am taking compliments galore.

'I love *coniglio*, but my mother doesn't know how to make it!' says Nicoletta, picking up a piece of rabbit with her hands to get all the flesh from the bone.

'An Australian who can cook one of the hardest dishes on Procida, *complimenti!*' gushes Rosalba, whose opinion I cherish most, given her prowess in the kitchen.

'I'm improving, but let's be honest, you saved my rabbit!'

My mobile rings and to my delight I see it's Alfonso, whom I haven't heard from all day.

'You answer, and tell him what you just told me!' I ask Rosalba, handing her the phone.

'Alfonso, your wife is becoming a damn good cook!' she gasps in a theatrical voice, making us all laugh before she hands the phone back to me.

'*Complimenti, Chunky*,' Alfonso says, prompting me to give him a step-by-step replay of my triumph.

'Hang on, did you wash the rabbit?' Alfonso interrupts.

'No,' I say, panic rising in my throat. 'Why?'

'*Madonna*, you should *always* wash it in water and lemon juice or with vinegar, to flush out the last traces of blood,' he explains.

'Okay then, *buona notte*,' I say before hanging up and smiling at my guests, who continue to gossip.

I ask Glorianna for a cigarette, which I puff with hidden dismay.

Bugger. Elisa must have washed her rabbit before I arrived. I assumed, like all the other meat I buy at the butcher's, it was ready to be thrown in the pan.

With a bit of luck, my girlfriends won't have any reason to suspect my innocent error, and the talk of Bar Capriccio the next day will be the fact an *Australiana* can make rabbit on a par with a *Procidana*.

LUGLIO

Coniglio alla Procidana
(Rabbit Procidan-style)

Undoubtedly my favourite local dish, this recipe can be served with or without pasta. If you don't want to go the full carbohydrates hog, serve with a salad or vegetables of your choice. Just one thing: don't forget to rinse the rabbit before you cook it!

Serves 4

> 1 kilogram whole rabbit, chopped into 8 pieces
> white vinegar and water mix (in equal quantities, enough to soak rabbit pieces) or 1 lemon, chopped
> 4 tablespoons extra virgin olive oil
> 2 teaspoons pig's fat or lard (if it's not a staple in your fridge just cut the fat off a bacon rasher or *prosciutto* slice)
> handful parsley leaves, torn
> 1 green chilli, finely chopped
> 2 glasses white cooking wine
> 20 cherry or tear-drop tomatoes
> 1 whole garlic head (sliced roughly but not entirely in half, with the outer skin left on)

2 whole garlic cloves, peeled
500 grams pasta; *bucatini* or *penne* are favoured by
   Italians, but any type is fine
rock salt to taste

Method

1. Place the rabbit pieces in a bowl of water with the white vinegar or lemon and leave for at least half an hour, then rinse well, in order to flush out the last traces of blood.

2. Drizzle oil in frying pan. Add the garlic cloves and rabbit. Cook in batches, so the pan isn't overcrowded, until golden brown and remove.

3. In a large, heavy saucepan, pour a generous amount of olive oil and toss in the rabbit with the lard, half the parsley, the chilli and the white wine. Bring to boil.

4. Cook until the white wine evaporates (smell to check it's gone), toss in the tomatoes, the garlic head (don't be afraid, it's good for you!) and the remaining parsley.

5. Cover the saucepan containing the rabbit and cook over a low heat for about an hour, checking frequently to ensure the sauce is not reducing too much. If it is,

add a little water. Keep the lid on, because rabbit can easily become dry.

6. Serve the rabbit on its own, or if you are cooking it with pasta remove it from the sauce and place it in a covered saucepan. While the pasta is cooking, keep the sauce simmering over a low heat, adding some of the salted pasta water if needed and, if desired, some rabbit meat pulled off any of the bonier and less presentable pieces. If the sauce is already bubbling, then remove from the heat.

7. When the pasta is almost cooked, take a few spoonfuls from the water and put it in the pan with the rabbit and gently reheat over a low heat. Drain the pasta and tip into the sauce. Stir for a minute until the pasta is coated in *sugo*.

8. Serve with a piece of rabbit alongside, garnish with chopped parsley.

This dish gets easier with practice; the trick is to keep the lid on during cooking and have enough *sugo* to coat the pasta thoroughly. Get hopping!

AGOSTO

Hot and bothered

Though clearly marked on the calendar, August is a Clayton's month in Italy. Agitated by the stifling heat and the influx of tourists, the Italians wisely choose to while away the month by preparing for, embarking upon and returning from their holidays.

Shops shut, tradesmen vanish and it's pointless trying to get anything done. You'll know normality is set to resume when the nightly news bulletins feature aerial film-footage of the *reintro*, the re-entrance of millions of Italians to their home regions, bringing the country's major highways to a standstill.

I don't have a car and absolutely no desire to go anywhere – living on an island in summer is holiday enough. Actually, it could be a longer break than expected. I receive a call from a former colleague to say my old company is definitely moving to Rome and my position has been made redundant. Don't I feel special?

I start to stress as I think of the financial repercussions. But given it's August there's no point getting in a tizz. I vow to chill out and use the month for sunbaking and constructive navel-gazing. At the very least I have managed – in the nick of pre-August time – to sort out my stay permit, thanks to the ever-helpful Sabrina of the Department of Foreign Affairs at the Australian Embassy in Rome. Two days of four-hour queues in an immigration office have given me another two years in Italy.

I only wish Alfonso were here to help me exploit the summer weather and my new-found unemployment. But he is already en route to Brazil. After finishing recording, his band caught a train from Milan to Rome for their flight to São Paolo.

Although I am enjoying long morning swims and walks and napping frequently, I often pine for Alfonso's company. I particularly notice his absence when I feel like dining out and can't manage to round up a friend or two. Practically everyone is busy preparing to leave or they've already gone to another beachside in Italy or somewhere else in Europe.

Around lunchtime one steamy day I sigh as I open the fridge. I don't feel like cooking, and I don't have the energy to walk to Elisa's house. So I head down to Bordero', so far our favourite restaurant on the island. It's hard not to eat well at the restaurants clustered around Procida's three ports. All serve fresh seafood and specialise in traditional dishes like *spaghetti con vongole* and *frittura*, a mountain of lightly fried fresh seafood. But Bordero' is our preferred choice for two reasons: it offers a far more adventurous menu than the others, and it's run by local lad Ottavio.

He was extremely professional and courteous the first time we walked into the narrow dining room, with beautiful black-and-white photos of Procida hung on its burnt-orange walls. He explained the menu with care and suggested a wine to accompany our choices. Clearly he was passionate about food.

Pretty soon we were dining at Bordero' at least once a week, keen to sample the ever-changing menu and get to know the increasingly hospitable Ottavio, who developed the habit of pulling a chair up to our table after lunch or dinner to wind down and have a chat.

Today, seated at the computer at the back of the restaurant, he seems a little glum. Earlier in the week I heard on the island grapevine at Bar Capriccio that the chef at Bordero', also Ottavio's business partner, had walked out. No one seems to know the reason for the split, but given the size of the island it won't take long for word to spread.

'So is it true you are without a chef?' I ask as delicately as possible.

Ottavio nods dismissively, obviously not keen to discuss the situation, but he assures me that he still has his regular team of sous-chefs to assist.

'Well, I'm without my chef too, and I can't seem to round up a table of friends. I don't really like eating alone, but I figured you'd keep me company,' I joke. I sit down at a table closest to the bench where Ottavio is working, and before long I am tucking into a new *primo* which Ottavio has cooked personally. He has replaced Alfonso's much-loved *sformato di melanzane*, an eggplant flan layered with *mozzarella* and a rich tomato *sugo*, with a flan with *alici*, anchovies, and ricotta.

'It's delicious!' I sing out to Ottavio, who is now dashing between the kitchen and tables of tourists dining outside, carrying wine and plates of food. I am tucking into my *secondo* of fresh fillets of *orata*, a white fleshy fish similar to bream, served with a gigantic salad, before he is finally able to join me.

Keen to avoid the subject of the chef's exodus, I ask Ottavio about his earliest memories of food.

His first recollection dates back to the age of four, he tells me, when his grandfather offered him a piece of mature gorgonzola. 'It had an even stronger taste than typical gorgonzola, and still today I can't manage to stomach it!' He laughs.

The family's meals were based around the produce from their garden. Every Sunday his mother would roast chicken or rabbit they had bred in their backyard.

Ottavio began to cook at an early age, beginning with a simple *sugo* of tomatoes after watching his mother prepare it daily.

When I suggest Procidan children have an idyllic youth, living in a tight-knit island community, Ottavio nods. Much of his childhood was spent playing in the garden with his younger sister, Antonella – who now waitresses at Bordero' – and other children in the area, but during summer the sea beckoned.

A favourite place was my own hideout, Punta Pizzaco, where Ottavio and his mates caught clams, which they'd cook with spaghetti. In winter, expeditions were organised to search for snails driven out of the island's gardens by the rain.

'Don't tell me you ate them!' I squirm, remembering my disgust at the slimy texture of the snails I once ordered while travelling in France.

'Of course! We'd cook them and pull them out of their shells with toothpicks!' says Ottavio, clapping his hands in glee at the memory. 'My mother used to cook them in a tomato *sugo* . . . they were delicious!'

Ottavio began working in the food game when he was thirteen, waitering at a local pizzeria, and before long he had landed a job at a restaurant at Chiaiolella.

'At first I worked as the barista, and then after a year I was setting tables, before I was finally allowed to start taking orders,' he says, adding that he was only around fifteen at the time.

'I liked the sense of control I had serving the tables, suggesting dishes and keeping everything running smoothly.'

To my surprise, Ottavio says that in his fifth year of high school he decided to enrol at the island's nautical institute. In Italy, there are two types of high school; in one students take subjects such as literature, history, maths and sciences. The other is the Technical Institute, where students learn a range of practical and vocational skills.

'I wanted to study the hotelier trade but the institute was at Ischia and my parents objected; I wasn't a good student and they were worried that if I went to Ischia I'd fall off the rails.'

Soon Ottavio was learning below-deck seafaring skills, but after he failed his first year he convinced his parents to let him study hospitality.

'Pretty soon my dream was to have my own bar or restaurant, but at that age it was all pie-in-the-sky stuff.'

Nonetheless, he kept dreaming of a restaurant offering *cucina procidana*, the local cuisine.

When I ask Ottavio how Bordero' came about he pours some more white *falanghina* wine in my glass and explains that he and two friends embarked on the venture in late 2005.

'We were all young so we were full of ideas and fantasy; we just had to put it all into practice.'

The trio was keen to give the local recipes a modern twist, rather than just opening a standard trattoria. The cuisine would be experimental but loyal to the flavours of the island.

'In the beginning, everyone said we were young upstarts making all the wrong decisions, but soon other restaurants started copying us,' he says with an air of smugness.

'But that is now the past,' Ottavio concludes sadly.

Keen to raise his spirits, I ask him what the secret is to being a good chef – maybe it will inspire me in my quest to overcome my trepidation of the kitchen.

'Passion,' he says simply. 'Even when you make a *sugo,* if you have the passion you stir it well; if you neglect it, it won't taste as good. You also need technique. Sure, you can take a recipe from a book, but a person with passion always thinks about how ingredients can be wedded; there is a marriage in the kitchen of love, food and wine.'

I laugh as I explain how, in our home, the food never tastes as good if Alfonso and I have had a fight, because he loses his passion for the job at hand.

I finish my *orata* and offer my compliments.

'Perhaps now it's time you turned your hand seriously to cooking,' I suggest.

'I've never cooked in restaurants . . . until yesterday,' Ottavio admits. 'It is so different from cooking at home. Here, the ovens are industrial and the quantities are bigger, and sometimes it's difficult to judge the right portion sizes. It's taking me a while to get used to it. But I've found a new chef who will start next week, and we'll put a new menu together.'

'I still reckon you should try and be the main chef.'

'Well, we'll see. It's fun, but it's a lot of work and I need more experience.'

'You just prefer being the star of the dining room,' I stir gently.

'Yes, Miss Penelope, you're right,' says Ottavio, looking at his watch. 'I'd better go, I have some things to prepare before tonight.'

I look out to the port and suddenly realise I am the only diner. I must lunch with myself more often.

A day before 15 August, the national *ferragosto* holiday, which marks the official start of the summer break when the last shops roll down their shutters, I stare out to sea from the lounge room with a sense of guilt. Alfonso's mother, Maria Rosaria, took her holidays in July so she is probably roasting in Naples now. Before I have time to reconsider I call and invite her to come over the next day to stay. There's no point inviting Alfonso's dad, Vincenzo, because he likes the comforts of home.

She gladly accepts, and I look around the living room in sudden anxiety. I must transform myself into a super *casalinga*, housewife, and make sure the apartment is spotless, just like Maria Rosaria's home, where you could eat off the floor. I sweep and mop, dust shelves and tables, and make up the sofa bed in the spare room with our best linen.

I am scrubbing the shower tiles the next morning when Maria Rosaria calls to say she caught an early ferry. I stifle a yelp. She is due in thirty minutes instead of an hour. I do a manic last-minute clean before I scurry down to the port.

As I walk I try to push aside images of buxom Brazilians fawning over my rock-star boyfriend while I entertain his mother!

Maria Rosaria steps off the boat, struggling with the sports bag in her hand.

'Have you done away with your husband and come here to scatter his remains?' I ask jokingly, as I wrest it from her.

'*Cara mia*, I've brought some things for you!' she says.

At home I watch nervously as Maria Rosaria scans the living room, which by my standards looks spic-and-span. Unzipping her bag, she pulls out a stash of goodies from Puglia, where one of her best friends lives: vine-ripened tomatoes, a bottle of red wine and some home-made *orecchiette* pasta. Finally, she produces a ceramic wine carafe and a matching serving tray. I hug Maria

Rosaria's cuddly frame before we put on our swimming costumes and head to the beach.

We walk up the street, slipping into single file when a car approaches. As Maria Rosaria stops every time a car passes, I realise how Procidan I have become, walking right up against the wall without stopping for traffic. Finally we reach the turn-off to via dei Bagni and walk down the stairs to the beach. To my dismay, piles of rubbish bags are stacked near the foot of the stairs.

We hire two beach chairs and I attempt to relax. Parked within arm's reach from us is a chubby family of four. At ten in the morning the mother and father and two children are already snacking on bread rolls filled with cured meat and cheese. I gaze at the loaded beach bag under their umbrella, wondering what other goodies they have packed to maintain their energy for a

High walls and narrow streets are typical on Procida

lazy day at the beach. A group of adults arrive and bicker over where to sit, and behind us the bar buzzes with the chit-chat of customers.

Maria Rosaria stands and wades into the water to cool down.

'I can't swim,' she says, on her return, 'but it's nice to put my feet in.'

I had not planned to spend the entire day at the beach, but suddenly the idea of staying at home for the afternoon is frightening. She'll probably want to iron my clothes and discover we don't even have an ironing board.

'I'm going to dash home to make a couple of rolls, I won't be long,' I tell her, sparking a small protest that I brush off with an insistent smile.

At home, I make our lunch and then reach for a cigarette. I don't smoke a great deal, usually only when I am nervous, and definitely not in front of my boyfriend's mother.

After less than two hours with her I am already stressed. Maria Rosaria and I have at least one thing in common: we are both restless by nature, a trait that is amplified in each other's company.

Try as I might, I can't overcome my suspicion that she is evaluating me as a potential daughter-in-law. I worry, too, about how long she plans to stay. I am quickly realising it might be a bit awkward without the buffer of Alfonso.

Back on the beach, the afternoon passes quickly between swimming, walking and napping and we return home to have a shower then walk down to Bar Capriccio for an *aperitivo*.

I have booked a table for dinner at nine at a restaurant at Corricella near our home, but by seven-thirty the minutes are dragging. I suggest a slow walk along the marina and on to the restaurant.

Half an hour early, we sit down at a table close to the waterfront, where a row of boats bobs gently. The air is soupy but every now and then a light breeze brings relief.

'It's so pretty here,' says Maria Rosaria and I smile in agreement. Streetlights illuminate the small port and its colourful buildings, which rise higgledy-piggledy up the hill. Above us the old prison is an imposing form on the cliff of Terra Murata.

We order an antipasto of seafood before the waiter rattles through the fish available that day as a *secondo*. The restaurant has no menu – and in any case in Italy it's always worth asking a waiter what is *fuori menu* (off the menu), since there is usually a special that is delicious and particularly fresh.

Our waiter recommends the *ricciola*, or amberjack, which he says is in season.

We both follow his recommendation and I order half a carafe of white wine. Just enough to keep me lubricated, but out of trouble.

The five or six tables nearby begin to fill and there is more than enough port action to keep a voyeuristic conversation afloat. On a small sailboat, a middle-aged couple sit eating dinner. Beside them, a large yacht resounds with the chatter of an extended family of grandparents, parents and children.

'I think they are Romans,' says Maria Rosaria, straining to hear the accent. Within seconds I hear a very Roman *aooooooo* and agree with her. While I can't identify all the different accents and dialects of Italy, the guttural Roman twang and the musical Venetian tones are two I can pick.

Our waiter appears with our antipasto plates, loaded with a seafood salad of clams, octopus marinated in olive oil, parsley and lemon, a frittata of anchovies, marinated anchovies and a swordfish *carpaccio*.

I take a sip of wine for courage before I broach the issue which, it occurs to me, has been the source of my anxiety since Maria Rosaria arrived: Alfonso and I plan to have a summer holiday in Australia in a few months' time. Though Alfonso has told his parents, I have not discussed the matter with Maria Rosaria, and I worry she won't cope well when we are away. Alfonso is, after all, her only child.

Alfonso has travelled and lived abroad and enjoys a very independent life, but that doesn't mean Maria Rosaria worries about him any less.

'*Cara*, I'm sure you will have a wonderful time. I'm sure your mother will be glad to see you,' she says, lifting a weight off my shoulders.

As Maria Rosaria breezily peppers me with questions about Australia I respond happily until our seconds arrive. The *ricciola* is delicious; moist and delicate in flavour, just as the waiter promised. Knowing Maria Rosaria's weakness for dessert, I don't have to work hard to coax her to have the *torta caprese*, which I help her demolish before we leave at ten o'clock. As we go, I notice that the restaurant is buzzing with customers who are only just arriving.

The next morning we return to the beach, but by midday the bay of bathers has turned the water into a suncream-streaked bath.

'How about I whip up a pasta?' says Maria Rosaria when we arrive home.

'It's a bit hot for pasta. Why don't I make a big Greek salad?' I suggest.

As we eat I realise my mistake. Maria Rosaria is never happier than when she is useful; I should have let her fuss and cook, but it's too late now.

Perhaps as tired of second-guessing as me, after lunch Maria Rosaria suggests we take a nap.

An hour later I wake to find Maria Rosaria reading in the living room, her neatly packed luggage nearby.

'I might get going, I promised a friend in Naples I'd visit her today,' she says, graciously.

I smile at her gratefully and pick up her bag.

As soon as Maria Rosaria's face on the outdoor deck of the ferry has become a speck in the distance I make a beeline for Bar Capriccio.

'One *spritz*, *subito*,' I ask Enzo, who reads my face and bursts into laughter.

'When's Alfonso due home?' he asks.

'I know it's been hard on you too, but you'll have to survive another month or so,' I joke.

An hour later Maria Rosaria asks me the same question via a text message.

I sigh out loud and reply that I am not exactly sure, but as soon as I have word I will let her know.

Sitting beside me on a bar stool, Glorianna gives me a sympathetic pat on the back. She's currently living with her mother because her lease dictates she must leave her small apartment for two months during summer so her landlord can charge a higher rent to holiday-makers.

In the evening I head back to Corricella, where the annual *Sagra degli alici* (festival of the anchovies) is due to begin. Being a huge fan of the small, pungent fish, I am looking forward to loading my plate up with them.

A rainbow of wooden fishing boats line the port, where groups of women in white aprons and blue headscarves assemble a long row of tables and drape them with colourful fishing nets.

In its maritime heyday, Procida was famous around the world

View from Terra Murata of the sunny Corricella port

for nets. Gilda's father was an expert in the trade. When he died, she said, the island lost its best netting artisan. At Corricella and down at Marina Grande, I love to watch men of varying ages mending nets they nurse on their laps.

As the women in the stalls slice bread and gossip, a bunch of children suddenly emerges from a house nearby dragging plastic bags. They set themselves up on the concrete near the water's edge and empty the bags, filled with Barbie dolls, hand-painted stones and clothes they obviously intend to sell in a spontaneous flea market. They soon begin arguing among themselves as to how to arrange their goods and who will act as vendor.

The sun slowly drops to make way for twilight and I hear a voice cry, 'Hey Pe!' It's Glorianna and Candida, who are generally inseparable.

I grin when I see Carlo, our Procidan friend who lives in Palermo, walking beside them. He occasionally comes back on weekends to visit his family.

We walk along the port to buy a ticket which will entitle us to a plate of *alici* and fresh tuna that are being fried on grills along the waterside. The heavy aroma of anchovies saturates the air and the port fills with families keen for a stroll and a feed. We pile our plates high with the seafood, buy glasses of locally made white wine and find seats at a table. Soon our friends Maria Grazia, Gennaro and Graziella join us.

As a half-moon hangs in the sky above the sea, Carlo reminisces about growing up on the island he obviously misses.

'When we were young, our favourite thing to do was to *fare i camponi*.'

'What do you mean?' I ask.

'Basically we roamed the island in search of a garden that we could get into,' he begins. 'We'd hide our bikes and climb over the gate then raid all the fruit and vegetables. We'd eat everything at the scene of the crime . . . even raw artichokes!'

He snuggles up to Glorianna in mock affection. She pushes him off and gives him a friendly whack. I know the two have a close friendship, and also that Carlo once dated Eliana, who sits nearby beside her boyfriend Gigi. Evidently, dating on a small island often means there are only three degrees of separation, or less.

'We used to be just as bad with seafood, eating everything we could get our hands on. We ate raw clams, and if someone was really tough they would eat live prawns and crabs! I had a forty-degree fever and food poisoning four times when I was young from eating them . . . but I still love it!'

Gennaro appears with another carafe of white wine as Carlo regales us with tales of the diving competitions of his youth. The higher and more dangerous the jump the better. One favourite spot was Punta Pizzaco, where Elisa told me the baby had been abandoned.

'We'd keep our sneakers on because the cliff was so high that our feet would hurt when we hit the water,' Carlo explains. 'Only the true professionals dived head-first, but you'd never do a really big jump that way, otherwise you risked losing your penis!'

The group dissolves into laughter, and the tales grow increasingly taller before we decide to head to Bar Capriccio.

I hitch a ride with Glorianna, along with Candida and Graziella.

'Whose car is that?' asks Candida, as she eyeballs the small silver car in front of us.

I stifle a giggle as, for the next few minutes, Glorianna and my fellow passengers try to confirm who is in the car ahead. In most places you wouldn't have a hope of knowing – or care about knowing – such a fact, but on Procida you can't sneeze without being noticed.

As the driver finally pulls over to park we pass and the girls exclaim in unison that it is Valeria, who has just bought a new car. With the puzzle resolved, they begin to chat about something else.

Already swaying in Bar Capriccio when we arrive, Carlo announces that the day Glorianna caves in to his advances he will erect a Christmas tree outside Bar Cavaliere.

We shriek at the absurdity of the idea and settle in for a round of drinks.

The next day I get a text message from Glorianna saying she is heading to the lighthouse to sunbake. Saved from a hangover by drinking three glasses of water before retiring the night before, I get dressed and head along via Faro in the hot mid-morning sun. A horn toots and I turn to see Carlo, who stops to offer me a lift.

Down on the rocks I spot Glorianna and Candida. As we spread out our towels Fabrizio arrives with Eliana, her sister Marina and Marina's boyfriend Rosario.

We laze on the rocks until Carlo, Fabrizio and Rosario stand and don wetsuits.

'We're off to see if we can catch some *ricci*,' says Carlo, adjusting a knife he's tucked into his belt.

A good hour later the boys return, exhausted, and I watch in delight as Carlo empties a canvas bag loaded with the black, spiky *ricci*, or sea urchins. He gives the bag one final shake and I squeal as an octopus falls onto the rocks. It appears Carlo has not managed to grow out of the mischievous thieving habits of his youth.

Glorianna grabs the knife and the women in our group begin shucking the *ricci*.

'Pe! Come and try one!' says Glorianna.

I look down at the urchin which she has carefully cut in half for my enjoyment. Lining the two shells are thin streaks of an orange roe which I scrape with my finger. It has a fishy, salty flavour I can only compare to a more sour version of anchovies.

Within an hour the group splits up to head home for lunch.

'What's *mamma* cooking for you today?' I tease Carlo, who had mentioned during the *sagra* that he loves coming home to be spoilt.

'Calamari with peas and I suspect she's whipped up a wicked dessert!' he says with glee.

That evening I wander past Elisa and Michele's home, headed towards Solchiaro. Our friend Graziella has invited the Bar Capriccio crew to her house for dinner, and asked everyone to bring a plate of food or a bottle of wine. I have learned that it's considered perfectly acceptable to ask guests to bring a contribution to the meal, especially if you're inviting a big group along.

I have made couscous spiced with mint, parsley and tomato, which I have no doubt will be appreciated but not devoured with as much gusto as the other dishes. Italians like nothing better than their own cuisine.

Graziella has jokingly organised the evening in competition with the other big event of the night, *La Graziella*, considered the highlight of the *Sagra del mare*, or the festival of the sea, staged annually at Marina Grande and now in its fifty-eighth year.

La Graziella is a fashion parade inspired by the book of the same name by a French poet, Alphonse de Lamartine. During a trip to Italy, he fell in love not only with Procida but with Graziella, the young daughter of a local fisherman. Forced to leave her to return to France, where he would eventually become the Foreign Affairs Minister during the second republic, Alphonse fails to fulfil his promise of returning to the island, where Graziella has fallen ill. Before she dies, she sends Alfonse a letter containing a lock of her hair that he will keep with remorse for the rest of his life.

Elisa's two daughters, Maria Pia and Paola, have both taken part in the contest, in which entrants wear traditional Procidan attire. Indeed, Procidan families have passed the dresses down as heirlooms over the generations, making the contest a true showcase of local culture.

The feature of the costume is the coloured *crespo*, a fringed silk scarf that is wrapped in a turban around the head. This was traditionally worn by women on the island on special occasions,

such as weddings or baptisms, while they donned a linen version
for everyday wear.

The whole costume comprises layer upon layer of silk and
cotton garments, covered by an embroidered silk coat and a
fringed linen scarf wrapped around the shoulders.

In the boiling August heat, surely contestants in the *La Graziella*
parade must wish they could strip down to the bikinis they wear
all summer long? However, unlike a modern-day beauty pageant
where looks are everything, Procida's *Grazielle* are judged by their
traditional costumes, their comportment and a certain youthful
freshness, which renders them most like Lamartine's heroine.

As I reach the contemporary Graziella's front door I half regret
not going to see *La Graziella*. With a bit of luck I'll be able to
make it back to the port in time for all the action . . .

Naturally, my best intentions are thwarted by a smorgasbord
of food and dancing, which lasts well past midnight. So the next
morning I am pleased when I hear *la macchina* – a car that circles
the island with a loudspeaker to make community announcements
– confirm that *La Graziella* will be televised on a local station
at midnight.

At eleven o'clock I struggle to keep my eyes open, but I manage
to stay awake until the program begins. As the contestants recite
parts of Lamartine's book and move awkwardly around the stage
in their heavy costumes, I am both amused and touched by what
is obviously a highly anticipated event, judging by the size of
the crowd.

I wake with a start to find myself still on the couch, the
morning news buzzing in the background. Damn. I fell asleep
before the winner was announced.

At my local newsagent a few days later, I buy the new issue
of *Procida Oggi*, the island's monthly newspaper, which has a
front-page photo of the winning *Graziella*. As I read the article, I

wonder if the judging panel were at all swayed by the fact that the winning brunette happens to work at Bar Graziella in Corricella. Talk about a happy coincidence.

In the late afternoon, when the sting of the sun has faded, I go for a long walk and a quick dip at the lighthouse before I inevitably find myself drawn to the port.

At the entrance of Bar Capriccio I stop short. There, in a small pot, is a fir Christmas tree with a small note on top reading *Grazie*. I burst into laughter, wondering if Carlo has finally had his wicked way. Within minutes Glorianna pulls up on her Vespa. As she approaches the doorway she shrieks in horror and races into the bar.

'It's not true, that cretin!' she protests, looking around for Carlo. Minutes later, he swaggers into the bar, where Glorianna launches herself at him with a flurry of punches.

'I never said I wouldn't put up a Christmas tree at all,' he protests.

He joins me at a table outside, and Gloriana – calmer now – comes and sits with us too. Carlo's long August holiday is about to end, but Glorianna will stay on the island. She rarely takes a holiday from her job as receptionist for Doctor Cardito.

Eventually Carlo stands up, ready to leave.

'Ah, so you're going back home, hey? No doubt your mother is slaving over the oven as we speak. What's on the menu for dinner?' I rib.

Carlo blushes, unusual since he can normally give as good as he gets. It is only when he links his arm through that of an attractive older woman who has been standing nearby that I realise my gaffe.

'Penelope, let me present you to my mother,' he says, doubling over in laughter alongside everyone else in earshot.

To her credit, Carlo's mother smiles graciously and shakes my hand before disappearing with her still chuckling son.

AGOSTO
Torta Caprese
(Capri cake)

Caprese (Car-pray-se!) on an Italian menu either means a salad of sliced tomatoes and *mozzarella* with basil and olive oil, or a flourless chocolate and almond *torta*, or cake. Both are said to have originated on Capri, where legend has it the sweet version was created by accident in the 1920s by a cook who forgot to add flour to her cake. Flat and crunchy on the outside and moist within, the *Caprese* also comes in a lemon version. I've included both, starting with the classic recipe:

Serves 8

> 300 grams blanched almonds
> 250 grams dark chocolate
> 250 grams butter
> 6 eggs
> 250 grams sugar
> 60 millilitres (1 espresso cup) Marsala cooking wine
> dash of vanilla
> ½ cup icing sugar

Method

1. Measure the almonds into a blender and grind to the size of breadcrumbs (or put them in a bag and stomp on them; a fun and healthy way to build up dessert appetite, but it might take you a while!).

2. Place the chocolate and butter in a bowl and melt by resting on top of a saucepan of simmering water. Don't allow water to touch bottom of bowl. Cool.

3. Preheat oven to 170 degrees Celsius.

4. Separate the egg yolks and whites.

5. Whip yolks with the sugar until creamy and light in colour. Add the cooking wine and vanilla, tip into the bowl with the cooled melted chocolate and butter and mix to combine. Then add the almonds.

6. Whip the egg whites into peaks and fold gently into the chocolate mix.

7. Pour the mixture into a 30 centimetre spring-form cake tin lined with oven paper and cook for an hour, or until a skewer inserted into the centre comes out clean.

8. Remove the cake from the tin, allow to cool, then dust with icing sugar.

For a finished *torta* that is less *umido* (wet) inside, a Procidan lady I met recommended adding a few extra measurements (such as an extra 100 grams of almonds, and *amaretti biscotti*). If you like sambuca you can substitue it for the Marsala.

To make the *Caprese al limone* (lemon Caprese), substitute the dark chocolate for white, then add a teaspoon of baking powder and the chopped rind of two lemons at stage 5. Instead of Marsala, use a limoncello liqueur (try your local Italian deli). If you can't source it, just add the juice of one lemon. *Semplice.*

SETTEMBRE

Doctor's orders

September the first is Alfonso's birthday, which would be smashing if only he'd cart himself back home. I've enjoyed a scorching August of *aperitivi* and beach time with the Bar Capriccio gang, but I am more than *pronta* for the return of my favourite playmate, chef and dialect translator.

Like the small boats I spy from the lounge-room window, tossing in the bad weather, I feel more exposed to the elements when I'm alone.

After an initial high of adventure, akin to the adrenalin rush I get whenever I set foot in a foreign country, I have ridden waves of nostalgia for my family and Alfonso, of exhilaration and appreciation for the rugged beauty around me, and of both pleasure and frustration as I get to know the locals, who are as generous and friendly as they are reclusive.

I have a vague idea it's just past midnight in Brazil when I call Alfonso to wish him many happy returns. My heart thumps in anticipation before I hear the familiar '*Pronto*'. I burst into a clamorous rendition of '*Tanti auguri a te*'.

Alfonso is on a bus returning to the band's hotel after performing another gig at the week-long ethnic rock festival. Some of the musicians around him have broken into a spontaneous jam session, so he yells to be heard as he fills me in on his impressions of Brazil, from the local food to his visit to the *favelas*.

'*Dai Chunky, ci manca poco,*' he says, reminding me he'll be home soon; in four days, to be precise.

Reassured, I hang up, but moments later my telephone rings. I am surprised to see my parents' number flash on its screen.

'Pen, I hate to be the bearer of bad news, but Pa passed away this morning,' my father says in a broken voice.

My heart tightens when I think of the last time I saw my grandfather. He was in a nursing home in Sydney. I had put on the brightest face I could manage as we spent the afternoon together, until I said goodbye and left his room to collapse into my father's arms. Seeing the strong man I always idolised reduced to frailty had not been easy, likewise the sense of guilt that is inherent with living so far away from loved ones.

'He had a good innings, it's mostly a relief,' says my father, reading my thoughts.

'We don't expect you to come home for the funeral, it's a long flight for what will be a few distressing hours . . . Just remember him in the reasonably good form you found him in last time.' As much as I want to fly home, I know my father is right.

After I hang up from Dad I walk into the lounge room to stare at the black-and-white photo on the wall. My grandfather is dressed in a smart suit and bowler hat, pacing a city street at

Circular Quay in Sydney, with my grandmother walking coyly beside him. The photo was taken before they were married, and shortly after they had met at the accountancy firm where Pa worked. Granny had been hired as a receptionist in the days when connecting someone meant pulling plugs in and out of a switchboard.

I open the bottom drawer of the cupboard in the lounge room and take out the transcript of an informal interview I did with my grandfather about sixteen years ago. I'd just finished school and had moved from country New South Wales to Sydney in search of work as a journalist, and I was glad when Pa agreed to let me stay with him for a while. Given that Gran had passed away months earlier, he was no doubt glad to have some company.

We chatted around a tape recorder in the leafy backyard, Pa's favourite place to do the *Sydney Morning Herald* cryptic crossword and listen to the cricket or talkback radio on his tinny transistor. In that hour, I caught a rare glimpse of his earliest years and his thoughts on various topics, like life after death, and whether he might see Gran on the other side. Pa was too much of a sceptic. As tears roll down my face, I can only hope he was wrong after living without his soul-mate for sixteen years.

I begin to dial Alfonso's number then change my mind. All things considered, it can wait until he returns. It's times like these I wish I had a magic carpet so I could fly home and into my parents' arms. I can't help but think the fact Alfonso's birthday is on the day Pa left the earth is somehow a good omen, but I am not sure if his Neapolitan superstitions would agree.

I head outdoors for a walk to distract myself and instinctively head to Elisa and Michele's home. Feeling resistance behind the gate I bump into Michele, who says he is off to visit his brother, who has terminal cancer. I tell him my news and he pats me on the back before casting me a weary look.

'Every time I leave my brother's house I feel so useless. There is nothing I can say . . . like "take care" or "things will be better tomorrow".'

'I know it's hardly a comfort, but I'm sure your brother is so grateful for your company every day,' I reply gently.

'I guess so,' Michele manages, his voice betraying his grief.

He leaves abruptly. There's nothing more heartbreaking than seeing a grown man in pieces. I drag my feet along the garden path, wishing I could bury death in the rows of vegetables around me.

I call Elisa's name before I let myself into the kitchen, where I find her standing at the table kneading some dough.

'Pe, how are you? I'm just making *pasta e fagioli* – pasta with cannellini beans – for lunch. Pay attention and you'll soon be a master!' she says with a smile, which makes way for a frown when she sees my flat expression. As I sit down, she pulls out a chair next to me at the table and I tell her of the morning's events and a little about my grandfather. She takes my hands in hers and simply listens, every now and then throwing in the odd *certo* (certainly) or *giusto* (right), without any of those platitudes that people often say to one another in times of grief, because they don't know how else to respond. I comment on how tough things are for Michele at the moment and she nods. Then in one shared glance we understand that, as is the way in life, there's nothing one can do but put on a bright face and move ahead.

Keen to be distracted I ask Elisa to fill me in on the culinary tasks at hand. She beckons me to the stove and raises the lid of a saucepan filled with simmering cannellini beans. *Pasta e fagioli* happens to be one of my favourite meals. It's made of a few cheap – or *poveri,* poor, as the Italians say – ingredients that combine to make a hearty and tasty meal.

'Buy the dried beans from your local deli and then put them in a dish of cold water to soak overnight,' Elisa says, her voice once again taking on an instructive tone. 'The next day, rinse the beans, put them in a saucepan and cover them with water then bring them to boiling point, and let them simmer for an hour.'

Elisa pauses, dips a spoon into the saucepan and tastes a bean she soon judges as cooked.

'Now you add a handful of cherry tomatoes, a few garlic cloves and a couple of sticks of celery.'

Traditionally, the pasta added at the end, when the tomatoes and celery have softened, is a hotch-potch of everything; whatever you can find in your pantry.

'Just make sure you check the cooking time of the different pastas and add them accordingly,' Elisa warns.

'When the pasta is *al dente* I add a drizzle of oil, a pinch of pepper and salt and a squeeze of lemon . . . delicious!'

With a cheery *buongiorno,* Maria Pia wanders into the kitchen. With wide green eyes and a dusting of freckles across her nose and cheeks, she radiates good health.

As Elisa keeps an eye on the *pasta e fagioli,* Maria Pia and I sit at the table and talk.

Maria's Pia's sailor husband, Stefano, is away for three months working on a cargo ship running daily from Messina, in Sicily, to Salerno, just south of Naples. A week earlier, she went on board for three days to spend time with him, a privilege that simply was not an option three decades ago for Elisa, who sometimes endured up to a year without seeing Michele.

'When I arrived I jokingly told the crew that I was ready to get to work,' says Maria Pia, who is a qualified mechanic, adding that Stefano's colleagues were impressed. While she was on board, Stefano's mother took care of their two young children, Eleanora and Pier Paolo. I have always suspected the elderly in Italy live to such a ripe old age not only because of their healthy Mediterranean diet, but because they are actively involved in the lives of their children and grandchildren. I feel a pang of guilt for being away from my grandfather for so long in his twilight years, though I remind myself that he always encouraged me to see the world.

When Michele arrives home at seven o'clock, just in time for dinner, Maria Pia and Elisa don't have to work hard to convince me to join their family meal.

'*Buon appetito!*' Elisa says, placing our plates of *pasta e fagioli* on the table.

I suddenly remember how, when I was living with Pa, I struggled to think of new dishes to cook him. Poor fellow, no wonder he drove to McDonald's once a week to enjoy a Big Mac.

'What are some traditional meals in Australia?' asks Maria Pia, interrupting my thoughts.

I smile as I think of how I might tell her about a lamington or a meat pie before explaining that while traditionally Australians served up meat and three veg, nowadays our cuisine is a multicultural melting pot, reflecting the traditions of scores of migrants.

'I love Italian food, but the thing I miss most about home is the choice.' I say that in inner-city Sydney, where my sister lives, 'typical' cuisine ranges from Indian, Thai and Vietnamese to Japanese, Chinese and Nepalese.

With dinner over, I try to help Michele wash the dishes but he shoos me out the door.

By nine o'clock I am standing in the kitchen in my own home, staring at a photo of my grandfather which I took at my sister Sally's wedding, when I remember something Elisa told me amid the flurry of activity in her kitchen.

'I never have a moment to spare, I'm always here, or in the garden, or embroidering!' she said exuberantly, wiping her large, wrinkled hands on her cotton apron. 'You have to always keep busy here, otherwise you enter a tunnel.'

Comforted by Elisa and Michele and their warmth and hospitality, I nonetheless feel at a loss as I mourn for my grandfather and my loved ones. I feel like I have one foot in the tunnel . . .

As I walk into our apartment building I hear the squeals of children from the *asilo,* or childcare centre, which recently opened on the ground floor. The door is wide open, so I seize the moment and pop my head inside. A slim blonde woman is holding a small dark-haired child on one hip. Snot drizzles from the child's nostrils, making me wish I had a tissue on hand.

Before I have time to change my mind, I introduce myself and explain that I live in the building and am keen to teach some English.

I feel my cheeks flushing wildly as I speak. The truth is I am scared witless by the idea of having to instruct, entertain or merely *be with* young children on my own for more than a few minutes. Before meeting Alfonso, I've enjoyed a mostly single existence with similarly childless friends, and while I have cherished playing with my five nieces and nephew on infrequent trips home to Australia, I've never had trouble saying goodbye to the little terrors.

On Procida, however, I've been more exposed to children, including Enzo and Gilda's twins, Michele and Angelo. When Michele first held my hand, after stubbornly refusing for months, my heart melted and I had to admit to myself that the idea of being a mum was becoming more appealing.

My fear of turning thirty is slowly being superseded by a mild paranoia about having children too late. I am not yet convinced my biological clock is ticking for the right motives.

Unlike marriage, to which I remain ambivalent, kids are for good, I keep reminding myself. No law can annul them, there's no refund or rewind.

As a result, while warming to the idea of having children, neither Alfonso nor I are sure it's for us. I figure teaching English to tots would be a fast way to find out. If worst comes to worst, my career will last just one petrifying hour.

The manager of the *asilo*, Anna, says many of the parents are keen for their offspring to learn English. Since the children at the centre are all under the age of four, she tells me that the best way to teach them is through games. When she invites me to hold my first class within a few days I hide my panic and smile confidently.

Con Calma. With Calm.

The title of a magazine article in one of the weekend newspapers draws me into an analysis of the global trend of downsizing.

Change the rhythm of your life. Work less, earn less, consume less.

Well, I have left manic Naples for a pebble in the sea. I have no permanent employment so, yes, I have a reduced wage, and since Alfonso has gone our food and gas bills have halved.

Choose quality over quantity and dedicate time to yourself and relationships with others.

After breakfast I wander up to the terrace with the magazine and stand in the sun with my elbows on the balcony ledge. At Chiaia beach below, the water is as flat as a plate, while directly out to sea, Capri is only a fuzzy outline beneath morning haze.

It might be good to live with more *calma*, and emails from my friends about their rat-race lives remind me how lucky I am. But now how am I going to fill all this flipping *calma*? When not pitching ideas to magazines, I find myself wasting hours on the internet and generally loafing around. I've never had problems with lack of motivation before. So what's wrong with me?

Some days pass with me barely uttering a word to anyone, and when I do socialise with my friends my inability to decipher their dialect makes me feel like a fish out of water so I usually head home early. I feel flat, so much so that I can't even bring myself to face the small island community.

And to think I was told that foreigners on Procida go batty in the depths of *winter*, not in September, when the weather is still glorious.

Fingers crossed, teaching English will help me to feel like I'm part of the community.

I pace about the apartment in a state of panic before Anna calls to let me know she is downstairs and would like to meet for a chat before I start my first English class.

I grab some paper, Textas and a few photocopied sheets of activities I've come up with after some web research, and walk down the steps with the trepidation of a bride-to-be.

Inside the childcare centre I swallow my mounting fear and listen as carefully as possible while Anna shows me around.

'You just need to repeat lots of words, like colours and animals and so on, and if they get bored, take them into the playroom. And obviously speak as much English as you can,' she says.

My jaw has already tightened from putting on a bright face as mothers and fathers drop off their children. I wonder if kids are like dogs, and have the ability to smell fear. At the very least I hope parents don't.

It is almost time for the class to begin when the only boy in the group of the nine fidgeting kids at my feet starts sobbing. He hides behind his mother.

'Cosmo, you can play some fun games now with your new *maestra,* Penelope!' says Anna, who takes advantage of Cosmo's momentary distraction at the word *games* to drag his mother out of the room.

I stare at Cosmo and will him to keep the peace.

'Let's start by writing our own name tags!' I say gaily.

As I stand on tiptoes to get some pencils from a high shelf I feel a cold hand pass over the skin above my jeans, where my shirt has slipped up. I swing around and see Cosmo, whose tears have evaporated to make way for what his mother would probably call a playful smile, but I recognise as the Evil Eye!

Somehow I manage to get all the kids sitting at the three miniature tables and soon they are scribbling their names with varying degrees of skill.

'*Ho finito!*' cries out a blonde-haired girl named Alessandra. She orders me to come to her and I put on an impressed look when I inspect the indecipherable scrawl on her tag. Obviously three-year-olds are too young to write.

'Very good,' I say, pinning her tag to her shirt. As I fiddle with the clasp I hear her little heartbeat and suddenly realise just how tiny and vulnerable children are. As Alessandra stares at me with enormous hazel eyes I feel a strange new weight of responsibility.

With shrieks at every turn indicating this game is over, I begin to panic about running out of things to do. I am an adult who enjoys a large degree of control over my environment, yet here I am with only a skerrick of authority over a writhing octopus of arms and legs.

I take a deep breath and give myself a silent pep talk. *Kids are nothing to be scared of. You are roughly thirty years older than them. They, not you, should be peeing their pants.* Cripes, come to think of it, Anna didn't tell me if they are toilet trained.

I clap my hands and announce that we are about to learn a song in English to sing to their parents later.

'Head, shoulders, knees and toes, knees and toes,' I sing with as much energy as I can muster. I can't believe I ever thought the antics of the *Play School* television presenters were ridiculous. I reckon they should get paid as much as the prime minister.

To my profound relief, the kids are soon at least mouthing the words and tapping their heads, shoulders, knees and toes (knees and toes), and my heart bursts as I see their little hands swinging without coordination and their eyes as wide as saucers. Even Cosmo can't get enough of it.

Better still, they keep calling me *maestra,* which seems to indicate that by some miracle they think I *am* in control.

I have only just let the kids dive into the plastic pool of coloured balls in the main play area when the parents start to stream in. I look nervously at Anna and note how slender she is. Now I know why. I bet she doesn't even have time to have a snack in her average morning.

I call out the kids' names in Italian and try to hustle them into a group as the parents look on curiously. Pushing aside nerves I start singing the song and to my relief the kids not only remember most of it, but practically exhaust their vocal cords while singing together. As the parents clap with joy and pride for their little tackers I visualise stepping onto a Lego podium to be given a pink plastic trophy for my efforts as Best New Teaching Talent for Kids. Watch and weep, Wiggles.

As I pack away the pencils and coloured playdough, I see Cosmo's mother approaching me to say thanks.

When she says she'd like her son to learn English once or twice a week, I nod with enthusiasm – silently vowing to always wear a belt – and tell her that I will arrange some fixed teaching days with Anna.

'Say goodbye to your *maestra*,' says Anna to Cosmo. To my surprise he strides over to me and gives me a kiss on the cheek. Bless.

'Now say goodbye to your other *maestra*,' says Anna expectantly. Cosmo makes a beeline for me and gives me another kiss.

'Well, you *were* a hit,' says Anna breezily as she scoops Cosmo up for a kiss.

I bid farewell to my class and head outdoors to get some air. I could be walking on the stuff, despite the fact my head feels like one of the deflated balls that lie in a corner of the playroom. I think of my older sister Lisa, a working mother of two with another on the way, and my middle sister Sally, who is a full-time mother of three kids under the age of seven. *Mamma mia,* indeed.

Around lunchtime I wander towards Corricella. Down at the tiny port, a banana tree sprouting from the hull of an abandoned boat turned enormous pot plant is flourishing in the unique microclimate. It's always a good five degrees warmer there, which explains why I visited so rarely at the height of summer.

Halfway along the port I notice a sign outside a restaurant indicating that it was featured in *Il Postino* (The Postman). In fact, many of the most memorable scenes in the film unfold down at Corricella. It was here that *il postino*, played by the late Massimo Troisi, first cast eyes on comely local lass Beatrice as she worked at her family's trattoria, now directly opposite me.

The trattoria has since been refurbished, but almost fifteen years after *Il Postino* won critical acclaim around the world, there has barely been a ripple of change at Corricella.

Orange and rust-red fishing nets are piled atop rows of simple boats in varying stages of decay. A child's plastic tricycle sits

Barbie dolls for sale at a spontaneous summer market at Corricella

abandoned on the concrete outside one of the narrow houses, with their beautiful arches and external staircases leading up to the second floor.

A much loved Neapolitan-born actor, director and poet, Troisi died of a heart attack shortly after the filming of *Il Postino* was completed.

My Procidan friends recall the excitement the film shoot generated on the island, when they would finish school and race to see the action.

'You could see Troisi was suffering from his heart problems. He had to swap hotels because the first one he stayed in had steps leading to his room and he just couldn't manage,' my mate Graziella recalled. 'When he passed away, we were all gutted. Troisi wasn't just an actor. He was an intellect, a philosopher. He had a unique way of representing Neapolitans.'

I hear a whistle and look up to see another friend, Eliana, standing at a window in the musk pink building further along the port. Keen to see the apartment she is refurbishing, I follow her instructions and enter the building via a narrow set of stairs leading from a dark passageway behind the marina.

Eliana is waiting for me in her doorway on the second floor. Dressed in a short denim skirt and a bright pink singlet layered over a bottle green one, her style is Madonna circa 1980.

Painted on the wall in the main room are pastel-coloured designs of Procidan houses; all arches and long staircases.

'You did those, didn't you? They're gorgeous!' I exclaim as I gaze around the spacious, split-level room. Still devoid of furniture, it has a beautiful tiled floor in a Mediterranean blue, curved white stone walls and a wood-fired oven. As Eliana shows me around, I can't hold back my gasps of admiration, my glance shifting from the bathroom with its enormous tub, to the two bedrooms and back to the living room, all with views of the port, the sea and Terra Murata rising from the cliffs.

Finally, we walk out onto the small terrace off the kitchen, where there is a small table with an umbrella, rustic marble sink with taps decorated with fragments of coloured tiles.

On the table I notice a bound blue leather book, which I pick up. It's Eliana's thesis on marine biology; she has recently graduated with a degree in environmental sciences. On the spine, I note her surname for the first time: *Altomare*, which means high sea. Appropriate for an island dweller.

I open the thesis and flick from the back, past complicated oceanic charts and scientific equations, to a short quote on the front page.

I often roam with my bicycle on my island, watching the sea that surrounds it, the distant lights and the boats that stop in the bay. There is he who thinks the island limits you, but I'll tell you the truth, it gives you a complete sense of liberty. To be born on an island is a fortune, you develop a love for the sea from a young age, and over the years you learn more and more to understand it. The sea becomes a part of you.

I suddenly envy Eliana's affinity with her surroundings.

'Why don't you feel limited by the island?' I ask.

Eliana sits down beside me on the warm terracotta tiles.

'When I come down here to Corricella it brings me all the peace in the world. I don't feel restricted, just lucky.'

I drop my gaze to watch a group of fishermen mending nets just below the balcony, then glance at the pretty confusion of pastel-coloured buildings that surround us. Eliana certainly is fortunate. Her grandmother left her not just her apartment but the whole building. During summer she rents a few units below her nest to holiday-makers.

'So you're filling in time here doing up the house as you look for work?' I ask, as she rolls some tobacco into a cigarette.

She nods.

'I want to find a job. I'd love to work on an oceanography boat, going out to take samples to monitor and protect the sea, or maybe in a marine park, but I always want to be able to return here at night. Even if I have nothing to do when I'm here it's a healthy lifestyle, just being by the sea,' she says, her emerald eyes skimming over the water below.

'Most of the apartments here have been bought by outsiders who use them as holiday homes, because the Procidans don't like living in Corricella.'

'Why on earth not?' I ask, incredulous at the idea that any islander wouldn't want to live in the warm, tranquil oasis.

'Because it's a bit isolated, and you can only reach it by the steep staircases. Procidans hate walking, and consider fifty metres on foot a tragedy. But I love it, because it's like an island in itself. It's not like the Marina Grande, with its traffic and shops and ferries; here there are just fishermen.'

Eliana falls silent and takes a final puff on her rollie.

'The sun rises here, in the east, and stays all day, which I love. In summer there's too much chaos with the motorboats and restaurants, but in winter it's beautiful, because there is no one here; at around four in the afternoon, not a soul.'

Eliana turns to me and asks if I would like to live permanently on Procida, perhaps even buy a house.

I shrug.

'Some outsiders fall in love with Procida, but usually strange types,' she says.

'I love it here. I love being near the sea and I don't want to live anywhere else in Italy,' I begin, struggling to collect my thoughts. 'There are just little conveniences that I miss. If I want to go swimming in a pool, for example, I have to catch a boat to Ischia or Naples, swim and travel back, and that's half a day gone, whereas in Australia I can do the same thing in a quarter of the time.'

'Oh, I see,' says Eliana. 'So you feel like you are losing time?'

I nod, asking her if I am an oddity in considering the minutes that pass in a day.

'No,' she reassures me. 'There are Procidans like you, but I'm different, I have another rhythm . . .' Her voice trails off, leaving me with no clue as to how I can find my own island mojo.

The day of Alfonso's return finally dawns and I hurry to the port to catch the early ferry to Naples. By chance, my dear Australian friend Daniela has travelled from Rome to Naples for work, and we've arranged to have lunch before I head out to Alfonso's parents' place to wait for their only son to come home. I plan to use the morning in Naples to run a few errands; in particular I want to buy some ingredients I can't source on the island.

Arriving early at the port, I buy my ticket and turn to see Nicola, our lawyer friend, who tells me he is catching the hydrofoil, which leaves half an hour after the ferry.

'Come on, you've got time for a coffee,' he says, dragging me into a bar.

As I listen to his chatter I soon lose track of time, and suddenly realise my ferry is due to depart. Waiting for Nicola, who is paying our bill, I am seized by panic when I see a ferry already docked.

'Nicola, isn't that my boat?' I ask as we walk out of the bar.

'Yes, hurry!'

I sing out farewell and quicken my step as I glance at the ferry. Hearing the familiar grind of the ramp, I begin to run and make a spectacular jump to land on the rising platform.

My jubilation at having made it onto my boat fades when I walk down the ramp to see a wall of people, mostly men, standing before me. I turn to face the port and my worst suspicions are confirmed. The ramp is lowering. The boat is just arriving. I blush wildly as I see Nicola's laughing face in the crowd. I brush past the passengers waiting to alight and disappear as fast as I can up the stairs to find a seat.

As the ferry makes its way to the mainland I read to contain my growing excitement at the prospect of seeing Alfonso again. I sneak a look at a happy snap of the two of us, before I bury my nose in my book again.

A few hours later I spy Daniela's blonde head pop out of a taxi and we give each other a lingering hug. I haven't seen her for a good six months, and it's a delight to converse in English. As we walk to an inner-city trattoria she fills me in on why she has come to Naples, her aim to score new business for the hotel booking website she works for, and other gossip from her life in my old home town of Rome.

Settled into a cosy corner of the trattoria, I take a deep breath when Daniela asks me how I am.

'I'm fine, I'm . . .' My attempt at a brave face collapses. 'I love Procida but I'm finding it hard now, without the routine of going to Naples for work.

'We've made friends with a great group of people but I realise more and more that it's difficult living on an island. Granted, Alfonso has been away. But I feel isolated, and I feel like I'm going crazy at times.'

Daniela looks at me with concern.

'You know, you don't have to live like that,' she reminds me as I fight back the tears.

'What do you mean? Are you saying we should leave the island?'

'Well, you do have a choice,' she suggests lightly.

My mind whirs. We still have six months on our lease and it's not like I'm unhappy with our island home. I've just been hit by waves of homesickness, more so since Pa passed away.

Over lunch, I listen to Daniela's calming voice. My move to teach English is a good one, she says, but perhaps it's not enough to keep me stimulated.

'Why not enrol in a course at university? Though enrolling in Italy as a foreigner is a nightmare – I tried it once and gave up,' she admits as I wonder whether my Italian skills would meet the university standard. 'But there are heaps of other courses you could do. Why don't you investigate in Naples? That way you can get your dose of the big city more often.'

Daniela's simple but constructive advice works wonders. I have always wanted to improve my photography skills, and a friend of Alfonso's works as a snapper in Naples. I'll have to make some inquiries.

I look at Daniela with gratitude as we finish a digestive espresso and I walk her to a cab so she can make it to her last appointment before she heads back to Rome.

We hug and I promise I'll be up to visit her within a few weeks, then I walk back towards the metro, passing my old office. As I stare up at the familiar building I momentarily pine for stability, but not the job itself.

On the metro my thoughts again turn to Alfonso.

The train emerges from a tunnel and I set eyes on the gritty northern suburbs, where the city's famous *faida*, or feud, between rival clans of the Camorra (the Neapolitan mafia) rages intermittently with tit-for-tat assassinations. Alfonso has spent half of his life in this concrete jungle, which I find so desolate and oppressive. I am counting down the months until I will be able to show him my own country. It will be the first time I have returned home with an Italian partner.

I step off the metro and see Alfonso's father, Enzo, waiting for me in his car nearby. Soon we are driving through the security gate of their large estate which contains about four tall apartment blocks.

Alfonso is due to arrive in time for dinner, at around eight o'clock.

I sit in the kitchen with Maria Rosaria, listening to her and the small television that sits on the corner of the kitchen work-bench. My phone beeps and I read a message from Alfonso saying that he is still in Rome, at the Fiumicino airport. One of their bags has gone missing, so they have been delayed, filling out forms with the police for compensation.

'Don't wait for me for dinner, I'll let you know when we get to the train station.'

I try to stay calm as Maria Rosaria serves us but her agitation is infectious.

Alfonso calls later to say the band has missed the last direct train to Naples. Instead, they'll have to take one of the slow regional trains to Caserta, where two of the band members' parents will pick them up and drive them back to Naples.

'Go to bed, I won't be getting in until at least two in the morning,' he says.

When I convey the message to Maria Rosaria she paces the room and asks whether she and her husband should go and pick up their son.

'It's almost midnight, it's not the best time to be travelling,' she frets.

I take a deep breath and look her in the eyes, trying not to let my frustration simmer over.

'Rosa, stay calm. If Alfonso was on his own perhaps it might be a good idea. But your son is thirty-two years old and he is travelling with four grown men. He'll be fine, and he'll get here as soon as he can.'

She nods, but looks offended. I bid her goodnight with a quick *bacio* and retire to Alfonso's room.

I watch crap television until two o'clock, trying to stay awake, but eventually drift off.

I awake to hear the bedroom door being pushed open and see Alfonso's figure illuminated by the corridor light outside. He dumps his luggage and collapses beside me before enveloping me in a hug.

'*Amo*', if it wasn't enough, the train broke down . . . total travel time from Brazil: sixty-six hours,' he says in a raspy voice.

I have barely clucked my condolences before his head is a dead weight on my shoulder.

The next day we sit on the ferry to Procida, holding hands like two teenagers.

Alfonso's return is cause for a rather late night at Bar Capriccio, where our small group of friends ambushes him with questions about his trip.

'I haven't seen you looking so happy for a while,' I rib Enzo, who stands behind the bar, rolling a cigarette.

'I could say the same about you,' he says, making me blush.

As I glance at Alfonso, halfway through a story about his band's visit to the *favelas*, I have an odd sensation that we have to get used to one another again. I feel inexplicably changed by the events of the past few months, my job insecurity and trying to make inroads into island life. I've lost a little of my usual confidence and at times I'm deliberately evasive.

Alfonso stops chatting and turns to me to plant a kiss on my cheek. The familiar scent of his aftershave strips away a layer of reserve I didn't possess before setting foot on the island.

We rise early and walk up the steep hill to Piazza dei Martiri, or Martyrs Square, a pretty plateau that sits below Terra Murata but is high enough to offer beautiful views over Corricella. We stop to catch our breath in the cobbled piazza, then turn down the walled lane which leads to La Vigna. I haven't been back to the delightful hotel since my friends Nic, Rob and Penny visited in June. At the reception, owners Vincenzo and Mara are looking tired after the busy August holiday period.

'The worst is over,' I say sympathetically as Vincenzo leads us out the back of the hotel to *la vigna,* the vineyard.

Today we are taking part in the *vendemmia,* or grape harvest that happens across Italy in September and October. We've been invited by Enzo, who I imagine must be exhausted after closing Bar Capriccio at three in the morning then rising only hours later.

Pressing business during *la vendemmia* organised by Loreto

We walk past the rows of vines where a team of locals is hard at work cutting the plump, pale green grapes, which tumble into plastic milk crates.

Vincenzo finds his father, Loreto, a local doctor who is leading today's harvest. A man of few words, he welcomes us with a smile and hands us some clippers before he disappears down another row.

Spying Enzo's head above the vines, we sing out to him in a reciprocal game of hellos which continues for the next few hours as we move quickly among the vines, clipping here and there and filling crates aplenty.

As I turn in to a new row of vines, I glimpse an elderly man whose tall, sturdy frame reminds me of my late grandfather. He is wearing a bowler hat like the one worn by my *nonno* in the photo in our lounge room.

Hard at work, the man doesn't notice me watching until he finishes a section of the vine and raises his head to meet my eye. Embarrassed, I look away, but spend the rest of the time stealing glances at him.

Just when I think I will pass out from hunger a cry goes out that the picking is done and lunch will be served at Loreto's home.

I walk to the edge of the vineyard to take one long last look from the cliff to the sea below before I rip off my gloves. My hands are sticky and dirty from the odd squirt of grape juice, mixed with specks of dust.

Alfonso and I jump into Loreto's tiny black Fiat and it roars off like an industrial lawn-mower over the cobblestones. After the *vendemmia*, tradition has it that workers retire to Loreto's house to have a late lunch and drink the wine of the previous year's harvest.

When I ask how much wine is usually produced Loreto takes a long drag from his cigarette before he negotiates a sharp curve.

Now in his fifties, it's not hard to imagine he was a catch in his youth. He still has the edge of a lean, older James Dean, a packet of Marlboro Reds never absent from his shirt pocket.

'We make about seven thousand litres of wine a year,' he says eventually before cranking down a gear and turning in to a steep driveway. I've walked past the property many times, but the wooden gate has always been closed.

In the garden beside the large grey brick house, a few men empty the containers of grapes into a pulping machine. We follow Loreto into the house, and the kitchen.

'This is the other labour force,' he says, gesturing towards his wife and the other women who are the partners of the men involved in the *vendemmia*.

Within minutes the women usher everyone to a small pergola outside, where three long tables have been set.

Alfonso and I sit down and soon a relay team of women begins delivering plates with two pastas – one with a rabbit *ragu*, the other with tomato, ricotta and basil.

Between mouthfuls of pasta and wine, we chat to Giancarlo and Lucia, a couple in their sixties sitting opposite us. Both architects, they live in Naples, but Lucia is Procidan, and every summer they come back to the island, where they stay in her late grandmother's home.

I discover that Giancarlo is the co-author of the book *Procida: A Mediterranean Architecture*, one of the tomes I have bought about our island home. It's full of beautiful photographs of Procida's architecture, brimming with colour and gentle curves.

Giancarlo explains that Procidan homes were not designed by architects but by master builders who worked closely with their client, more often than not without a blueprint sketch.

'The client would simply say how many rooms they wanted

and the builder would draw lines in the soil on site,' Giancarlo tells us.

'Then, as families grew,' chimes in Lucia, lighting the first of many slim cigarettes, 'extra rooms were added on.'

Procida's style of architecture was largely determined by the hot climate. Using the local, yellowy stone called tufa, the builders' main challenge was to protect homes from the sun, says Giancarlo.

'Corricella attracts far too much sun, so windows are small and the external staircases are an added protection against the light,' he explains.

When I mention how much I love the staircases, he explains they were built outside for another reason as well.

'A standard Procidan room has a high vaulted roof. If someone wanted to put in stairs it would have meant losing space and the vault would have to be broken. So the stairs went outside. It's very logical.'

So too, points out Lucia, is the design of the island's narrow roads.

'The lanes are all boxed in with walls, which protect them from the wind in winter and makes them cooler in summer,' she explains.

As the army of women serve chunks of roasted rabbit, beef and lamb, Giancarlo curses the locals for not respecting the island's architecture and making unsympathetic renovations.

'There are idiots who cut the high ceilings, where hot air gathers, to make a loft. Then they realise they can't live there any more!' he says. 'Apart from the fact that their renovations are illegal, they destroy the enormous benefit of the vault, which maintains the interior climate of the house.'

Another wine bottle is placed on our table and our conversation stops with the sound of a wine glass being tapped loudly. Women move from table to table to top up wine glasses as Lucia explains that a poem celebrating the day's hard work is usually read out at Loreto's long luncheon. Behind us a man stands and, swaying slightly, begins to read a poem entitled '*Preghiera a Padre Bacco*' – Prayer to Father Bacco, or Bacchus, the God of Wine.

'Our father in the cellar, hallowed be your medicine, may your good wine come as long as it's good and genuine,' the man begins. 'Give us today our daily dose and fill our glasses, as we fill those of our drinkers. Don't ask us to be teetotallers, and deliver us from water.'

Laughter and applause erupt as the man solemnly says, 'Amen.'

Passing our table, Loreto fills our glasses for the umpteenth

Locals mix with guests at the long summer lunches at
La Vigna hotel

time. He tells me that our chances of a hangover are slim because the local drop has only seven grams of preservatives in each one hundred litres compared to one hundred grams in commercial brews. Let's hope so, because we are downing it like water.

As I pick up a *biscotto* my eyes rest on the old man who resembles my grandfather, sitting at a table to my right. I have noticed that he hasn't spoken a word to anyone, but he has obviously seen me observing him.

He picks up a biscuit and, checking that I am watching, dunks it in his glass of white wine, and gestures to me to do the same.

I follow suit and smile at him before he looks away.

A large, bosomy woman strides from the kitchen with an enormous, creamy white *cassata*, the ricotta-rich cake for which Sicily is famous.

As I clutch my stomach Enzo plonks a plate of it before Alfonso and me, and looks at us sternly.

'You have no choice, it's the best I have ever eaten,' he promises.

It's been years since I tasted the Sicilian version during a trip to the island's capital, Palermo, but Enzo is right.

Everyone else must agree, since the cake's creator suddenly makes a dash home on her Vespa. Within ten minutes she reappears with a second, smaller *cassata* and she places it in front of Loreto, who leans forward to inhale the aroma.

Jokes fly thick and fast and suddenly the man who read the poem stands and pushes Loreto until his aquiline nose is dipped in the thick icing. The afternoon only gets messier and night has fallen by the time we leave to drag our swollen bellies home, singing out cheery *ciaos*.

Just what doctor Loreto ordered, the *vendemmia* couldn't have come at a better time.

SETTEMBRE

PASTA E FAGIOLI
(PASTA WITH BEANS)

Pasta and beans, this classic dish is often found on Italian menus, and not just in winter. You can cheat and buy canned beans, but the dried ones you can find at your supermarket or health food store are healthier and tastier; all you have to do is soak them overnight, or for at least ten hours first. Impress not only by making this classic dish, but by pronouncing it right, too (fadge-ol-ee).

Serves 4

> 300 grams cannellini beans
> small amount pork rind or a little fat off a slice of
>   *prosciutto* (optional)
> 100 grams cherry tomatoes
> 2 celery sticks, diced
> 2 whole garlic cloves, peeled
> 250 grams various kinds of short pasta, whatever is
>   in your pantry
> salt, pepper, extra virgin olive oil, lemon juice (to taste)

Method

1. Rinse the <u>soaked</u> beans and put them in a saucepan with plenty of water. Bring to boil then turn heat down and cook for about an hour. For extra flavour, add the pork rind, or *prosciutto* fat at this point. Every now and then you'll have to skim foam from the top.

2. When the beans are cooked, toss in the tomatoes, celery and garlic and simmer for 20 minutes or so, until they form a nice pulp.

3. Throw in some odds and ends of pasta. Importantly, should you need to add water at any stage, make sure it is boiling hot.

4. When the pasta thickens* add salt, pepper and olive oil to taste and, if you like, a squeeze of lemon.

*Note that some of the pasta will be over-cooked and other bits chewy, but that's what makes the texture interesting!

For a different version of this winter warmer, substitute the beans with chickpeas (soaked and boiled) and instead of adding tomato and celery toss in garlic, rosemary and parsley. Easy peasy.

OTTOBRE

Trouble on the rock

I am reading the morning papers as Alfonso strums his guitar in the next room, when a photo of my father suddenly springs to mind. Snapped in the early seventies, he sits with the same instrument on his knee and wears pants that flare almost as much as the ends of his handle-bar moustache.

Just before I was born, Gough Whitlam's federal Labor government proposed the construction of an international airport in Galston, the north-western Sydney suburb where my parents lived. The residents were outraged by the plans, fearing they would ruin what was then a rural hamlet, and my father took it upon himself to record a protest song, with the punchy title 'Galston International Airport – A Rural Tragedy'.

A one-man band, my dad strummed and crooned to create a rousing acoustic moment I like to think left Dylan for dust.

He must have been good, because the airport plan was scrapped, and for years after my sisters and I would crowd around the record player, drop the needle over Dad's increasingly scratched record and belt out the lyrics, ecstatic to be able to say 'bloody hell' without getting smacked on our behinds with a wooden spoon.

Dad's protest song has been rattling in my head since rumours began to spread around the island that the council is set to build a *dissociatore molecolare*, a type of incinerator, to process the island's mounting rubbish heaps.

Waste collection on Procida has suddenly dipped because of the situation in Naples, where the fifteen-year rubbish 'emergency' has taken another turn for the worse. Put simply, the Campania region has run out of space for its rubbish and the government's attempts to build more incinerators are being opposed by irate Neapolitans and undermined by the Camorra, which makes millions of dollars each year by illegally burying the waste from Italian and foreign industries in the countryside around Naples.

No longer able to ship all of its waste to Naples, Procida's council has ordered residents to separate their rubbish, putting all recyclable material in a special yellow bag for collection twice a week.

The move has caused general chaos: from the elderly residents who are used to lowering their rubbish bag tied to a piece of string from their windows down to the street, and have no concept of recycling, to housewives who can't work out if a teabag qualifies for recycling. And many people simply can't remember what day to put their yellow bag out.

Procida's biggest problem, however, is that it has no mechanism to process the *differenziata*, recyclable material, and as a Bandaid solution is stockpiling on vacant land.

To top things off, Naples' latest crisis means Procida's *umido*, or non-recyclable rubbish, isn't being collected as often as it should be, rendering my morning walks increasingly stinky. The continuing degradation on *lo scoglio*, the rock, as many Procidans affectionately refer to their chunk of land, makes me both sad and angry.

I check my email to find a message from our friend Graziella, whose family's business of Hotel Solcalante will, like other tourist operators on the island, suffer enormously if the crisis isn't quickly resolved.

She has attached a document about an incinerator similar to one that may be built on Procida. A chemicals expert claimed that tests in Alaska on an incinerator prototype there found not only that it emitted pollutants, but that the dioxins and furans content was ten times higher than the level set by the Alaskan authorities.

Struggling to decipher the scientific terms in Italian, I am surfing the web looking for an English version when I hear the unmistakable sound of *la macchina*, the car that blasts recorded community messages from a megaphone roped to its roof.

Alfonso stops playing and joins me on the balcony overlooking our street. Today being Sunday, the message bleats, traffic is banned from ten in the morning until six at night. I'm pleased, but the move will no doubt enrage my friends Glorianna and Candida, who consider being able to drive their cars a basic human right. The second message is less welcome: residents are kindly asked not to place their rubbish on the street, so as not to aggravate the current crisis.

'What the hell are people meant to do?' I snap at Alfonso.

'Come on, I heard there's a meeting about the council plans in an hour. Let's call Alessandro and go with him,' he replies.

Alessandro is in a local band Alfonso has been jamming with recently in an abandoned former convent high on Terra Murata.

The group had already organised a concert the following weekend at Chiaiolella when rumours of the incinerator spread like wildfire. According to Alfonso, Alessandro now intends to use the performance as a chance to collect signatures against the council plan, and he has also invited Alfonso's Neapolitan band, 'A67, to perform.

Alfonso arranges to meet his friend in a nearby piazza. When we arrive I shake hands with Alessandro, a lean man with an intense gaze who explains that Procida's mayor is in America examining technology for the incinerator project.

'He only speaks two words of English,' he scoffs, before claiming that the council has practically signed off on the deal.

When I suggest that an information day should be organised to show the public how to recycle properly, Alessandro nods.

'I was thinking that I could go around and show people, what can be recycled and what can't,' he says. 'It will be hard, because there are so many houses to canvas, but we have to try.'

We arrive at Piazza dei Martiri, where Alessandro turns down a tiny alley. We step over rubbish bags and around a dumped washing machine before walking up a staircase. Alessandro knocks furiously on a blue door adorned with beads.

'Peppino sometimes can't hear because he's in his studio out the back,' he says. Apparently Peppino is a local who is hosting the meeting.

A tall man with a long, unruly beard and spectacles opens the door and ushers us past a kitchen and into his studio, complete with a loft sleeping area.

Around us the bookshelves groan with volumes on everything from philosophy, cinema and politics to origami and gardening, and there are sculptures and paintings everywhere. My eyes rest on a black-and-white photo showing the back of a naked man plunging off a cliff. He has the same wiry build as Peppino.

He introduces us to the five or six people gathered in the room, and the next two hours are spent deciding what to write on a flyer Peppino will design. He reads the final slogan – *si alla differenziata, no al dissociatore*, yes to recycling, no to the incinerator – before Alessandro mentions his idea to take to the streets and show Procidans how to recycle.

'My son, it's too personal a campaign, and the next thing you know people will start clogging their homes with ugly recycled art,' says Peppino, making everyone laugh. He gently convinces Alessandro to think a bit more rationally about the problem.

The group breaks up, but Alfonso and I take the opportunity to chat to Peppino for a little longer. Given Procida's size, it's strange that in the six months we have been on the island I have never before set eyes upon him, nor his wife Saara, who has just arrived home.

When I mention this fact to the couple, who I would guess are in their late fifties, they share a little chuckle.

'We have a good rapport with Procida,' begins Peppino.

'But then perhaps you could say only a cordial one with the Procidans. We keep a certain distance,' interrupts Saara, with a smile.

'Our great fortune is we are good together,' continues Peppino, as Saara excuses herself from the room, 'so we don't need to be sociable. And we both work from home.'

'Are you Procidan?' I ask Peppino.

'I was born just across the road, but Saara was born in France, to Spanish parents,' he says.

'Come upstairs for a coffee,' Peppino suggests, and we follow him back out the front door and up a steep set of external stairs to another door. Inside, Saara sits in a small kitchen, nursing a baby girl. Peppino explains she is the newborn daughter of the couple's son, Tadzio, and his Indian wife, Chrysann, who met while they were both employed on the same cruise boat.

As the conversation returns to the council plans for the incinerator, I ask Peppino if the characteristically sluggish locals are easily stirred to protest.

He gives an emphatic shake of his head.

'People just want quick solutions without thinking about the future,' says Saara.

Peppino tells us that Procida's council has almost always been right-leaning, and has always enjoyed particular control because of the island's maritime industry.

'The problem is that the sailors go away for four months, in the old days even longer, and when they come back to dry land they don't understand a damn thing,' he laments. 'At the first sign of a bit of confusion, the easiest choice is a quick fix, totalitarianism, Fascism, order with discipline.'

Peppino views the Procidans' 'not in our backyard' attitude to rubbish in general as a huge problem.

'Until a few months ago, their attitude was, "Here, I pay you to take my rubbish away, do what you want with it and I don't care. The important thing is that I don't see it."'

According to Peppino, the best solution for Procida's waste is a mechanical biological treatment plant, where rubbish is sorted and treated in an environmentally friendly system, including composting. He also backs the idea of a local engineer to build a sea platform just offshore. It would deal with household waste via an anaerobic digestor, which could also produce gas to service the platform, making it self-sufficient.

Peppino explains that he and a small group of locals have

presented the council with a plan for recycling which he says is vital for the island's future.

'There is no reasonable urban plan because people have built illegally all over the island, and now they are the ones demanding rubbish collection and other services!' he scoffs. 'It's hardly surprising the situation's such a mess.'

Peppino finishes his diatribe and laughs despite himself.

'But look, at the end of the day, if we went to another place, like Spain, where Saara's family is, maybe it would seem so much better at first, but after five years I might think, Shit, it's worse than Procida!'

Alfonso and I laugh alongside our friendly host before we stand to leave.

'Thanks for having us, I guess we'll see you in a year or so.' I wink.

'Every now and then we meet people who make coming outdoors worth the effort,' Peppino says with a grin.

He waves us goodbye before closing the door and he is no doubt at peace again in his private universe, far from the Procidans.

I walk down to the port with Alfonso, who is going to Naples for band practice.

As the hydrofoil leaves, I head to Bar Capriccio and I am about to order a coffee when I feel a tap on my shoulder.

I swing around to see Vittorio, otherwise known as *Bottone,* or button – Italian slang meaning someone who is always looking to corner someone for a chinwag. While Bottone lives up to his nickname, he was given it for another reason: as a child, he told me, he always tore buttons off his shirt to use in a playground game, causing his mother to screech, '*Vittorio . . . il bottone!*'

Ottobre

He barely comes up to my shoulder, and I smile down at his round, tanned face and toothy grin.

Bottone points to the cloudless sky and, before I have time to argue, orders that our coffees be served outside. Bottone used to work on the oil tankers, and I am impressed that he always seems to know how the weather will behave over the next forty-eight hours.

As we sit down, I jokingly raise my index finger to gauge the wind.

Obviously encouraged to share his seaman's knowledge, Bottone pulls a paper serviette from its holder on the table, produces a pen from the inside of his light jacket and begins to draw an eight-pointed star.

'Procidans have the weather in their DNA; as soon as they wake they look out to see what the weather is doing. Then, every sailor knows the *rosa dei venti*, the rose of winds,' he says in his gravelly voice.

Bottone touches the eight points of the star and tells me the names of the winds. Tramontana, at due north, then moving clockwise to the Greco, Levante, Greco Levante and the southern Sirocco, then the Libeccio, Ponente and Maestrale.

'So, that's how you know what the weather will do,' I say, even more impressed.

'No, every night I watch the weather on every possible channel to get an idea of what it will do the next day. And I'm usually right.'

I burst into laughter.

True to his nickname, Bottone is on a roll, counting on his stumpy fingers all the countries he has lived in, or at least those he can remember: Guatemala, America, Brazil, Taiwan. His eyes suddenly light up with mischief when he mentions his posting to the Swedish city of Halmstad.

'We worked on board during the day but went onshore every night to have fun. We'd go to a nightclub with a beautiful dance area. The first floor was for the old people, the second for couples, and the third for the singles. Obviously, I was on the top floor.

'There were more women at this place than men, and I would work the whole room, asking them to dance, but they all turned me down because I was short and they thought I couldn't dance. But I was really good at the tango, the *cha cha cha*.

'I was always sad when I went back to the ship because all I wanted to do was dance. Anyway, one night I was on my way home and I saw a car that had ended up in a ditch after veering off the road. I ran over and I saw a girl inside. She was half-conscious, so I dragged her out. The car's battery had started to leak and I thought the car would go up in flames.'

Bottone goes on to recount how he then tried to flag down a car, but no one would stop. The only people who did react telephoned the police, who promptly arrived to arrest him on the spot, suspecting he had somehow harmed the young woman.

I tried to explain, but they couldn't understand me, so they put me in a cell until the next day, when the girl woke up and told them I had saved her.

'The girl found out where I was and came to thank me, and she said, "Can I do anything for you?" and I said, "Yes, can you come and dance with me?"

'She looked me in the face and said, "That's all?", and when I nodded she said, "Sure, tomorrow I'll come and pick you up." So we went back to the nightclub and when the other girls saw how well I danced they kept coming up and asking me to dance, and this time it was *me* who was saying no!'

I chuckle alongside my elderly friend, who shakes his head when I ask if he finds himself at a loss now he is retired and not sailing the world.

'The first thing I did before I went on the pension was to build an office under my house, with a television, radio and tools. But I don't have any time to myself. There is always someone who needs a hand.'

As Bottone explains how he spent the entire morning restoring electricity to a friend's house, I stare at his thick hands, scarred from a life of manual labour.

The abrasive sound of a pop tune breaks the morning calm and Bottone answers his mobile phone. He chats for a few minutes, then eases his squat frame out of his chair.

'Be good. I have to go and fix a washing machine,' he says before tipping the brim of his baseball cap and ambling down the street.

The big day has finally arrived. After months of waiting for the right moon, and thus the right weather conditions, we are going fishing with Gilda's uncle, Gerardo, who has a fishing trawler moored at Chiaiolella port. When she learnt I was interested in making such a trip, Gilda was kind enough to ask Gerardo on our behalf.

I have learned that there are two main types of fishing on the island.

The first is called *paranza*, which means a long net is dragged along the bottom of the ocean to catch whatever is in its wake. The word *paranza* is also found on every restaurant menu on Procida; it is a dish of fried fish. The *paranza* boats are usually moored at Marina Grande, where they throw their red and orange nets over chairs and bins along the port to air in the sun.

In Procidan dialect, the second type of fishing is called *zaccalea*, which stems from the Italian term *saccaleva*, literally meaning 'sack

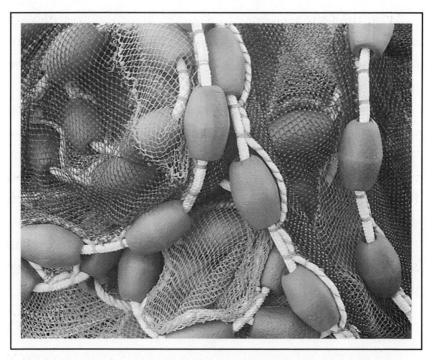

Fishing nets are untangled, mended and dried in every Procidan port

lift'. A trawler is equipped with two small dinghies, each known as a *lampara*, which means both fishing lamp and a boat with fishing lamps. The *lampare* are dropped into the ocean and fishermen use their spotlights to lure the fish to the surface. The trawler drops a net weighted with iron rings and a cable, and circles the *lampare*. Eventually the net is pulled closed to form a big sack, which is lifted onto the fishing trawler. The *zaccalea* boats are generally moored in the ports of Chiaiolella and Corricella.

Some locals, like our lawyer-cum-fisherman friend Nicola, argue that the *zaccalea* method is better than the *paranza*, because it drops a net in a specific zone rather than trawling the bottom of the ocean and damaging the marine environment in the process. While the *paranza* tends to catch an array of fish, the *zaccalea* usually hauls in anchovies, herring and tuna.

With the October weather still mild, Alfonso and I dress in old T-shirts and track pants and carry jumpers to Chiaiolella for our 9 pm appointment with Gerardo. About five metres off the jetty is a sea trawler with *San Giuseppe* written across the bow.

'That's Gerardo's boat!' I say to Alfonso with excitement as a voice sings out '*Ciao.*'

We wait on the jetty in the dark as some figures lower a dinghy into the water to come and pick us up. As the boat approaches I see it is being steered by a young, pimply boy with buck teeth who looks too young to drive a car, let alone a sea vessel.

We jump on board and within minutes we are being helped up onto the *San Giuseppe*. A tall man with snow-white hair and a large beer belly approaches us and introduces himself as Gerardo.

He explains that tonight we are going to try our luck off the coast of Ischia.

'We went there last night and there were plenty of fish, mostly anchovies,' he says.

When I ask how long he's been fishing Gerardo says he's had the *zaccalea* operation for almost thirty years. Until 1980 he was, like so many Procidan men, a sailor.

'Until around 1950 fishing was very simple, but then we got all sorts of new technology to help,' he says, pointing to the cabin behind us, where there is a sonar to measure sea depth and highlight schools of fish, a radar that scans the entire sea zone showing all the landmasses, and a global positioning system, which keeps track of the location of the *lampare* as the trawler circles the sea.

'In the old days, fishing was much more fun and there was more money to be made.' He explains that new technology means more competition, while the introduction of fridges at the market means that the fish can be frozen, allowing boats to come from further afield with their catches.

'Excuse me, it's time to get going,' he says, disappearing into the cabin. The motor starts with a jump as a few men lift the second dinghy back onto the boat.

Alfonso and I sit on an upturned crate used to store fish. I scan the crew, numbering eleven. There are about four young men – all students at the island's nautical institute, we learn – who are earning a bit of cash before they are qualified to go to sea. The rest of the crew are former sailors now on the pension, most of whom sport paunches to rival that of Gerardo's.

The young man who picked us up appears with a pot of coffee and a stack of small white plastic cups. I gratefully accept an espresso shot, as Gilda has predicted we won't be home before one or two o'clock – well past our bedtime.

Standing nearby, the leanest of the elderly crew offers us a handshake, introducing himself as Guido Vittorio. He tells us he retired from sailing five years ago, but has been helping out on *San Giuseppe* for the past ten years.

'On Procida you either have a passion for the sea or the land; I have both,' he shouts above the motor, explaining that he has a huge garden where he grows just about every vegetable imaginable.

'The water is calm, it will be a nice night on the boat,' he says, casting his gaze to the sky. 'But the moon is high, so we'll have to wait for it to sink a little, because when there is too much light the fish don't come out. When it gets darker, the lamps will be able to attract more fish.'

San Giuseppe chugs on and by ten o'clock the drone of the motor is the only thing keeping me awake as I am lulled by the gentle rock of the boat. Guido Vittorio stands nearby making a woven sack from fishing line. He will put a large rock into it to create an anchor for the two dinghies which we are yet to drop.

Rather than use a regular anchor, they simply cut the net when finished and the boulders stay on the bottom of the sea.

'What time do you normally finish fishing?' I ask him.

'The market opens at three in the morning, and we usually get there just before,' he says. Like all of Procida's trawlers, *San Guiseppe* sells its catch at the fish market at Pozzuoli, a small port south of Naples, which is about twenty minutes by boat from Procida.

With impeccable timing, another young boy appears from the cabin with some more coffee. I finish mine in one gulp and I'm looking for a rubbish bag when I notice two of the older crew members toss their plastic cups into the sea. My blood boils, but I bite my tongue. It's not my place to tell these old salts what scoundrels they are. They might chop me up in pieces and use me for bait.

I step into the cabin where Gerardo steers the boat. I stare at the radar, a series of green rings, and make out the island of Ischia to our left. The sonar shows one direct line measuring the depth of the ocean. Seeing me staring at the screens, Gerardo yells above the roar of the engine to explain that the yellow mass on the sonar indicates fish, and the mass will grow and turn red if there is a large school.

At eleven-thirty the trawler drops down a gear and the first *lampara* is lowered into the ocean. I watch the small dinghy edge away, its three spotlights sweeping the sea and transforming it into an iridescent blue.

Our trawler moves away and for the next hour we chug along the coast, the lights of Ischia flickering in concert with the stars above our heads.

'*Delfini!*' shouts a crew member, spying a pair of dolphins.

The second *lampara* is dropped. From the first dinghy an old man calls out, 'Just sardines.'

The crew throw him a rope to tow the dinghy to another spot.

More minutes pass until we reach the second *lampara*, which is now surrounded by about ten other boats with lamps, lighting the sea like giant fireflies.

We press on and find a new place to drop the first *lampara* then return to the second boat to see fish jumping out of the water. I would have thought it was a good sign, but the sonar is still not indicating big schools.

By two o'clock, Alfonso and I have lost all sense of bearing and logic as our trawler chugs back to the first *lampara*. We have been crisscrossing the ocean for five hours, and I'd be willing to dynamite the fish out if it meant going home.

As we draw to a stop Gerardo appears from the cabin to yell out to the man on the second *lampara*. The answer is disappointing: only a few sardines. It appears we will be turning back to Procida without a single fish. I glance at my watch and see it is three-thirty.

Just then a large trawler from Corricella comes into view. Amid a great deal of shouting, the crew of the other boat haul up nets that are writhing with anchovies.

In an exchange of grunts between the two captains, which Alfonso generously deciphers for me, it is agreed that our boat will try its luck in the area once the other boat leaves.

In the time it takes to round up the *lampare* we sip our third, sugary coffee. With our two dinghies trailing us, ready to be dropped, we return to the Corricella trawler as it finishes loading its haul. Its dinghy stays in position until one of our own *lampara* can slide into place, leaving a constant source of light to keep the fish around. Soon our trawler drops its large net, weighted with iron rings, and sails in a huge circle around the dinghy. Standing on the outer deck, Gerardo barks the order for the *lampara* to cut its lights and leave the area so the net can be closed. He then turns the wheel of a machine that reels in the net, closing it into a tight sack.

The crew, now dressed in fluorescent yellow plastic overalls and wellington boots, lean over the boat to help as the sack nudges the hull. From a safe distance, we look down into the ocean to see countless silver anchovies. In the moonlight they sparkle like diamonds in the bright blue sea.

Nearby the young boys prepare the overturned containers we have sat on for the past six hours, throwing in large slabs of ice as other crew members use a long stick with a net to scoop the fish out of the sea and toss them in.

Alfonso and I stand in the cabin and watch as the containers fill with silver fish. The crew stack small wooden crates on top

The early morning catch aboard *San Giuseppe*

of the containers and load the catch into them until they have ninety crates brimming with fish.

Satisfied, Gerardo jumps back into the driver's seat and we start to move towards Procida. It is five-thirty in the morning.

Exhausted, we have told Gerardo that we'll skip the market experience and head home.

The sun rises as we reach the waters just off the port. Shaking hands with Gerardo and thanking him for letting us come aboard, we scramble into one of the small dinghies with three other crew members and go back to Chiaiolella.

Too tired to talk, we sit at one end and watch the coastline of Procida pass by. We round the lighthouse corner and pass Pozzo Vecchio beach, counting down the minutes until we are on dry land.

At the last cliff before Chiaiolella I raise my head, puzzled, as the motor of our small boat cuts out.

'We have to get some boulders for the anchors for tonight,' one of the crew explains, pointing at a beach nearby that is littered with rocks.

I purse my lips and sigh.

It is six-thirty when we finally moor at Chiaiolella and we say our prayers when two of the crew offer to give us a ride home on their Vespas. Sitting behind Guido Vittorio, I close my eyes and fight dizziness as we whiz along the streets.

Thanking our sea comrades for the experience, we haul our bodies up three flights of stairs, strip out of our fishy clothes and have a welcome hot shower.

I have enough energy to shut the windows in our room before we collapse into bed.

Wiped out from our fishing adventure, it takes us two days to recover our sleep patterns. Now I understand why fishermen are a somewhat silent, gruff bunch. It's not the work that is exhausting, it's the long periods of waiting without any guarantee of finding fish to sell at the market and pay their wages.

After a trying afternoon teaching toddlers for two hours, I go for a stroll and decide to call in on Elisa and Michele.

I find Elisa and two of her three sisters sitting around the table in the sunroom, fingering some linen that Elisa no doubt plans to use to make something for a member of her family.

I join them and listen to Elisa chat with her sisters Margherita and Antonietta. When the sisters are together it's like being in a hen coop as their voices grow more and more shrill in their attempts to be the rooster. Usually I pick up a small snippet of folklore, and today is no different. According to the women, their mother taught them that Procidan women left alone by their sailing husbands should not sweep the floor near the dining table after meals, out of respect for their absent partners.

'I don't know how to explain it – it was as if sweeping would have kept the men away,' says Elisa with a shrug.

Margherita and Antonietta cluck their goodbyes and I follow Elisa into the kitchen. When she tells me she is about to make a dough for a *pizza di scarole*, pizza with endives, I clap my hands with glee.

'Finally, I am not too late to see you make a dough from scratch!' I say. Pretty soon Alfonso won't have to buy his pizza.

I sit down on one of the green kitchen chairs and watch Elisa in action. First, she pours around half a bag of flour onto the marble tabletop. She then makes a well in the centre and drops in a tablespoon of butter.

'If you don't have butter just drizzle in some olive oil,' she says, while placing a small cube of yeast into the well.

She sprinkles a pinch of sugar on one side of the flour and two pinches of salt on the other.

'Don't put the two near each other, as it will affect how the pizza rises.' She pours in roughly a glass of boiling water and with a knife she slowly blends the wet and dry ingredients. Eventually she uses her hands to deftly knead the dough.

As she kneads, Elisa gives me little tips and shares some advice from her own mother.

'She used to tell me that bread is like a child, because you have to look after it and help it grow, and that is why bakers never go on holidays,' she says with a gentle smile.

'She said it should always be covered with a cloth at night like a priest covers communion bread. If you make good use of bread it's considered to bring good fortune.'

Elisa uses a jar of marmalade as her rolling pin. I am always amused by her short-cuts. She doesn't believe in utensils like spatulas; when she needs to scrape the last trickle of cake mix from the bowl she just tears the cardboard top off a pasta packet and runs it along the rim instead.

'Look, see how I am pressing my finger here, and then the yeast springs back again straight afterwards . . . it's *alive!*' she says, prodding and pulling at the dough.

Seeing my worried expression, Elisa is quick to add that if I don't think I am up to the job I can always buy freshly made dough, ready to cook, from any bakery on the island. I shake my head. While that's reassuring, I want to try to make it from scratch.

Elisa flattens two wide circles of dough the size of her baking tray, which she has already lined with oven paper.

'Pe, you can put all sorts of fillings inside this pizza, like eggplant and *provola*,' she chatters.

'What do you mean *inside* the pizza? Don't you mean on top?'

'We say *pizza* for all sorts of savoury snacks including savoury pies,' she explains, adding that a standard pizza dough has no sugar. Hmmm. Alfonso might still have to get his pizza from the bakery for some time yet.

Elisa drains the endive and squeezes it with all her might.

'You really have to squeeze it tight, otherwise the water will ruin the pizza,' she warns.

She puts the greens in a bowl and adds roughly sliced olives, some slivered almonds, a few salted anchovies and a sprinkling of capers.

'I'm using almonds because I don't have pine nuts . . . you know me, I use whatever's on hand,' she says briskly.

She lights the stove and pours olive oil into the pan with a few cloves of garlic. She mixes the endives with the other ingredients and tips the lot into the pan, stirring it for about five minutes.

Finally, she has everything ready and I watch her line a pie dish with one of the pasta circles, add the endive mix and then seal it with the second pasta circle.

Before she places it in her oven I watch as she drizzles a generous amount of oil on top.

'I thought you were on a diet!' I rib her, and she blushes.

Elisa and I go into the lounge room to watch the 24-hour cooking channel on cable TV as we wait for the pie to cook.

Every now and then she leans forward and clucks her approval of a particular dish, usually describing it as *invitante*, or inviting, or *interessante*, interesting.

After about fifteen minutes, Elisa takes the pie out of the oven and Michele sweeps in carrying a plastic bag holding two medium-sized fish.

'Not much, but better than nothing,' he says, sitting down at the dining-room table.

I join him and show Michele my photographs from the fishing trip, and ask if he has ever been on a *zaccalea*.

He nods, saying that in his youth he went out on the trawlers now and then to earn a quid.

He explains that his grandfather and father were farmers, and they traded some of their produce with the island's fishermen, in a transaction traditionally known as *lo scambio,* the exchange.

Michele's grandfather bought batches of silkworms in small towns on the outskirts of Naples and sold the thread for fishing lines.

'He stored the worms in rectangular crates this big,' says Michele, stretching his arms along the length and breadth of the large dining table.

Silkworms live on mulberry leaves, which explains why the trees are everywhere around Procida: in the school grounds opposite our house and in the isolated path around the tip of Solchiaro, where I often go on a morning walk.

'Those trees at Solchiaro were planted by my ancestors,' Michele says proudly. 'There was often a crowd of women sitting in the courtyard outside our house, all wearing plastic aprons and opening the silkworm cocoons.'

The cocoons would be opened when the silkworms had grown about eight centimetres long and had turned a pinky colour, indicating their maturity. The women would remove the silk then toss the pupa into a bucket at their feet. Measuring just over a metre, each piece of silk was cleaned then hung to dry like fresh spaghetti. They were then bundled up and tied in bunches weighing about a kilo each.

'My grandfather sold them to wholesalers who then used the silk to make reels or made nets to sell.'

Scoffing at the modern fishing technology, Michele explains that when he worked on a *zaccalea* as a child the work was far more exhausting. 'In those days, the nets were made of cotton; nylon hadn't been invented yet, and silk was only used for fishing line. The nets were huge and heavy, and there weren't any machines or cranes to haul them in. It took at least eighteen men.'

Back then, Michele adds, the trawlers could only fish on alternate days because on the off days they had to dry the nets. They would spread them out over the main sea wall at the entrance to the port, and along Marina Grande, where shopkeepers put out large bins on the jetty so the fishermen could string the nets over them.

'Then every fifteen days the fishermen had to dye the nets, which I think reinforced them, using tree bark so they became a browny colour,' he remembers.

I could sit for hours reliving the old days through the stories of my two friends, but my stomach is rumbling and I know Alfonso is cooking up a surprise lunch at home.

With my fresh dough bundled safely in one of Elisa's home-made tea towels, I thank the couple and wander home. As a gust of wind buffets my path along the narrow street I think of Bottone and wonder if he's already forecast the weather for the next two days.

The day of the rock concert at Chiaiolella dawns and Alfonso paces the house, killing time before he goes down to meet his band mates off the ferry.

'You're going to wear the marble out,' I say, gesturing at the floor.

'I'm nervous – it's the first time I've played in front of a lot of people I know.'

A day earlier, when I said I wanted to tell our friends that his group was playing at Chiaiolella, Alfonso begged me to keep a lid on it. I agreed not to send an SMS alert, but that isn't to say the island grapevine didn't bear fruit regardless, nor that I didn't answer inquiries from interested friends . . .

Alfonso leaves me in peace and goes to greet the band at Marina Grande, from where they will go to a bar called Agave, run by the cousin of our mate Gennaro, to watch Naples' soccer team face Juventus in the national league.

Happy to avoid the grudge match between southern and northern Italy, I stay home and catch up on the Sunday papers. To my surprise, Procida has made national headlines. Accompanied by a beautiful photo of Corricella, *La Repubblica* reports that tensions are rising on our island thanks to the council's plan for a *dissociatore*. Mayor Gerardo Lubrano, back from a trip to America to examine the technology, tells the newspaper that not only does

Fishermen check their overnight haul

the incinerator not pollute, it runs as quietly as a new fridge: 'I'd install it in my own home if I could. It's a very virtuous project that would make Procida a happy island.'

Later I walk to Chiaiolella, skirting along the *lido*, or beach front. I arrive just in time to see a young boy on the beach setting fire to a scarecrow dressed in Juventus player Del Piero's jersey. As the scarecrow goes up in flames amid the honking car horns and random cat calls, I confirm that Naples has downed the northerners three to one.

Around the corner at the port a small crowd is gathering when the first band, an instrumental group from Naples, takes the stage. I find Alfonso standing with the band and kiss my hellos before joining a large number of our friends nearby. Looking around I see more familiar faces, Gilda and her twin boys, Enzo's sister Paola and her husband Michele, and a host of others I have come to know through Bar Capriccio. I wave to Alessandro and Peppino, who are standing near an information stand across the road. I have already noticed Peppino's flyer protesting against the incinerator in the hands of many in the crowd.

Finally 'A67 take to the stage and Daniele, the lead singer, introduces the band.

'Alfonso is practically Procidan, so too his *ragazza* Penny,' says Daniele, pointing to me in the audience.

I blush wildly as the girls around me wolf-whistle.

I watch Alfonso's nerves fade as he finds his groove. When singer Daniele announces the end of the set I shriek with laughter as Rosalba and Nicoletta, the cheeky girls from Bar Capriccio, rush forward to throw a couple of G-strings at Alfonso.

Later I sit down at Crescenzo, one of the restaurants at the port, which has generously offered dinner and a night's stay for Alfonso's band.

In between courses – a fresh seafood antipasto, pasta with pumpkin and cuttlefish, and fried calamari and fish – I flit to the nearby table where half of my friends who attended the gig are munching pizza.

I eventually leave Alfonso to chill out with his band and I walk home along the deserted streets without the fear that gripped me in Naples. I realise it's my father's birthday, so I give him a quick call.

'Good news, Pen, we've decided we're not too old to visit,' my father says.

'Fantastic!' I say, glad my nagging has paid off.

'When are you coming?'

'In two weeks, and we're staying for just over three weeks.'

Gazing at the rubbish piled high outside our door as I listen to my father's voice, I wish for a miracle resolution that will turn my island home into the paradise it could so easily be.

At seven o'clock Club Napoli, a small room on Marina Grande that is a meeting point for Procidan fans of Naples' football team, is crammed with locals sitting patiently in rows of white plastic chairs. Hanging on the back wall is a huge poster of Maradona wearing a Naples jersey, and a sombre painting of Jesus. Some Neapolitans and other residents of the Campania region may well rate Maradona the higher power.

Peppino clears his throat and flicks a switch to start a slideshow with pictures of the type of incinerator planned for Procida, alongside the various ways of recycling.

'Until now we haven't thought of the rubbish as our problem, but that attitude must change. We don't want to be guinea pigs,'

Peppino warns as an image of five extremely cute white rodents flashes on the screen.

A chair scrapes and I see the hotelier father of our friend Graziella stand up to have a say. His voice rises in anger. 'It's an incinerator, a polluter, whichever way you look at it. I am convinced that even the council has no idea what harm it will do to us and future generations,' he says, his face reddening. 'If this thing is built, you can forget about people wanting to come here for a day trip!'

By the end of the meeting there is not only talk of a referendum, but the word *revoluzione* is being used. It is agreed that the following Monday residents will stage a street march, which will culminate with a peaceful sit-in of the council chambers.

'Why are you so quiet?' asks Alfonso as we walk home.

'I'm not used to being so actively involved in the community,' I say. I have lived in a place where council plans have directly affected me. But there is another factor which is unsettling.

'As a journalist, I am used to being on the sidelines and just reporting the facts.'

'Yes, but you are a resident of Procida,' Alfonso points out.

Half an hour later, checking my emails I smile as I read a new one that has popped into my inbox.

Dearest Penelope
The other day you asked me what the Procidans were like. Well, I think you will be now able to understand how they are: they sleep for years, electing the worst administrations, and then suddenly they wake up and applaud the first person who yells 'Revoluzione!' For someone who has the itches at the stench of easy demagogy, you can only imagine how I feel!
A huge hug,
Peppino

OTTOBRE

Pizza di scarole

(Endive, olive and caper pie)

A hearty winter warmer, in Italy this flavoursome pie is most commonly cooked around Christmas time. I reckon it tastes good whatever the weather and it can be eaten cold, too. If you add sultanas their sweetness contrasts nicely against the salty olives (and anchovies, if you choose to toss them in, too). Don't forget to squeeze the endives really well, because no one wants seconds of a watery pie ...

Serves 6

Pastry:

    500 grams flour

    25 grams (1 cube) beer yeast (dry yeast)

    ½ teaspoon sugar

    1 heaped teaspoon table salt

    250–300 grams tepid water (use less or more
        depending on dough consistency)

    60 millilitres (1 espresso cup) extra virgin olive oil

Filling:

    4 bunches (1 kilogram) endives, washed

    4 tablespoons extra virgin olive oil

2 whole garlic cloves, peeled

50 grams black olives, pitted

50 grams capers (or less if you prefer the pie less salty)

25 grams sultanas (optional – for sweeter taste)

25 grams anchovies (optional – for saltier taste)

30 grams pine nuts

table salt and pepper (to taste)

Method

1. Start with the pastry: pour the flour onto a tabletop and make a small, rough well in the centre. Add the yeast and then put the sugar and salt on opposite sides of the *vulcano*. Add a little bit of water and begin to mix and knead, adding the water until the pasta is smooth and stretchy. (Hint: you can also dissolve the yeast and sugar in the tepid water and add gradually).

2. Shape the pasta into a ball, dust with flour, cover with clingwrap or a tea towel, and let it rest for up to an hour. If it's in a warm spot 30 minutes should suffice.

3. Put the cleaned endives in a deep frying pan with a little water to boil for about 15 minutes.

4. Drain the endives, let them cool and squeeze them really well with hands to drain excess water.

5. Add the oil to another pan and fry the garlic until golden, then add the olives and capers*.

6. After about 2 minutes add the pine nuts and endives, salt and pepper to taste. Stir-fry until the water in the endives evaporates as much as possible. Remove from the heat and leave to cool.

7. Grease a pie tin then take the ball of dough and divide in two, with one part slighter bigger.

8. Take the bigger ball and roll it into a rough circle. Use it to line the bottom and sides of the pie tin.

9. Take the other piece of dough and roll it into another circle before putting it aside.

10. Pour the chilled endives mix into the pie tin and spread evenly across the base. Moisten the edge of the dough with water.

11. Roll out the second dough circle on your rolling pin and gently place it over the endives to cover the mixture. Moisten the edge with water, then use your fingers to close the pie around the edges.

12. Pierce the pie top with a skewer a few times then cook in oven at 200 degrees Celsius for about half an hour or until golden.

*If you love anchovies, you can now also add a few of the pungent, hairy fish, as well as a few sultanas!

NOVEMBRE

All in the family

The orange-and-white striped hydrofoil powers out of the port with Alfonso aboard. As I watch it disappear I think of all the Procidan wives who have stood where I have to say innumerable farewells, and I count myself lucky not to be in their shoes. Not only does Alfonso return to me after no more than a few days, he always leaves me well supplied: stacked neatly in plastic bags in our freezer are *polpette* (meatballs) with *provola*, pine nuts, and a slightly healthier version of zucchini *polpette*. Spoilt? Me? Nah.

I turn and walk to Bar Capriccio. It's one of those mornings when I need two espressos in quick succession to jump-start my motor.

I sing out *buongiorno* to Giuseppe, the barista – Gilda's brother. He's chatting to his wife Valentina, who is nursing their youngest child, Marco. On the verge of walking, he is – like every Italian child – the centre of attention, reducing men and women of every age to a mass of cooing babysitters.

I step into the bar and stop short at the counter. Five or six empty espresso cups rest there, the customers nowhere in sight. It's like a scene in a Western where a gunfight has drawn the town's population out of the saloon and onto the street.

'What's going on?' I ask Giuseppe.

'Do you know Salvatore?' says Giuseppe, his big, expressive eyes flashing with excitement. He is referring to one of the many men who hang around outside the cafe all day.

'Well, this morning, he was in the post office, and when he saw an old woman with cash in her hand ready to pay a bill he grabbed one hundred euro and began to run.'

I begin laughing uncontrollably. Given the size of Procida, the chances of anyone getting away with such a robbery are non-existent.

'So then what happened?' I ask.

'Naturally, he came straight to Bar Capriccio and sat down outside as if nothing was wrong. Ten minutes later the police showed up and nabbed him.'

Giuseppe shakes his head.

'What drama, this will be the talk of the island for about a week!' he says. 'It's a shame they got him – I mean, we *need* people like this on the island, otherwise we don't have anything to gossip about.'

Talk of the heist has reminded me I have a few postcards to send to my family, which have been sitting in my handbag for at least a month waiting until I am in the right mood to face the post office.

With an hour to kill before the peaceful protest march against the incinerator, I make a beeline for the plain brick edifice close to Piazza della Repubblica. The usual crowd hovers inside.

Of all the post offices I have visited in Italy, Procida's is best designed to encourage outright bedlam. It has a first-in-first-served electronic ticket system, invaluable given Italians are simply not capable of forming a queue, and there's even seating for customers who are waiting. Unfortunately, once seated your view of the electronic screen is blocked by a thick concrete pillar, resulting in a never-ending game of musical chairs from the moment the post office opens its doors.

I lean on a wall and finish the last two pages of *Il Panno di Lino*, or *The Linen Cloth*, written by local woman Clelia Ambrosino. I also have a copy of her first book, a collection of the island's most typical recipes. Her novel is the tale of a solitary sailor, Salvatore, married to Mariuccia, and they have two daughters. When Mariuccia dies suddenly, Salvatore is persuaded by his family to marry her sister, Matilde, who bears him another daughter. But Salvatore, still mourning his first wife and racked with guilt for marrying a woman he doesn't love, flees to France, where he marries a third woman with whom he has another child, a daughter who eventually comes in search of her Procidan family. I finish the book and glance at the picture of the author on the back cover. I read the text below to learn that, lo and behold, Clelia Ambrosino works at the post office. I scan the counter and notice that the only woman working does indeed match the photo in my book.

When it is my turn I take it as destiny that Clelia is the one to serve me. I waste no time in flashing my reading material.

She blushes with pleasure and in the time it takes to serve me she establishes that I am living on the island and invites me over for dinner. Happy to avoid cooking when my chef is out of town, I suggest a day and we exchange phone numbers.

As I leave the post office I notice Salvatore lingering outside, perhaps too embarrassed by the events of the morning to assume his regular position inside. Obviously the police had better things to do than keep an unstable but harmless person behind bars.

Within a few steps I arrive at Piazza della Repubblica, where the march is set to begin within half an hour. Most of my friends have told me they will come along, but I don't see anyone I know.

To my relief, Maria Grazia, Rosalba and Nicoletta soon arrive, as does Bottone. We listen to a recorded message being blasted from a small minivan. Before long the call goes out for the march to begin.

At the front of a crowd I estimate conservatively to be two hundred, three people carry a banner with the words, '*Si alla differenziata, no al dissociatore*' written in bold red.

The chanting crowd passes along the street, past manicured gardens and rubbish bins piled high, before it finally reaches the council building.

With barely a protest from the council workers, the crowd surges up the steps and enters the building, clambering up more steps to a large room on the second floor to stage a peaceful sit-in.

It appears the mayor, who only a day earlier said he was ready to talk with the locals, is out of town for the day. He is not the only one. I scan the crowd for Peppino.

I listen for the next hour as a microphone is passed between various speakers, from hotel owners to a young schoolgirl who earns whistles of support from the crowd when she says she and her friends managed to attend even though their teachers forbade them.

The bulk of the speakers support continued recycling, but slam the council for having awarded a collection contract to a company they view as useless and expensive.

The sit-in winds up with the crowd being urged to attend an upcoming council meeting at the invitation of the mayor, where a panel of experts will address the community.

Rubbish protestors fill the streets

Everyone flows back onto the street and marches resolutely down to the main port, stopping in the piazza for a barbecue lunch. In the end, I can't help but think with a smile, the Italians just want to do what they do best: eat!

Tired of the throng, I bail out along with my girlfriends.

I feel strangely flat as I start up the hill towards home. It was good to see the community turn out in decent numbers, but without Alfonso by my side to translate it was often hard to understand the speakers. When Procidans get passionate they automatically slip into their dialect. As much as I want to attend the mayor's meeting, I have a feeling I will be a no-show unless Alfonso can join me. After all, it's not like the issue will come to a vote. Besides, I can always get an update from my friends or read about the proceedings in the local newspaper the next day. Call me a defeatist, but sometimes practicality reigns supreme.

As I go for my morning stroll along the street leading to the port, I notice an unmistakable figure ahead of me. I quicken my step and find myself within a metre of Evangelista. With a small, lithe build and one of the most spectacularly obvious wigs I have ever seen, the elderly Procidan is a living piece of island history. Bowled over by his theatrical hair the first time I set eyes on him, I tapped my island friends for information and learnt that Evangelista is a costume maker who once worked as the servant to Vera Vergani, a star of Italian comic theatre in the 1920s.

I have been keen to talk to him ever since, but due to his old age – or perhaps that Procidan reserve – he doesn't seem to get out much. Now that I am so close, I don't intend to let this showstopper get away.

I stretch out my hand and tap him on the shoulder, marvelling again at his head of thick silver-grey hair.

He turns and my fascination deepens as I look into his eyes, which have that slight milkiness of old age, and notice the wrinkles incised in his pallid face.

When I mention as casually as possible that I have heard he is a fabulous costume maker, a wide grin spreads across his face.

'*Vieni*,' he says, beckoning me to follow him as he opens a door a few steps away. Inside is a beautiful potted garden. We pass a rose-pink building and walk under an elegant arched staircase leading to the roof terrace of the sprawling house which, my host explains, once belonged to Vera Vergani, his glamorous former employer. After her death, the house was divided into apartments and sold, but Vergani's granddaughter, Elisabetta, an award-winning Italian costume designer and author, kept the apartment with the terrace.

Evangelista opens the door to his small, ground-floor studio.

I enter a room crammed with piles of material; frocks and ornaments scattered everywhere. I admire two elaborate dresses – one in a shiny olive-green fabric and the other a deep pink, both embellished with strips of gold material – which drop elegantly from coat hangers.

Instinctively I touch the fabric in appreciation and Evangelista nods when I ask him if he made them for the *Graziella* fashion parade.

When I ask Evangelista why the legend of Graziella is so strongly celebrated in Procida, he shrugs.

'Procida is an island of culture and richness, and the story of Graziella resounds because she is a *bella ragazza*, the daughter of a fisherman,' he says. 'The young girls today know about it but they lack the elegance of the old days.'

He points to a wall where some framed photographs of women in traditional costumes hang.

'See that photo at the bottom? That's my niece. She won years ago, now she has three daughters of her own.'

Evangelista beckons me to sit down then drops gracefully onto a small stool, upholstered in cream-and-gold fabric, positioned in front of a black Singer sewing machine on a small table.

'This would be at least one hundred years old. It was my mother's and I brought it here when she passed away,' he says of the Singer.

I look around the tiny room in awe. I feel as if I have been given special access to one of those priceless displays that are cordoned off in a museum. I am sure none of my Procidan friends have been where I am now sitting.

Extravagant hats hang from walls draped with dresses, all dripping in silver, coloured beading and tulle. An antique doll of the Madonna is encased in protective glass, while oriental fans are framed on another wall alongside some autographed black-and-white photos of Italian acting greats, including the late Marcello Mastroianni.

Evangelista smiles when I ask him to tell me a little about his life, given I have heard so much of his talent.

'You want to know my history? Well, there's a lot – I'm eighty-five years old. I was born on Procida but I worked from the age of sixteen as a fisherman, and I travelled to Trieste, Ancona and Fiumincino,' he begins, after lighting a cigarette.

One of ten children, Evangelista fished from a young age to help support his ever-expanding family, until he turned thirty-eight.

Evangelista at work in his studio

'That's when I met *la signora* Vergani . . .'

Evangelista pauses as if to emphasise what a momentous occasion it was.

He leans forward and reaches into a cane basket to retrieve some yellowed newspapers, and I read about Vergani, who was born in Milan in 1894 and died at the age of ninety-five. She was twenty-one when she began to act for the famed theatre company of Ruggero Ruggeri, a noted film and stage actor of the late nineteenth and early twentieth century.

At only thirty-four she abandoned her stellar theatre career – she had performed in no less than one hundred and sixty comedies – for love. Aboard a ship en route to a foreign destination for a theatre production, she set eyes on the Procidan-born captain, Leonardo Pescarolo, and the pair were instantly smitten. Marrying and moving to Genova, the couple had two children, Leo and Vera. Vera would grow up to marry respected Italian director Giuliano Montaldo.

Vergani and Pescarolo eventually moved back to his island birthplace, where he passed away in 1978. Vergani died just over ten years later.

I look at the newspaper image of Vergani in her acting days. Her dark wavy hair cut in a chic bob, she wears an off-the-shoulder dress which was no doubt very racy for the time.

'How did you meet Vera?' I ask Evangelista.

'She saw me in a local theatre production here on Procida, and she asked me to come to work here,' he says, waving his arm to indicate the *palazzo* around us. 'I said yes immediately, because I knew she was a wonderful woman and I was tired of fishing. I came and lived here, and I basically did all her errands. I looked after the sixteen rooms in the original villa, I cooked and took care of the garden. I worked for her for another thirty years . . . and now I'm the one on the pension!'

I stare at Evangelista, sitting by his beautiful sewing machine, and ask him if he learnt his trade from his mother.

'No, I taught myself,' he says, lighting another cigarette and immediately apologising for smoking 'like a Turk'.

'I always dabbled, but when *la signora* passed away I had more time on my hands so I started to sew more. I just wanted something to do because I don't know how to be inactive.'

I know how you feel, I think.

'When I worked for *la signora* I never had time for anything. The house was enormous and I was working from early morning until midnight. *La signora* always had famous guests to stay, like Mastroianni. I met him in Rome and he said to *la signora,* "What good fortune that you have Evangelista – he knows how to do everything!" I was like a son to her.'

As I comment on the beauty of the elaborate costumes hanging on his walls, Evangelista tells me he has sewn dresses for the *La Graziella* parade for over three decades.

He assisted with costumes on the film of the same name, inspired by the book, starring Maria Fiore, and he helped with the costumes and had a cameo role in the film *Francesca e Nunziata*, starring Sofia Loren.

'Sofia Loren liked my hats,' he says proudly, adding that he has won a few trophies for his efforts, one of which sits on an antique dresser beside me.

When I ask Evangelista how much the island has changed since he was a child, his eyes light up.

'When I was young it was so beautiful, there were no cars, and fruit and vegetable sellers sold their wares on the street. Now there is so much traffic, and the road work on the street outside is a nightmare. Procida has so much more to offer than the other islands nearby. Capri, what does it have? A small piazza. But there you live well, because there are no cars and you breathe fresh air. Ischia is like us. Invaded by traffic.'

I glance at another news article in the collection he gave me and read the headline 'Evangelista, let us dream!' It's a response to Evangelista's announcement at the time that he would no longer design costumes for *La Graziella*. It urges him not to abandon the island's creative scene.

'So, you've decided to keep going?' I ask with a smile.

'Yes . . . Look, back then I was tired so I said, "I'm getting too old" but everyone kept insisting. So now here I am. It's tiring, but it's fun.' Evangelista looks at all the fabric around him. 'I have clothes everywhere, in cupboards and drawers. And albums, too.'

He takes one from a pile of photo albums gathering dust in a cane basket and we flick through the pages, looking at photos of everything from curvy *Graziella* contestants and models in vibrant designs to Evangelista himself, dressed in heels and fishnets for a local theatre production.

Always inspired by someone who has lived to a ripe old age and still has energy to burn, I ask him what the secret is to a good, long life.

'I thank the Lord for my long life and for making me able to do what no one else is capable of – so much so that the whole island knows me,' he says proudly. 'How do I do it? I don't eat a lot, I don't drink, and I look after myself. And then I think the key to life is to always be carefree. I have always been like that. Now I am old I want to die in peace without bothering anyone,' he says with a chuckle. 'Old age is ugly. If you are sick, better to die than bother someone. Who knows how long I have before I go to the other world?'

I consider this, then ask Evangelista if he has ever thought of leaving the island.

'I'm happy here, and besides, I'm too old now. I don't want to go anywhere. I used to go to Rome to the theatre with *la signora*, but only because she wouldn't have been happy if I didn't accompany her. And she introduced me to so many personalities. Famous people.'

Outside the afternoon light is fading. 'I must go, I have a dress fitting for a girl around the corner. She wants to marry in a traditional Procidan costume,' Evangelista says.

We shake hands. I feel honoured to have met someone who is a part of the island's history.

My very casual career as an English teacher is proving challenging. Which would be fine if the children, not the parents, were the problematic ones.

Less than half of the reminder text messages I send to parents a day before my twice-weekly classes elicit any response. Explaining the situation to Anna, I tell her I will teach just one class a week, because I am tired of planning lessons to have only one or two kids turn up.

'I completely understand; unfortunately it happens to us at the childcare centre too,' she says with a shrug.

Some days I love teaching, especially when the kids are responsive, but when my flock is tetchy there are times when I wonder what the hell I am doing singing 'Old Macdonald had a Farm'.

What validates my efforts is hearing one of my little pupils chant numbers, colours and words at random. I will never again ridicule new parents who rave for hours about the moment their child spoke his or her first word. At the end of each teaching day

I recount cute tales to Alfonso, who usually appreciates them as much as I do.

However, when Gilda calls to say she wants her twins, Angelo and Michele, to come to me for English lessons with two other kids, I stall for time.

'Let me check my schedule,' I say, realising how ridiculous that sounds, given I don't have a full-time job.

I call her back within the hour to accept, thanking her for thinking of me. Even though I am not convinced teaching is my calling in life, it's important to keep busy – with winter approaching it's all too easy to hibernate.

As I put on a coat and prepare to head out for dinner at Clelia's house I think of Gilda with fondness. I've been spending more time with her lately; we go swimming together at the pool at Ischia, along with her younger sister Loredana. Hanging out with the two sisters is always fun. Their sense of humour and mock rivalry reminds me of my relationships with my own sisters.

Clelia is waiting outside to pick me up. I jump into the passenger seat of her small two-door car and say *buonasera*. I would estimate Clelia to be in her early forties, with steely blue eyes softened by a plump face. She explains that dinner will be at her parents' house, where she has been living with her young son since she split with her husband a year earlier. Her older son, a sailor, is rarely home.

As we set off, she admits that she is missing her freedom and is looking for a flat she can afford to rent on her own.

'I've invited two of my girlfriends, Caterina and Daniela, to dinner – I hope you don't mind,' she says.

'The more the merrier.'

We drive through a gate along the Panorama, the coastal stretch of road heading towards Solchiaro. I have walked past the closed gate a million times and now, finally, I have a chance to see what lies beyond: a two-storey brick-and-timber house with a pretty garden.

I follow Clelia past the ground floor. Through the window I see an old man with a young boy, eating dinner.

'That's my son, Gabriele, and my dad,' says Clelia as she walks up the stairs to the top storey. She opens a door to lead us into a small kitchen with a dining area.

'*Mamma mia!*' I exclaim as my eyes rest on the table.

Clelia points from dish to dish to explain the smorgasbord: *musetto di maile* (pig's snout) marinated in lemon, salt and parsley; a savoury bread with sausage and *friarielli*, a spinach-like vegetable found only in the Campania region; *pizza di scarole*; a savoury bacon-filled bread; marinated capsicum, salad and tripe.

'I thought I'd cook you some hearty winter dishes,' she says with a smile.

Telling my host I also have her cookbook, I ask if food has particular importance on Procida.

'Well, being a small island without the usual distractions, often the only thing to do is to meet and eat,' Clelia says as she opens the bottle of red wine I brought.

I love talking about food and Clelia is soon nominating the most common *terra e mare* (land and sea) ingredients used in local cooking. From rabbit, artichokes and *parmeggiana* to cuttlefish and pea stew and pasta with eggplant and swordfish.

'Who taught you to cook?'

'My mother is a fabulous cook, so I learnt a lot from her, but I have always had a passion for the kitchen.'

I remember that in Clelia's second book, featuring the sailor Salvatore and the women in his life, one of his Procidan daughters, Archina, used her grandmother's old recipe book. Clelia nods when I ask if she has her own grandmother's recipes.

'She was an exceptional cook, but she was extremely jealous and she never gave a recipe to anyone!' Clelia laughs. 'In fact, it was only when she died that my mother and our nieces and I could read them.'

I ask whether the character of Salvatore is based on a real person.

'Yes, Salvatore is my paternal grandfather,' she says. A respected naval commander, he had some children with his first Procidan wife. When she passed away, he married her sister, Clelia's grandmother, before vanishing into thin air.

'My family tried to track him down and they discovered he had a whole new family somewhere else. My grandmother couldn't raise her kids alone so she was helped by her brother.'

Clelia looks sad as she tells me her family still suffers from her grandfather's disappearance.

'My father is a walking wound. When his father abandoned Procida, he had to get his navigating diploma immediately to go to sea and bring in some money for the family. In those days the contracts were for more than a year, and he worked hard. He didn't have a youth. And he doesn't want to know about his father.'

Clelia is philosophical about the impact the sea has had on the life of her family.

'I think Procidans are a bit like shellfish,' she says. 'To a certain point, the island protects you like a womb, and it brings you economic benefits. But at the same time it isolates you and robs you of loved ones. Women on Procida have a love–hate relationship with the sea. I watched my mother from a young age and she just accepted the status quo. I think women here are stronger than most, and more sensitive.'

While I remember, I ask Clelia to sign my copy of her new book. As she searches for a pen, I comment on the cover photograph, showing a young girl dressed in a traditional dark smock with a cream linen cloth draped like a shawl over her shoulder.

'The shawls were made by the prisoners serving life sentences in the jail at Terra Murata,' says Clelia. 'They were given big rolls of thread which they wove on a huge loom to create rough linen. Then they cut it up to make everything from handkerchiefs to towels and sheets, which Procidan women bought and then embroidered.' There is a knock on the door and Clelia ushers in her friends Daniela and Caterina, the latter bearing a plate of sweets wrapped in pretty *pasticceria* paper held together with a ribbon. Clelia pours them each a glass of wine and hands around plates.

I load mine with spoonfuls of the dishes before me and sample the *musetto* with trepidation. To my dismay, it is as slimy as the tip of the nose of a pig that has just slurped from a trough. I push the image out of my head and swallow.

I stab at some tripe, which has the same texture as the pig's snout. Fortunately I fare much better with the others dishes.

'This savoury bread is great,' I tell Clelia, adding that the bacon gives it a delicious flavour.

'There are specks of crackling and lard in it, too,' she says, with a hint of guilt.

'All in all, there are probably forty different types of animal fat,' chimes in Daniela, just to make me feel lighter. She cuts a generous slice of the *pizza di scarole* and plonks it on my plate.

'Here, in the south, we cook very rich foods, cover them with heavy dressings, and we fry so many things, and then occasionally we go on diets,' she groans.

'We have tried ten thousand diets, but none of them suit us,' Clelia says, making us all laugh. 'Do you remember that time we saw a dietician in Pozzuoli?'

She turns to me.

'Four of us went to the appointment and took all the advice on earth, and then we went back to the port to wait for the ferry. The only problem was that there, in the *piazza*, was a fabulous *pasticceria*. Well, given we had a month before the next weigh-in, we bought a huge tray of sweets and demolished it in five minutes!'

I laugh as Clelia pours me some more wine and talks of how one of the things she loves about Procida is the fresh produce.

'You can't find everything in the supermarket here so you just use what is in season. Everything is more flavoursome.'

She opens the freezer and pulls out a bottle of green alcohol I realise is a digestive.

'It's made from bergamot orange; it's a little like *limoncello* but it's more floral, more aromatic,' she says, pouring a small amount into a plastic espresso cup. I take a sip and find it is too bitter for my palate. 'I love it because it takes me back to my childhood. My grandfather had a bergamot orange tree.'

'Speaking of sweets, let's make a dent in them,' says Daniela, opening the parcel at the end of the table. She selects a typical Neapolitan, ricotta-filled pastry called a *sfogliatella,* while Clelia and I opt for the rum-soaked *babà*.

Caterina reaches for the cream-filled *coda di aragosta*, which takes its name from its lobster tail shape.

She finishes it and declares that she would love to lose a few kilos.

'The problem is I eat, and eat, then think, Oh well, tomorrow,' she sighs as she stands to leave.

Later, as I walk up the steps to our apartment, I can't help feeling that an extra kilo or two are making the journey to the front door increasingly difficult. Chunky indeed.

I fidget with excitement as the train speeds through Rome's outskirts to Fiumicino international airport. I haven't seen my parents for a year and now they will meet the first Italian serious boyfriend I have lived with.

Alfonso sits quietly, staring at me from time to time with tangible anxiety. Perhaps it was churlish of me to compare my father to the restless and highly competitive father played by Robert De Niro in *Meet The Parents*.

'You'll be fine,' I reassure him before throwing a newspaper into his hands for distraction.

Finally, my parents walk through the arrival gate and after I hug them I watch happily as Alfonso kisses the cheeks of my mother before turning to my father who, to his credit, takes the local culture in his stride.

To help my parents get over their jetlag, we stay in Rome for two days, seeing a few tourist sites and eating at my favourite haunts in the city I once called home, before catching the train south to Naples.

The hydrofoil to Procida lurches in big seas, forcing my dad to stand and walk outside to the back, but by the time the boat slips into our home port the colour has returned to his face.

At the taxi rank I am pleased when one of the drivers points us in the direction of an older style cab, called an *ape* after the Italian word for bee – perhaps because they have a noisy drone. These three-wheeled cars are generally used by the island's farmers, who load produce into the back, but a few taxi drivers have fixed on a tarp roof and converted the back into a primitive seating area.

'Yikes!' Mum yelps when her head knocks the tarp roof after the taxi hits a bump.

'Hang in there, Nel,' I say, using my family's pet name for her.

At our apartment Mum's face lights up at the sea views from the lounge room and the terrace.

'I can't believe you have so much space, and so much light for Italy,' she says, reminding me of my first shared house in Rome, where natural light was not exactly abundant.

We rug up and go for a long walk, eventually arriving at Bar Capriccio, where Enzo extends a warm welcome to my parents.

'Come to our house tomorrow for lunch,' he orders, adding that his own parents will be coming. 'Are you sure we won't be too many?' I ask Enzo, who merely waves us out the door.

'What a lovely man!' says my mother when I tell her of our lunch invitation. I nod, thinking how Enzo and his parents have a special gift for making everyone feel *a casa*, at home.

Elisa's husband Michele with a freshly netted *polipo* (octupus)

On the way home we buy some fresh clams at the fish shop and Alfonso is soon busy in the kitchen, whipping up his signature *linguine alla vongole*. Dad stands in the doorway, chatting and allaying Alfonso's concern about the number of shark attacks in Australia. For some reason, Italians think they happen as often as car prangs Down Under.

After I set the table with a red-and-white gingham cloth like those found in many a *trattoria*, I put on Billy Joel's early album, *The Stranger*, which is one of Dad's favourites. When the song 'Scenes From an Italian Restaurant' begins, Dad and I start to sing, hamming things up with exaggerated harmony, making Alfonso grin.

Mum retires with a bad headache, leaving Alfonso, Dad and me at the dinner table.

'*Chin, chin,*' says Dad, raising his glass of white wine.

I take a mouthful of pasta and throw Alfonso a panicked look.

'It's too salty,' he says, somewhat of an understatement given the pasta seems to have been boiled in water from the Dead Sea.

'*O dio!* The pasta is undercooked!' he continues, his face reddening.

'Didn't you test it?' I ask, suspecting he had been distracted by the conversation and trying to impress my dad.

'No,' he says sheepishly. 'I am mortified.'

Dad and Alfonso decide to go out, but I opt to stay home with Mum.

It's well past midnight when I hear the door open and feel Alfonso's weight drop onto the sofa bed we have pulled out in the spare room.

'Argh, you smell like a brewery,' I groan.

'I walked into Bar Capriccio and everyone said, "*Whoahhhh!* How's it going with Penny's parents?" he says with a laugh. 'I turned around and introduced everyone to your father . . . that shut them up!'

According to Alfonso, my father was the hit of the evening, surrounded by all of my girlfriends. I don't have to work hard to imagine the scene.

The next morning I hear Mum and Dad stir and stick my head in their bedroom door. Dad looks up and grins like a cat who's swallowed a sizeable budgie.

'I was surrounded by women,' he says, winking at Mum, before rolling off the names of all my girlfriends.

Just after midday we join Gilda and Enzo for lunch, starting with a glass of wine on their roof terrace, with its spectacular view of Terra Murata and, further in the distance, Marina Grande.

Back downstairs we find Michele and Elisa just arriving. I introduce them to my parents, who ask me to tell my elderly friends how much they love our island. Michele is just starting to use his somewhat rusty sailor's English when Enzo tells us to sit down at the table. Gilda dashes around the kitchen with her mother, Clara, who has perfected many a recipe from watching the midday television program *Prova della Cuoca*, Cook's Test, in which teams of chefs compete to create their dishes in record time.

Today the mother-and-daughter team of Gilda and Clara serve a lunch fit for a royal family: an antipasto of marinated anchovies and capsicum and ricotta-filled zucchini flowers; pasta with zucchini and prawns; and calamari stuffed with egg, parsley, breadcrumbs and bacon.

When Gilda places some roasted chestnuts on the table my mother throws me a look which tells me she cannot cope with any more food. As if on cue, Clara places a huge chocolate *caprese* cake alongside a mountainous plate of chocolate profiteroles.

'Can you tell Gilda I just can't manage?' Mum pleads before I do my best to translate in Italian a joke Dad has just remembered, causing the table to dissolve in laughter because there is a similar version in Italian.

We leave the island to embark on a week of travelling, with the first stop being the port of Pozzuoli to meet Alfonso's parents.

I spy Maria Rosaria waiting for us on the dock as we walk off the boat. She shakes my parents' hands and kisses them as Alfonso's father, Enzo, appears. He stands on his tiptoes to kiss my mother's cheeks before jokingly jumping like a kangaroo to reach my father.

Over a coffee Alfonso and I translate, both feeling a little nervous in front of our respective parents.

Before we leave, Mum gives Maria Rosaria a small purse with a kookaburra design on it and a T-shirt with 'G'day Mate' on the front to Enzo, who appreciates the gift more when I explain its significance. We hop in the car and wave goodbye to Enzo and Maria Rosaria. When they have disappeared from sight Alfonso and I exchange a look of relief. Considering the language difficulties, our parents' first introduction went swimmingly.

After a trip to Pompeii we drive to the mountains in the nearby region of Abruzzo, where Alfonso's grandfather left him a little house in a hilltop village.

For the next two days, we make scenic trips to nearby towns. In the evenings we head home to light the small log fire, cook dinner and play cards around the cabin's small table.

'Four aces,' declares Alfonso jubilantly, reducing us to tears by pronouncing the word like a rude term for buttocks.

I bask in the fact my parents and Alfonso seem to have hit it off.

The next day, with band practice scheduled in Naples, Alfonso leaves us at the nearest station to catch the train to Tuscany, where we plan to make a quick visit to see Dad's brother. Stopping en route in Florence, we are holed up in a cosy *trattoria* when my Dad suddenly gets serious.

'So, Pen, is Alfonso *the one*?' he asks, pouring me some more wine as if sensing I might need some assistance.

I take a sip and my thoughts spill out randomly. I explain how Pa's death sent me into a spin, and that I worry about the fact our careers hardly put us on a secure financial footing as far as future plans go.

'What I do know is that he is my best mate and we love each other a great deal.'

'Well,' says Dad, throwing me a stern look, 'let's just hope there's nothing underneath the carpet.'

'What do you mean?' I ask, jokingly adding that Alfonso is not a member of the Camorra. I had forgotten just how cynical my father can be.

'There are no guarantees in life, that's all I am trying to say. Everything is always a risk.'

'Robert, we barely knew David and Craig before they married Lisa and Sally,' says Mum, referring to my sisters' husbands.

'True,' says my father, casually scanning the dessert menu in a sign that he's finished his sermon.

My father's words rattle in my head almost as much as his snores as I lie in the dark of our small hotel room. When cultural differences flare in my relationship, I can't deny that I have often thought it would be easier to return home and – who knows –

maybe hook up with a local lad. But in Australia I never found a man who was as open and sensitive and affectionate as Alfonso. Confused, I turn on my iPod and tune out.

After a week on the road, my heart skips as I scan the port of Procida from the deck of the ferry. As we wait for the ramp to lower, I am suddenly hit by a wave of exhaustion brought on by playing tour guide and translator. The sight of Alfonso is a comfort, so too is his long embrace. He wrests my mother's backpack from her and we stroll home to relax for a few hours.

Maria Grazia and Gennaro have invited us to have an *aperitivo* that evening before Procida's annual *Sagra del Vino*, wine festival, gets under way. We huddle in their kitchen nibbling on olives and cheese and sipping *prosecco* as more of our friends arrive.

'How many people can you fit in your kitchen?' Dad asks Gennaro with mock annoyance.

'We're having a competition, actually,' jokes Gennaro, handing Dad another Campari.

Departing en masse for the festival, we walk up a sloping, narrow street and past the church of Madonna della Libera to enter a large field where the *sagra* is lit up by fairy lights strung between trees. There are already long queues leading to the sausage sizzle and a few bands are swinging into action. The traditional Neapolitan music attracts young and old couples who perform the *Tammuriata*, an energetic dance involving lots of twirling and finger-clicking. Gennaro and a few of our other male friends lock arms to do a jig, and our friend Ramon, a short man with his head shaved in a number-one cut, is being whirled around by a woman twice his height and age.

After nibbling a plate of sweets my mother is happy to call it a night, so we walk home.

The faint boom of the music echoes across the island as I lie in bed. Within a day or so my parents will be gone, and I struggle to subdue the mounting sadness.

We awake to a beautiful clear day and, as Dad and Mum pack, Alfonso and I busy ourselves in the kitchen making fresh ravioli filled with ricotta, pumpkin and a sprinkle of cinnamon, and some chicken *involtini* for lunch.

We carry everything up to our rooftop terrace, where we are joined by seagulls that strut along the edge of the balcony wall.

'Strewth, they're enormous,' Dad says, throwing some bread to the nearest seagull as I translate the first word for Alfonso.

Later we go down to Bar Capriccio for an *aperitivo*.

When we make to leave, Enzo steps out of the bar to kiss my parents goodbye.

'You look after them,' my dad says in a tone I read to be half serious.

The next morning we take the early hydrofoil to Naples then catch a train to Rome in time for my parents' afternoon flight. My heart heaves as I turn to hug them on the platform at Termini station before they board the train for Fiumicino airport.

'It was great to meet you,' my mother tells Alfonso, and my dad gives him a hug.

On the train back to Naples, Alfonso holds my hand as I weep silently. Never before has homesickness struck me so hard.

'Don't worry, we'll be in Australia soon,' he says.

Suddenly three months seems like an awfully long time to be without my own family.

For the next few days I can't seem to manage to start or finish anything; my mind keeps replaying moments of my parents' trip and flashing to thoughts about my homeland.

After a quick telephone call to Alfonso, who is still in Naples, instinct drives me out the door and up to Elisa and Michele's home. Admittedly, it's just before seven o'clock, when the couple have dinner.

'*Mangi con noi,*' Elisa orders me to join them in dining and swiftly sets another place at the table.

Michele pours me a glass of wine as Elisa dishes up fresh fish and *finocchi al gratin,* or fennel baked in white sauce topped with parmesan.

The tasty dish is the perfect comfort food, and is exactly what I needed.

After dinner, I take out some photos from my parents' visit.

'How are you feeling, Pe?' says Elisa, her voice softening with concern.

'I miss my family . . . and when I see them I just always get confused as to where home is,' I say. My eyes rest on the photo of lunch with Mum and Dad, Alfonso and me on our terrace, when I was lucky enough to have the best of both worlds.

'That's to be expected,' Elisa says. 'Won't it be great to see your parents and sisters again soon, in your own country?'

I look at Elisa and Michele's caring faces and realise how much I have missed their company in the weeks I have been distracted with playing host.

As I walk home the streets are deserted and the yellow-and-white churches I pass glow beneath fairy lights, which signal the approach of Christmas.

NOVEMBRE

FINOCCHI AL GRATIN
(BAKED FENNEL)

I mostly eat fennel raw, sliced up and dressed with lemon, salt and olive oil, but this recipe makes a nice change in the cooler months for those addicted to its aniseed-like tang. My bad memories of white sauce – hiding boiled silverside that always remained dry anyway – are banished by this winning recipe.

Serves 4

    8 fennel bulbs, trimmed at ends and roughly sliced
    ½ litre milk
    2 tablespoons butter
    2 tablespoons flour
    3 tablespoons parmesan cheese, grated
    sprinkle of nutmeg, table salt and pepper

Method

1. Boil the fennel slices until they are tender but still crisp, roughly 5–10 minutes.

2. Make the white sauce: melt the butter in a saucepan then remove from the heat for a minute to sift in the flour, stirring vigorously so lumps don't form. Return the saucepan to a low heat and add the milk little by little, stirring with a wooden spoon until the milk thickens to form a sauce. Add the nutmeg.

3. Grease a baking tray or glass dish with butter and a few teaspoons of white sauce. Layer the fennel slices on top, cover with white sauce, then sprinkle with the parmesan.

4. Bake for about half an hour at 180 degrees Celsius, putting under the grill for the last 5 minutes if a golden crust has not already formed.

This dish is typically served as a *contorno*, or side dish, and is probably best teamed with meat *secondi*. However you choose, it's *delizioso*.

Decembre

'Tis the season to be a glutton

In winter, we have been warned, the Procidans retreat into their shells. However, as the temperature drops, our contact with our friends on the island continues, albeit in fits and starts.

On a biting cold morning I walk into Bar Capriccio and see Bottone, his short frame rendered even more round by a padded windcheater.

'No fishing for you today!' I say to him.

'Bah! I have my means,' says Bottone. My elderly friend tells me that a few winters ago, tired of being trapped on land by the dismal weather, he decided to convert his seven-metre fishing boat.

'I found an old Telecom Italia telephone box, and I sawed it in half and fitted it on to my boat,' says Bottone with a smug grin. 'When I go fishing now I can stick the line out and stay in my cabin, as toasty as can be!'

I laugh out loud, imagining what a strange sight that must be for other fishermen circling Procida.

I farewell Bottone and wrestle with my umbrella against the wind as I pop into the butcher's, our local fruit and vegetable store, and deli to stock up for what I imagine will be a raucous evening at our house.

Playing *tombola* (bingo) and cards in the weeks before Christmas is something of a tradition in Italy, and Procida is no exception, and we have invited our friends around for a few hands.

I spend the rest of the morning cleaning our apartment before I feel stir-crazy enough to face the chill outside for a walk, and end up at the port to meet Alfonso.

He embraces me and pulls a small bag out of his backpack.

'A little gift for you on our special day,' he says in an exaggeratedly soppy voice.

In a flash I realise that today is our first anniversary. Oops.

I open the bag to find Dante's *Divine Comedy* in an edition that has English on one side of the page and Italian on the other. In another bag is the CD of the soundtrack to *Into The Wild*, a film directed by Sean Penn about a young American's decision to drop out of society and find peace in the Alaskan wilderness. When we saw the film in Naples, I was moved to tears by the true-life story and the evocative music by Eddie Vedder.

'I'm sorry, I've been too busy getting ready for tonight to buy you a present, but how about I treat you to dinner at Bordero' later in the week?' I propose, hoping he won't realise I had completely forgotten about the momentous occasion.

'Deal,' he says as we start to walk home.

Happily, after two fairly average replacement chefs, Ottavio has found a new cook, who is slowly bringing Bordero' back into favour, so the prospect of dining there soon is once more appealing.

We do the grocery shopping and Alfonso is soon hard at work preparing the *polpette.*

I assist only when called upon, because in our house two cooks can definitely spoil the meatballs. Though I'd love to help Chef Fonz, somehow I always get under his feet. After countless squabbles – during which I have to restrain myself from taking a skewer and using the chef as my voodoo doll – I have managed to extract a confession from Alfonso that he is far too territorial about the kitchen. In exchange, I have conceded that my clumsiness and generally distracted nature could become a real fire hazard.

Tonight, however, I ask to watch as he makes the meatballs.

'I might want to make them when you're away one night,' I say, sitting on a stool in the corner.

'Fine, but you have to help me,' he replies.

Alfonso takes a big loaf of bread, cuts it open and uses his hands to remove the soft inner dough, which he drops into a bowl. He then pours in about a cup of milk to soften the bread.

He asks me to dice some fresh parsley and I am halfway through my task, when he demands that I stop.

'Why are you using that?' he says with a scowl, pointing at the filleting knife. 'Sometimes you are so stupid!'

'There was no other decent knife. And if I'm so stupid you can do it yourself!' I storm out, into the lounge room to look out over the orchard to the sea.

'Come here!' Alfonso says, his somewhat arrogant tone grating.

Not willing to let a filleting knife come between us, I walk back into the kitchen and resume chopping, until he starts ribbing me about not knowing my knives.

'*Basta!*' I snap before striding out again.

'Chunky, sorry, come back,' says Alfonso, pulling me back into the kitchen. 'I know I become unbearable when I am in the kitchen, but I have a million things to watch, and you have this habit of always getting under my feet!'

He gives me an apologetic hug and tells me to sit in the corner. On my best behaviour, I watch as he squeezes the bread with all his might to drain the milk.

I follow his instructions to put the mince into the bowl, as he cracks an egg into it and tosses in a fistful of grated parmesan, some pine nuts and my perfectly diced parsley, and we keep working in peace.

Finally, he adds some salt and pepper before we begin to roll the mixture into balls.

'That's not a meatball,' says Alfonso, staring at the lump in my hand. I watch as he rolls a perfect specimen.

At nine o'clock our door buzzer sounds and we hear the soft pad of feet on the three flights of stairs up to our apartment, a delicious scent of meatballs wafting from the kitchen.

Graziella sweeps in and heads straight to the kitchen with a spinach and ricotta pie and a plate of *crostini* with melted cheese.

'What's that?' I ask curiously, pointing to the bowl of dip next to the *crostini*.

'It's an onion dip, a bit of an experiment,' says our friend, adding that she made it with onions, butter and a dash of Cognac.

Maria Grazia arrives next with a bottle of whisky and *nocillo,* a hazelnut liqueur her father made. She's followed by Fabrizio, our shipbuilder friend, and Carlo, who is back for the weekend from Palermo.

Fabrizio puts a big square box of *pandoro,* the buttery cake which is a favourite at Christmas, on the table.

'So what's your mother cooked for us?' I ask Carlo, eyeing the plastic bag he is carrying with care.

He produces a savoury pizza with tomato and *mozzarella,*

which Chef Fonz decides to sample immediately to make sure it is up to standard.

Gennaro, a hurricane of nervous energy, comes in carrying a huge box from the *pasticceria* of Bar Cavaliere, where he works with his wife, Maria Grazia.

I raise my eyebrows and look at the box with pleasure.

'*Una torta caprese,* your favourite,' he confirms.

The door is pushed open and we greet Ramon, who works alongside Gennaro, and his partner Antonella, who is a waitress at Bar Capriccio. Ramon produces a packaged chocolate cake as Glorianna and Candida walk through the door, brandishing a large bag of Lindt chocolates and a box of *zampone,* or preserved pig's trotter. A typical Christmas and New Year dish, it is served with lentils which are said to be symbolic of money and other good fortune. We haven't prepared any lentils, so we place the box on top of a kitchen cupboard for the next time we have a sudden craving for pig's trotter.

At ten o'clock we decide to start eating from the large spread on the table. Alfonso's meatballs soon win compliments from all our guests.

'How did you learn to cook so well?' asks Gennaro, who is also a decent chef.

Alfonso explains that he took the initiative when he grew tired of eating the lunch his mother prepared for him every morning before going to work.

My only lasting memory of my mother in the kitchen is the day she singed her eyebrows when lighting a cantankerous oven. I still have memories of her wearing burn cream on her face for days after the accident. It occurs to me that childhood trauma is at the root of my kitchen phobia.

We are opening the fourth bottle of red wine as Maria Grazia's brother Nicola and his girlfriend, Maria Rosaria, buzz our front door. They enter puffing from climbing the stairs, carrying their bike helmets and a bag of *roccoco*, a crunchy biscuit also traditional at Christmas.

Last but not least, Claudia and Angela, two Procidan friends who study and work in Naples, complete our group, plonking three bottles of red wine on the table.

It is almost midnight when we finally start shuffling the cards. We are playing *Mercante in Fiera*, an Italian game which, in my increasingly sozzled state, I struggle to remember.

It involves a lot of swapping and wheeling and dealing, and I watch as my friends bid up to ten euro for a hand of cards.

As I bid five euro I stare at the smoke rising from our guests' cigarettes to fill the domed lounge-room roof. Our apartment is starting to look like a smoking room in a Las Vegas casino.

In the early hours the winners scoop up their takings, and our friends decide to continue the party at Bar Capriccio.

When I first arrived in Italy, I made a point of not socialising with English-speaking foreigners. I don't regret being so strict with myself. Why bother to move to another country if you hang around with people who speak your own language? Only when you communicate in the local language can you appreciate the finer subtleties of a new culture.

Six years on, and with a fair amount of Italian under my belt, I now know that it's important to meet up with people who speak your language and have shared similar experiences. Because sometimes the yearning to totally relax, not to have to think and rephrase words in Italian, is so strong that your very sense of being, and happiness, hinges upon it.

I love the company of my Procidan friends, who are generous in their invitations, but I have reached the point where I crave the companionship of foreigners who, like me, have found themselves washed up on *lo scoglio*, the rock. So I am pleased when Marie-Claude, the fifty-something French woman who rents a part of Elisa and Michele's house with her Italian husband, Giulio, telephones one morning to invite me to a gathering of foreign women under the pretext of sharing *ninna nanna* (lullabies) of different cultures.

In the past, I would have considered all-women events to be somewhat twee. But right now, following a dinner I cooked for my Procidan girlfriends only to sit for two hours at the table understanding barely a third of the conversation and silently willing them to go home, I can't think of anything nicer.

Marie-Claude has asked me to bring an Australian dish, so I decide to cook an apple crumble, one of my mum's more successful dishes.

I while away the afternoon chopping and stewing apples and making the crumble of oats, brown sugar and butter. When I take it out of the oven I stare at its golden, crunchy top with satisfaction.

'*Vieni!*' I follow the voice to Marie-Claude's kitchen. Maria Pia kisses me hello and I place my crumble next to her offering, a rich chocolate cake made with red wine.

Then Marie-Claude introduces me to the other women. There is Sari, a Balinese woman, and her toddler, Jennifer, and Gina, who hails from the Congo. Beside her is Erica, from Rio de Janeiro, with her baby girl, and Alina, a fellow Brazilian from the Amazonian region, with another tot in tow.

There is a knock at the door and I am introduced to South African Duzu, who holds a cute *bambina* in her arms.

As we sit down to eat I stare at the faces around me, wondering why I haven't seen these women before. Most of them have young children, so I imagine they spend more time indoors than loafing about Bar Capriccio like I do.

Soon my plate is loaded with a French zucchini and mint terrine, spicy Brazilian chicken and an Indonesian stir-fry.

From the discussion – mainly in Italian, with a bit of English thrown in – I learn that most of the women met their sailor partners or husbands in their home countries. Then they moved to Procida to create new lives with their men.

Marie-Claude explains that she decided to start the group when she befriended another foreign woman. 'She told me that for the first two years on Procida she was really lonely; she used to go down to the beach to cry in private,' she says, as the women around me nod in unison like an Oprah audience.

'I wanted to unite all the lonely women who live here, to give them a chance to talk about their own culture.'

As rain begins to patter outside the conversation turns to the weather and Alina recalls the climate shock of leaving the Amazon for Procida.

'The coldest weather I have experienced at home is twenty degrees, so when I stepped off the plane in Milan in winter I almost died.'

'I find it really hard in summer, too,' says Gina, to our surprise. 'Everyone thinks it's funny, because I am African, but summer here is so humid, and at home it's dry. My sister visited and said, "How do you cope with this heat?"'

We all laugh at this and the chatter continues as we nibble on dessert.

'Let's start the *ninna nanna*,' says Marie-Claude. Suddenly I realise I didn't think of an Australian lullaby. I got sidetracked making my crumble.

I rack my brain as our host starts singing one of her own national songs.

Then Duzu's rich voice rings out with a melodic tune in her native Zulu, giving me goose bumps.

When my turn comes around I choose a lullaby my late grandmother, Oriel, wrote herself and used to sing to my sisters and me.

As the last note is sung we all clap hands and once again I feel like I am in some cheesy form of self-help group. But unexpectedly this sudden dose of solidarity is doing me good!

As we stand to clear plates two of the women begin dancing the *Tammuriata*, a swaying and circling dance, popular in the Campania region, which I never grow tired of watching. Then Gina takes centre stage, moving in time to clapping hands to perform a traditional Congolese dance, which begins innocently enough before transforming into quite a sensual number.

Later, I stroll home with Sari, who tells me that her husband will be home for Christmas after three months at sea.

'It must be hard, raising Jennifer alone without your own family. But I guess your husband's parents help?'

'Yes, but . . .' Sari stops, obviously wanting to be diplomatic.

'They have different views on things. I want to feed Jennifer rice, which we eat in my country, but they don't think it measures up to pasta.'

I smile understandingly. 'If you ever need anything, don't hesitate to call us,' I tell her, giving her my mobile number.

'If I don't see you beforehand, have a merry Christmas,' she says, gently lifting Jennifer out of the pram she leaves in the entrance to her apartment.

The little girl stirs and Sari begins to sing a lullaby in her native tongue.

'It's the only time I get away with it; my husband's family doesn't seem to want her to learn Indonesian,' she says, rolling her eyes. *'Buona notte.'*

A few days later, we head to Bordero' for the dinner I promised Alfonso for our anniversary. Our friend Ottavio is in a particularly cheery mood now that business is booming again. He leans over and lights the candle at the centre of our table before we order. We manage to squeeze in two delicious courses then walk ten metres along the port to Bar Capriccio.

As we listen to the banter of our group of friends, Alfonso and I lock eyes and grin. Despite the warnings of Enzo upon our arrival, we have survived on Procida for nine months – better, we still seem to have a good thing going.

We are almost home when we move to the left as a young boy on a scooter approaches. Just before he reaches us I notice that he quickly crosses himself as he passes the candlelit Madonna that perches in a small box on the wall.

As we walk up the stairs to our apartment I stare at our own little Madonna with appreciation. Living in Italy hasn't made me any less agnostic, but her serene presence is always welcome.

We had vowed not to indulge too much before the feasting we will have to endure at *Natale*, when Gilda and Enzo invite us to lunch two days before Christmas Day.

En route to their house, we pass a nursery and buy our friends a poinsettia, a Christmas plant which boasts yellow leaves rather

A Madonna on a street wall in the Casale Vascello neighbourhood

than the typical red ones. Over the festive season, the plants change hands as often as the ubiquitous *pandoro* and *panettone*.

Michele and Elisa have been invited too, and they hug Alfonso and me as if we were their own children. Soon we are enjoying *antipasti* of marinated anchovies, capsicum and pumpkin. Next, Gilda's mother Clara dishes up *penne* pasta with a minced veal *ragu*. I undo one button as we begin the second course: rabbit cooked Procidan-style with tomatoes and herbs, some spicy beef *involtini* stuffed with *provola* and vegetables and Alfonso's favourite, eggplant and parmesan cheese *parmeggiana*.

I have sworn off dessert but soon find myself tucking into the chocolate profiteroles, which Gilda has drizzled with a sticky toffee sauce.

Stuffed like sausages, we sit around the table chatting until Enzo stands.

'Let's go for a *secret* walk at Vivara,' he says, widening his eyes to fuel the enthusiasm of the twins – and managing to get me just as hyped. I've been wanting to explore the remote islet – the tail on the bull of the map of Procida – since our adventure-loving friend Carlo told us how much he loves it.

Vivara is a nature-lover's paradise, with hundreds of botanic species and migratory birds tracked intermittently by ornithological observatories. In the seventies, it was also the operational base of the Clover Association, which Carlo belonged to in his youth.

The group, which set up a hermitage in an abandoned building on the islet, was viewed with suspicion by some locals, according to Carlo. The fact that it was a male-only club, and that its residents would only come to the mainland to get provisions were both considered extreme, so too its charter to protect the isolated, three-kilometre stretch of bushland. Eventually, Carlo's mum banned her son from going to the secluded bush location and in time the Clover Association folded.

Vivara is still off-limits to the public. Under the control of various authorities including the national Environment Ministry and Procida's Municipality, it was declared a State Nature Reserve in 2004 and is patrolled daily by the Civil Protection Authority to keep trespassers at bay.

All of which makes our trip with Enzo more appealing.

We grab our coats and hop in the car. At Chiaiolella, Enzo climbs up a small hill and parks in front of a set of padlocked gates beyond which lies the rugged bushland. I push images of *The Blair Witch Project* from my mind and follow Enzo.

We haul ourselves up and over the wall beside the gate and follow a path that takes us down a hill towards Vivara. It is linked to the mainland by a concrete bridge which doubles as an aqueduct for water pumped from Naples to Procida and on to Ischia. Before the bridge was built, a long rocky cliff connected Procida to the islet, a strategic landing point for Mycenaean ships and, in later times, a vast hunting ground for the Romans.

'A few years ago a group of archaeologists dived in the grottos there and found remains dating back to the Bronze Age,' Enzo says, pointing to the closest shore of the islet.

At the end of the bridge we climb a slope and arrive at another padlocked gate, protecting an abandoned stone building which, Enzo says, was built for the guards of Charles III.

We scale another wall and walk along a bush track. Rounding a curve I start when I see a figure ahead. To our collective relief, it's Michela, a young woman who used to work at Bar Capriccio. She's doing a quick patrol of Vivara as part of her voluntary work with the Civil Protection Authority.

Alfonso and Enzo with twins Michele and Angelo, walking from the mainland towards the rickety bridge that leads to Vivara

'Don't worry; being Procidan we have a right to be here, too,' Enzo reassures me with a winning smile.

As we loop one side of the island, passing the crumbling ruins of a French watchtower and a hut where olives were ground to make oil, Michela tells us about the area. In the 1990s various local and international groups had designs on turning Vivara into a tourist village, but the World Wildlife Fund and local green groups successfully blocked the move.

We pass rows of olive trees on the hill which slopes down to the sea facing Ischia, then on through a clearing to arrive at Punta di Mezzogiorno, the southern-most tip of the islet.

'This is the King's Table, built by Charles III, which was mainly a lookout point,' Michela says, pointing to a large, round concrete slab on the ground in front of us.

Enzo and the twins scramble on top and Alfonso, Michela and I follow, taking in the mesmerising views of Ischia, Procida and Naples.

We follow the bush trail back to the bridge. Alfonso and I hold Michele's hands while Enzo keeps Angelo under control as we cross, the wind lashing our faces and the waves crashing onto the shore at Chiaiolella. Back on Procida, we thank Michela for her impromptu tour and accept a ride from Enzo down to Bar Capriccio, where he is due to start work.

We stand by the bar under the Christmas lights draped from the ceiling and catch up with a few of our friends before calling it a night.

We are just about to hop into bed when we hear what seems to be Scottish bagpipe music. I open our window and look down onto the street, where I spy two men blowing into single pipes.

Alfonso explains that they are *zampognari*, or pipers, who traditionally play around Christmas. I am about to shut the window when the sound of a man's angry voice blasts from the apartment block opposite. I don't catch his precise words, but it's clear he has told the pipers in no uncertain terms to beat it.

The seasonal merrymaking continues the next day, Christmas Eve, as we rug up and walk to the home of our friend Eliana, who has organised a dinner for the masses, with everyone bringing along a dish.

Try as I might, I fail to resist the food delights, and enjoy some drunken dancing.

'I can't take it any more and it's not even Christmas,' I groan to Alfonso as we topple into bed.

On Christmas morning we pop in to Bar Cavaliere to offer season's greetings to Maria Grazia and Gennaro before repeating the gesture at Bar Capriccio, where Gilda's barman brother, Giuseppe, and the rest of the staff are wearing Santa hats. We have

Traditionally dressed locals make merry at a Christmas *festa*

a quick chat to Bottone outside Club Napoli then we catch the ferry to the mainland to join Alfonso's parents and some family friends for an enormous lunch and dinner. Alfonso dresses up as Santa Claus to hand out gifts. Patting my belly in discomfort, I feel I could have performed Alfonso's role without the cushion he has stuffed under his red suit.

In the days before New Year's Eve the island buzzes in preparation. We decide to go to the restaurant in Chiaiolella called Agave, after a plant of the same name that grows in abundance around the island.

We arrive at nine o'clock and are greeted by our friend Gennaro, who thrusts glasses of *prosecco* into our hands. The main dining room is filled with one high buffet table, and we join the queue to fill our plates with *antipasti*, including fresh and fried seafood, *prosciutto* and *mozzarella* and savoury cakes and mini pizzas. The staff then clear the table and bring out huge plates of pastas, followed by grilled seafood kebabs.

We save ourselves from the dessert by taking to the dance floor with our friend Dino, a Procidan who lives in Milan, playing DJ.

A cry goes out that it's close to midnight and we join the crush to walk outside, where bottles of *prosecco* are being shaken vigorously.

'*Dieci, nove, otto . . .*'

The countdown culminates in a shower of *prosecco* which, by a stroke of luck, doesn't reach me on the small balcony where I stand with Alfonso overlooking the street. Across the bay, fireworks explode into the sky on the mainland and on the island of Ischia.

I kiss Alfonso before we are smothered in *baci* from our friends and total strangers.

Fireworks whiz and bang for the next twenty minutes near the beach, casting flashes of light across the sea, which is otherwise cloaked in darkness.

'*Buon anno nuovo*, Chunky,' Alfonso murmurs as we sink into the comfort of bed.

'*Buon anno nuovo,* sweetie,' I reply, happy to have my one constant at my side.

DECEMBRE

POLPETTE AL SUGO

(MEATBALLS IN TOMATO SAUCE)

My love affair with meatballs was fed by my late grandmother, Oriel, who made enough to feed her six sons and grandkids. The best thing about these little balls of savoury joy is that you can change the mince mix to taste, or even put a piece of soft cheese inside. Yum. There's not a song about meatballs for nothing!

Serves 5

Meatballs:

500 grams minced meat

400 grams white bread, or roughly a large loaf of
    unsliced bread, with crust removed*

1 egg

½ litre milk or water

1 whole garlic clove, finely chopped

½ cup parmesan cheese, grated

½ cup pine nuts

handful parsley

table salt

* You can use dry bread that is a few days old

Sugo:
1 garlic clove, finely chopped
extra virgin olive oil
800 grams peeled tomatoes (canned)
1 large onion, diced
2 teaspoons vegetable (or cooking) oil

Method

1. The longer the *sugo* cooks the better, so put the garlic and a generous drizzle of olive oil in a saucepan and simmer for a few seconds before adding the tomatoes and the onion. Cover with saucepan lid and leave to simmer over a low heat.

2. Pull the soft inside of the bread out of the loaf and put in a bowl with the milk until it becomes soft. Pick up the bread and squeeze the life out of it so no milk is left.

3. Beat the egg in another big bowl then add the bread and meat. Mix with your hands, using your fist to clench the meat and blend with the bread, until it becomes compact.

4. Add the garlic, parmesan, parsley, pine nuts and salt and use your hands to once again blend thoroughly,

rolling the mixture with the palms of your hands to form golf balls.

5. Add the vegetable oil to a saucepan and fry the meatballs until golden (or bake in the oven for a healthier alternative), then place on a paper towel.

6. Drop the meatballs into the *sugo* and let them cook for 10–15 minutes before serving.

You can serve your meatballs with pasta, too. If you have too many meatballs, just put some in the freezer for a rainy day, or the next *polpette* craving.

GENNAIO

Worlds apart

G iven the over-indulgence of the festive season, perhaps one New Year's resolution should be to curtail our pasta intake. But there is nothing quite like a steaming bowl of the local staple to warm us as the weather gets wilder. Besides, it would be impossible to follow one of those no-carb diets when we have at least three bakeries within walking distance.

Alfonso is a whiz at making pasta *fresca*, armed with only his agile hands and the rim of a drinking glass he uses as a dough cutter. But when we spy a pasta-making machine in the window of our favourite general store, his head is turned.

We lug it home, and, as a compromise for making buckets of pasta, we have decided not to use any eggs in the hope of keeping our dinner lighter.

Alfonso pours a packet of flour into a bowl, adds tepid water and salt, then kneads until he judges the dough adequately smooth and elastic.

He quickly whips up a filling of spinach and ricotta, then we approach the pasta machine clamped to our dining table.

I watch as Alfonso feeds in the dough and turns the handle. By switching the rollers to make the pasta progressively finer each time, he eventually produces five long rectangles of thin and very professional-looking pasta.

We grin at each other in glee, feeling particularly talented. Next step: creating the ravioli.

Alfonso feeds one of the pasta sheets into the machine and carefully spoons the spinach and ricotta mix into the hole allotted for ravioli.

I watch in excitement as he turns the handle to compress the spinach into the little pockets of pasta.

'Look! They're coming out!' I cry, peering beneath the pasta machine like a mechanic.

Within seconds it is obvious that something is going awry. Alfonso curses as the ravioli begins to droop and the pasta sticks to the machine.

'Damn, I knew we should have put egg into the dough . . . Or at least I should have added some extra oil to make it more elastic!' he moans.

The first batch of ravioli is ruined, and try as we might our second, third and fourth attempts are no better.

Increasingly hungry and irritated, we salvage the spinach and ricotta mix from the mangled pasta and knead some of it into the pasta dough, which soon takes on a green colour.

'I'll make some ravioli by hand and we can use the rest of the pasta to make tagliatelle with the machine,' sighs Alfonso.

He sets about using the old-fashioned technique his mother taught him: cutting circles of pasta with the rim of an upturned glass, putting a small blob of spinach and ricotta into the centre, placing a second circle on top and sealing it with his fingers then using a pasta cutter to neatly trim the edge.

He cuts the rest of the pasta into tagliatelle, which he hangs in strips over the backs of the chairs around the table. Soon the room resembles a scene out of a Dr Seuss book, with pasta draped across every surface.

It's almost midnight when we slump into chairs at the table ready to eat some tagliatelle that Alfonso serves with a minced veal *ragu*. The pasta is definitely lighter on the stomach, but we're so famished we eat more than usual. Exhausted from four hours in the kitchen, we shelve our plans to drop into Bar Capriccio. I ignore the few strands of pasta that we forgot to cook hanging off a chair and make a beeline for bed. Tomorrow I'll make more of an effort to be a domestic goddess.

Fresh from an afternoon watching Elisa making *polpette di pesce*, I head down to the port to buy some fish to try making the dish myself.

On Procida, you can buy the catch of the day at Marina Grande at around three in the afternoon, when the *paranza* trawlers edge back into the port, attracting flocks of squawking seagulls.

I reach the first of the three fish shops along the port, swallow my nerves and walk in. The pungent smell fills my nostrils. With no other woman in sight, I attempt to look inconspicuous and not slip on the wet floor. It has just been hosed down or it's sludgy from the water dripping off the fish being flung about at lightning speed.

Fisheries at the port always draw a crowd in the early afternoon, when the fresh catch comes in

'*Prego*,' says the man behind the counter, on which white Styrofoam boxes are filled with various fish, calamari, mussels and other unidentifiable slimy objects.

I order the *pesce bandiera*, whose name is derived from the fact it is long and flat like a flag, but the man shakes his head.

'*Invece un po' di merluzzo?*' I ask for some cod, the other fish Elisa said I could use.

The man thrusts his hand into a box, pulls out two silvery fish and flops them onto a set of old-fashioned scales.

'Four hundred grams, *va bene?*'

I nod meekly, mentally rehearsing the most important part of the exchange.

'*Me li potresti pulire?*' I say, asking the man if he can clean the fish for me.

He whistles to an old man standing at a work bench that is made for filleting, judging by the blood and water staining it.

In the time it takes me to pay, my fish have been wrapped in paper, placed in a bag, thrust into my hand, and the old man has moved on to another customer.

I stare at the man behind the counter again and build up the courage to ask him if it is possible to *spinare,* or debone, my cod.

With a sigh, he begins to unwrap the parcel then stops short.

'What are you cooking?' he says. When I explain he hands the fish back to me and rattles off instructions.

'The bones will come out easily enough after you boil the fish.'

Flustered, I ask how long I should cook it, conscious that a few customers are looking at me with amusement.

The man patiently explains that I only need to boil it for a few minutes, at which point it will all but debone itself.

Thanking him, I leave quickly, holding my head high.

Not only have I just been to the fish shop, but I was able to name two fish and ask them to be *cleaned.* Not bad for a girl from the bush.

I've invited our friends Gennaro and Maria Grazia over for dinner. We've eaten at their place more than a few times, so I figure it's high time the pleasure was returned but the cooking is all up to me as Alfonso is in Naples for music practice.

I do a bit more shopping and walk home planning the menu: breadsticks wrapped in *prosciutto crudo* to nibble on, Alfonso's spinach and ricotta ravioli, followed by my fish balls with a salad of locally grown *rucola*, rocket, much spicier than the usual variety, and *radicchio*, the dark burgundy, slightly bitter lettuce largely cultivated in the northern Veneto region, which adds kick to any dish.

Preparing the nibblies and first course will take mere seconds, but the *polpette* are my main concern. I put a saucepan of water on to boil, and take my fish by their slippery tails.

I gingerly drop them in the water but to my annoyance they're so long their tails stick out. Risking third-degree burns in my initial attempts to sink the fish, I grab a fork and with some difficulty manage to push them down.

I count four minutes then turn off the flame.

I'm scooping up the first fish when a white ball – evidently a cooked eyeball – bounces from nowhere.

I stare at the fish I have placed on a plate and think of the army of waiters on the island who can fillet a fish faster than I can say *merluzzo*, or cod. I take a deep breath and prepare to operate. To my relief, the main spine comes up cleanly. I flip the fish over and remove the rest of the white flesh with relative ease. I toss the fishbone, head and tail onto some newspaper and carefully pick the remaining bones from the meat. When I am satisfied not a scale or bone has escaped me, I repeat the process with the second fish. What seems like hours later, I look with satisfaction at the fillet which, in my search for bones, has become a white, stringy pulp.

I work quickly to mix the fish with some bread, eggs, *pecorino* cheese, basil and parsley. Just before I begin to roll up the little balls I remember to add some fennel seeds, stealing the idea from the menu at Bordero'.

Before long I am tossing the neat fish balls into a frying pan generously filled with virgin olive oil.

Soon my beautiful little *palle d'oro*, golden balls, are sitting on paper towels and the air in our small kitchen is heavy with the smell of fish and the delicious scent of fried garlic. I eat one of the cooked cloves without hesitation. I can never smell garlic on others and I don't even care if others notice it on me. My naturopath sister Sal has long extolled its healing properties.

I pour some tomato *passata,* or sauce, into a saucepan and add the fish balls. A handful of capers and I'm done.

I jump in the shower to wash the fish right out of my hair before my guests arrive.

I have barely finished dressing when Gennaro and Maria Grazia buzz from downstairs. In the time it takes them to walk up four flights of stairs I have prepared the plate of nibblies and checked my delicious fish balls once again.

The idea that I have just cooked a new dish from scratch with not even a hiccup makes me want to bow before my guests. Instead, I feign natural efficiency and hug Gennaro and Maria Grazia. Then, unable to contain my triumph, I spoil the impression by blurting out the details of my afternoon of preparation.

'Gennaro, you'll have to help me with the pasta, though,' I say, my inherent fear of cooking for Italians finally rising to the surface. If Alfonso's idea to dress it with butter and sage backfires, at least I'll be able to blame someone else.

As soon as the water is boiling I throw in some salt and add the ravioli. They chat and sip wine in the kitchen until we deem it to be cooked. I drain it carefully before Gennaro dollops some butter on top and stirs in the sage.

I serve it up and we sit down at the table.

'Not bad,' says Gennaro.

Bolstered by this success, I clear the dishes and ban my guests from entering the kitchen, where I quickly reheat the *polpette* and arrange them on a large dish, which I bring out along with a big salad.

'The form seems perfect, let's see how they taste,' says Gennaro, helping himself to two fish balls . . . 'Mmm, *complimenti!*' he says, helping himself to more.

'Do you know, I have never bought fish from the fish shop,' says Maria Grazia. 'My dad fishes, but I don't know how to tell one from the other.'

Maria Grazia explains that when her father, a retired sailor, was young, he and his brother were the first to use scuba tanks to dive for mussels around the island. Procida now has a scuba-diving school, but for years Maria Grazia's father and uncle were called out when a boat sank and they had to dive to search for bodies.

She tells us her grandfather was also a sailor and was aboard the Italian oceanliner SS *Andrea Doria*, which sank in 1956 when it collided with another liner. Almost fifty people died, but her grandfather was among the survivors. 'He called his daughter Doria after the tragedy,' she says.

As we eat, I ask my friends about the rumours I have heard that they are leaving the island.

'We've applied for work at Ancona, a town that has teaching opportunities for both of us,' says Gennaro. The couple explain that there are fewer jobs in the Naples area to suit their qualifications; they both have language degrees from the university there.

'The other day,' I say, 'I went for a walk to the lighthouse and it was so beautiful. And I thought about all the things I could do to stay here – the work and things to make life more fulfilling.' I add that the longer we stay the more remote the idea of leaving Procida becomes.

'I know,' says Gennaro. 'I mean, where else can you call a friend and meet them in thirty seconds?' He laughs. 'You will miss it, but life goes on.'

'I worry sometimes that if we move to Australia we'll regret it,' I admit. As our holiday to Australia approaches, Alfonso and I have touched upon the possibility.

'Well, you can always come back,' says Gennaro.

The view from our lounge room

'Do you think Procida is a good place to raise kids?' I ask. Maria Grazia is three months pregnant, and I'm keen to hear her opinion in particular.

'I think it's a good place until the kids are eighteen, but then they have to leave, to have better opportunities,' she says.

Gennaro sighs.

'In essence,' he continues, 'all Procida's problems are due to the sailors. Because they go to sea, they earn well and when they return they don't care about tourism, or the islands woes. They think only of themselves.

'Then, to revive their relationships with their families after a long absence, the first thing they do is buy presents for their kids, usually motorbikes and cars. My dad did the same – when

I was sixteen he bought me a scooter, two years later four wheels. That's why you see too many cars around this place.'

I refill our glasses and, keen to change the tone of the discussion, I ask my friends what they treasure most about the island.

'We have a true love for the sea, which puts food on our table, and the beach, which surrounds us,' says Gennaro simply, pointing out that Ravenna, where the couple both lived for a time, and Ancona, where they are set to move, are both seaside towns.

'I don't know many Procidans who have moved to inland cities,' he says. 'When you have grown up by the sea its impact on you is enormous. If you wake and there is a storm, or if the waters are calm, it has an effect.'

'And Procida has a unique character. It's so small that you would think it would be closed and conservative, but because there are so many sailors who have had so much contact with the world, the opposite is true. I mean, here we don't care about tourists, and we are much more open-minded than other places.' Gennaro mentions Evangelista, the old man with the spectacular wig, as a case in point.

'Evangelista was openly gay from the 1940s and you would think on an island measuring four square kilometres that would be unthinkable at the time, but he has never had any problems. Procida is strange. I mean, maybe people feel you shouldn't have kids before you marry, but then you ask a gay man to be your son's godfather. They go to church every day but then at home their prayers are a mixture of religion, devil, spirits and so on.'

I raise my eyebrows with interest. According to the numerous books on Procida, the island folklore is full of strange old legends. At Terra Murata, for example, stories have it that in the 1300s there was a 'witch's windmill' where a witch was known to practise her spells. She apparently met her death when she fell from the steep cliffs of the hilltop neighbourhood after failing to make it home on her broomstick before dawn. In days gone by, indeed, people would place various objects at their doors – such as spikes, brooms and sand – to block the entrance of bothersome witches.

Perhaps the most widespread Procidan practice was the use of the *quadrillo,* a small, round mirror in which the future could be read by those with magical powers. Fortunately for the Procidans – many of whom wanted to consult the *quadrillo* to find out if their loved ones at sea were safe – there were two witches living at Corricella. I remember, too, Elisa speaking of local women who would concoct remedies for ailing locals.

'Yes, historically we have always had *moglie-streghe,* or wife-witches, who would cure you in times of trouble, using methods the church totally opposed,' says Gennaro.

'When I was little,' Maria Grazia tells me, 'I had an upset stomach so my mother took me to see a woman who rubbed some garlic on my belly, and I felt better immediately.'

On another occasion, when Maria Grazia was suffering from sunstroke, her mother took her to see the mother of our friend Glorianna.

'She put a piece of cloth on my head, then poured a glass of water on top. I don't remember getting wet, but the water began to bubble and Glorianna's mum was chanting things. And when she took off the cloth the pain of the sunburn had gone.'

Gennaro recalls the time his friend Dino had a wart on his foot that wouldn't go away.

'He went to an old lady who took a broad bean and made three crosses over his wart while chanting. She told Dino that he had to throw the bean somewhere where he would never come across it again. I think he threw it in the sea. It worked.'

I listen in amazement as Gennaro and Maria Grazia chant little spells that use garlic as a means to ward off ills.

As the church bell strikes midnight I farewell my friends. It's early by local standards, but as the wind whistles I abandon my plan to head down to Bar Capriccio. I'll find the same crowd there tomorrow.

On an overcast afternoon I stroll towards La Rosa Dei Venti, the hotel perched on a plot of land skirting the ocean at Cottimo, near the lighthouse. The hotel is run by the family of our friend Erminia, who has recently been granted a working holiday visa for a year in Australia. I've bought two Italian-language guidebooks about my country so Alfonso can read up on the places we'll be visiting, and I promised Erminia I'd lend them to her.

Just before I reach the steps that lead down to the lighthouse I catch sight of the old woman who lives opposite, in a crumbling pink stone house with a green door. I have often seen her standing on her doorstep, looking out to sea, but I've never managed to elicit a greeting from her, or sneak a peek inside her home. In my wildest imagination, she is a witch who kidnaps children that pass her isolated home and fattens them up for her winter stew.

I weave through the lush garden of La Rosa Dei Venti to Erminia's apartment. She greets me with a kiss, and I ask about the old woman.

'Oh, that's Gioconda, you know, like the name of Leonardo da Vinci's *Mona Lisa*. Gioconda means joyous.'

'She seems anything but,' I say.

'She's a farmer and she's lived there for years. She tends to land entrusted to her by other islanders. I often see her walking past here early in the morning carrying a big bag of zucchini or other vegetables. She's actually not that old. I'd say around sixty-five.'

Cottimo is known for its agriculture, and Erminia's grandfather was also a farmer. But her father made his living from the sea, building the hotel during his brief spells back on the mainland. When he passed away, Erminia, her mother and one of her brothers took over the hotel, which is a collection of garden cottages with private access to the coast.

Erminia flicks through the guidebooks and tells me she's excited and petrified about her departure.

'You'll be fine. Think of the summer you're about to enjoy! And who knows, you might meet your knight in shining armour and never come back!'

'Whatever happens, I will definitely return, because I love this island,' she says. 'I think our pride comes from that sense of belonging. Practically all Procidans own their homes, but that's not all that binds us here. It's also that we know the history of our homes and our families on the island. I have my own house because my grandfather stooped over a hoe twelve hours a day to cultivate the land, and it was his passion. Then my father went to sea for many years to build our hotel. So, I am here because of people who worked very hard with love and passion. I'm convinced it is the history of my family over generations in the one place that makes it difficult for me to think about living a long way from home.' I think of how many Australians, my parents included, make money in the property market by moving frequently without great thought about the history of the land.

I glance at Erminia, her face tender with emotion, with sudden appreciation.

'So many island families have stories of men who faced bad weather and disasters at sea and it was only thanks to a miracle that they made it home. You have to understand and appreciate the sacrifice that they made.'

After talking to retired sailors like Michele and Bottone, I have some idea of what Erminia is talking about. I have heard that there is a chapel in the church of the Madonna della Libera dedicated to the Procidan sailors lost at sea. When I ask my friend about it she nods and picks up her telephone to call her uncle Nicola, a retired sailor who founded Il Tirreno, the hotel just around the corner. Within minutes Erminia has arranged for me to meet him and he will take me to see the chapel.

I kiss Erminia goodbye, telling her to call me if she has any questions about Australia. Then I take a shortcut through orchards and vineyards to reach the hotel, where a tall, bespectacled man is waiting at the arched entrance on his Vespa.

'I'm one of those baddies with a Vespa. Hop on,' he says.

As we ride towards the church, Nicola shouts above the engine to explain that since he went on the pension a decade ago he has dedicated his time to preserving Procida's maritime history. He is the former president of Pio Monte Dei Marinai, an association that gives assistance to the orphans and widows of Procidans killed at sea. I've seen its headquarters at the Marina Grande, where old salts gather from early in the morning to play cards. It was set up by local mariners in 1617 to raise funds to pay the ransoms demanded by the Saracens who kidnapped local women and children during their frequent raids on the island. The association also built the bright yellow Santa Maria della Pieta church just near its headquarters. Without any formal links to the Vatican, the church's priests have all been former sailors or sons of sailors.

We pull up at the Madonna della Libera church and Nicola leads me into the chapel. One wall serves as a shrine to Procida's missing sailors. There are scores of black-and-white photographs of the dead or missing, each accompanied by a name, details of the ship and the year of the tragedy. Their wooden frames are bordered by sailing twine.

Hanging near them is a series of oil paintings depicting sailing boats in ferocious seas. At the bottom of each is the name of the ship, its captain and its bearing at the time of the disaster. Nicola explains that when a Procidan sailor escaped death at sea, he would commission an artist to capture the miracle on canvas and dedicate the painting to the Madonna.

As we leave, Nicola gestures to the statue of the Madonna della Libera, from which the church takes its name.

'When our men were at sea and the ship encountered bad weather, they would pray to the Madonna, saying *liberarmi dalla tempesta,* or "free me from the storm".'

Outside the church I thank Nicola profusely for his time. He starts his engine and roars off, a cloud of black smoke streaming from his muffler.

Barely a day passes when I don't find myself gazing up at Terra Murata. Ringed by grey stone walls and perched high on a rugged cliff about ninety metres above sea level, Procida's oldest village dominates the skyline. Whether I'm on the ferry, standing on our rooftop terrace or walking around the island, it draws my attention like no other landmark.

It was settled in the Middle Ages by residents who fled to the highest point on the island to protect themselves, first from barbaric invasions then from Saracen attacks. Terra Murata was fortified in 1563, after which time the population began to leave the walled community and spread to the rest of the island.

Terra Murata

There is an air of desolation on the clifftop, where access to pretty much everything is off-limits: from the remains of the prison and sixteenth-century castle to Santa Margherita Nuova, the crumbling church perched at its feet only metres from where the cliff drops away into the ocean.

The only place open to tourists is the Abbey of San Michele, which houses a gold-and-silver statue of the island's patron saint, San Michele, an impressive library and a secret chapel overlooking the sea.

One afternoon I ditch my regular walking paths and find myself standing at the lookout within the walls of Terra Murata, gazing down on the scores of small, barred cell windows in the oldest section of the prison. I wonder whether the sight of the sea would have brought consolation to inmates, or merely added to their torture.

I do a lap of the settlement but don't encounter a single person, which only fuels my curiosity about the inhabitants – if, indeed, there are any.

I decide to find someone who can tell me more about life in arguably the most unwelcoming place on Procida. After consulting a few friends I track down a woman called Vanna, who once worked as a guide in the abbey's museum but now runs her own computer school. I am especially keen to talk to her after hearing that her late father worked in the old jail.

On a chilly winter morning I rug up and tackle the steep hill leading to the old settlement. I stop to catch my breath at the small lookout at the top; complete with two ancient cannons, it has a stunning view of Corricella. Then I continue along the steep road, passing under the first arch in the wall circling Terra Murata.

I veer left and find the faded yellow building where Vanna lives. At the entrance the electrical wires of the intercom have been pulled loose and a handwritten sign warns strangers to keep away. I phone Vanna to tell her I have arrived, and step into the courtyard where I see a woman with long, straw-blonde hair approaching me with a smile.

Vanna ushers me into a spotless kitchen, where I gravitate to a large window and look out to a prison watchtower at the end of a long wall. Vanna opens the window and tells me to lean out and look left. I follow her instructions and see a second watchtower about five metres from the window ledge. Down below are prison cells.

'When the jail was still open this window was fitted with one-way glass, so we could look out without being seen,' she says, adding that the window was also protected by a grate. 'It was important we had privacy, given my father's job.'

'What did he do?' I ask, my feet still planted at the window as I stare at the long wall where the sentinels used to pace.

Vanna explains that her father, Giovanni, a brigadier, was in charge of protocol and prison correspondence. The inmates were largely political prisoners considered dangerous by international authorities, who wanted to isolate them from the mainland.

Giovanni met his future wife, who was from another part of the island, during a stroll one Sunday at Marina Grande, and the newlyweds eventually moved into the home where Vanna lives now.

'Did you ever visit your father at work?' I ask, never having set foot in a prison.

'Yes, a few times. But he didn't want us hanging around – he was very strict. He banned my sister and me from going to the bar that used to be just down the road from here. Back then, Terra Murata was full of men – like the guards and sentinels – and there were always inmates being accompanied around the area to do odd jobs, like gardening and painting houses.

'Once there was an old man who was cleaning our garden and I said, "Papa, how did a good man like this end up in jail?" Papa said, "*Attenzione!* That man is serving a life sentence." It turned out that the man used to be married and had a son. When his wife died, he wanted to remarry but the boy didn't fit in with his plans. So the man killed him, cut him into pieces, put him in a suitcase and buried him.'

Vanna leans forward, her eyes widening. 'I never waved to that man again.'

In 1986, her father died of cancer, and within two years the jail was closed.

'After Dad died, the director of the jail said we could stay here until we found other accommodation, because Mum was alone and I was only thirteen, my sister Clara a year older and our brother only six.

'Then the jail shut and now, more than twenty years later, we still live here, along with ten other families. No one has ever told us to leave.'

'But are you still paying rent?' I ask, wondering if I am being too nosey.

'No, we don't know who to pay. My father was paying rent to the jail administrators, but since the jail is no longer here . . .' She shrugs.

'What is it like to live on Terra Murata?' I ask, explaining that the view of the clifftop community has always fuelled my imagination.

'It's a little closed,' she says.

According to Vanna, Terra Murata is not only cut off from the rest of the island, but split within.

'There are those who live high up near the abbey, and then others, like us, who are down on this lower level,' she says. 'Up there they call us the *guardiani*, or custodians. And we just call them "those up there".

'I worked at Terra Murata when I ran guided tours of the church, but I don't really like it. The people are closed, and you feel that in the air.

'Another thing unique to Terra Murata,' she continues, 'is our dialect. Now, we're speaking in Italian, but if I speak our dialect to someone in Chiaiolella, on the other side of the island, they won't have a hope of understanding me. They have their own dialect.'

While I can understand Italy's many regional dialects, I had no idea that a small island like Procida would have numerous dialects of its own. Now I feel better about feeling so confused at times.

In Vanna's opinion, when the prison was still operating, Terra Murata – and, indeed, Procida – was better for it.

A rabbit warren of seventeenth-century houses in the Casale
Vascello village near Terra Murata

'There was a management of the island that no longer exists,' she says simply. 'The jail brought business – the people who worked here would shop locally, and the relatives of the prisoners who visited each day, would use the island's taxis. It was so much cleaner. I have always believed that if the jail were still here Procida would be better off. When it closed, the restaurant and bar here closed too. It's such a shame.'

I tell Vanna I have heard that car manufacturing giant Fiat was once interested in developing a casino on the jail site.

'There have always been rumours of people who wanted to invest, entrepreneurs from northern Italy and even Switzerland, but then there have always been obstacles,' she says. 'Look at Ischia. All it took was one man, Rizzoli, to build a hotel, and now there are four hundred hotels on the island. All we need is a clever entrepreneur.'

She dismisses the idea that Procida doesn't need tourism because of its wealthy sailors.

'Something serious is happening on Procida,' she warns. 'The young people are leaving for cities on the mainland to get jobs. I stayed, because I am close to my family, but I had to set up the computer school to make a living because there is no work.

'Procida is becoming an island for the elderly. If there was more tourism, if the jail was redeveloped, maybe kids would stay. But today, apart from a few exceptions, no one wants to do what used to bring in money: work at sea.'

Still captivated by the view from Vanna's kitchen window, which reminds me of one of my favourite prison-break movies, *The Great Escape*, I ask if any inmates had managed to scarper.

'As far as I remember, there was only one person who somehow managed to get as far as the sea,' says Vanna. 'He started to swim to the mainland, but they nabbed him pretty quickly.'

After thanking Vanna, I wander back down the steep hill towards Piazza dei Martiri and head home. Reaching the Corricella lookout, I stare back towards Terra Murata and decide it is no surprise it has a unique dialect. It really is a world apart.

I finish up an afternoon English class at home and all but push the little terrors down the stairs in my haste to get to the port. After months of technical hiccups and delays, tonight Alfonso's band, 'A67, is launching their new CD at La Feltrinelli, the biggest bookstore in Naples.

I am not sure whether his superstitious nature or his nerves are to blame, but once again Alfonso begged me not to tell our Procidan friends about the event. I ignored him, but as many of them have work and study commitments I am not sure what the turn-out will be like.

As the hydrofoil bumps its way across the bay, I realise I can't remember the last time I went to Naples. I have to remind myself that leaving the island is essential for my mental health. Winter has been trying, despite our busy social calendar. I'm not sure which scenario is worse: being a slave in the office, or trying to make a living as a freelance scribe. Despite my friend Daniela's pep talk, my intentions of enrolling in a vocational course somehow fell by the wayside. Deep down, I know my failure to commit is because I'm not sure whether we will stay on Procida or move to Australia when our lease expires in little more than five weeks.

My thoughts are interrupted when I feel the hydrofoil nudge the dock of Naples.

I leap off the boat like the Flying Nun and follow my nose to La Feltrinelli, where I have arranged to meet Alfonso's parents. Much to his annoyance, they read about the event in the paper and insisted on coming.

I kiss Maria Rosaria and Enzo and we walk into the bookshop.

Being half an hour early, we are just in time to see 'A67 being interviewed by a local television crew. Seated on a black leather couch under bright spotlights, the band play their rock-star roles to perfection. As soon as the interview ends Alfonso sails across the room to give me a hug and his parents a nervous kiss.

About ten minutes before the band is due to start playing I turn to see Enzo, Gilda and their twins arrive. I catch Alfonso's eye and tilt my head towards them. I notice the delight on his face when he sees them, knowing that Enzo has never taken a night off from Bar Capriccio, apart from his own wedding night.

My smile widens as I watch more of our Procidan friends arrive – Glorianna, Candida, Gennaro, Nicola, Maria Rosaria, Claudia, Amalia, Angela and Rosella, among others.

After a brief introduction by a local author, the band launches into a five-song set which has everyone in the crowd tapping their feet and whistling at the end of each one.

As the final song draws to an end the mother of Daniele, the lead singer, jumps to her feet.

'*Amore mio,* you are the best!' she says, her eyes welling with tears from the emotion of seeing her youngest son perform. The entire room bursts into laughter and applause. At times like these I love being in Italy's south, where the locals are famous for their passionate displays of emotion. I lock eyes with Alfonso and tilt my head towards his mother, as if to say 'Count your blessings she's shy'. He grins as Daniele, not in the least perturbed by his mother's outburst, thanks the audience for coming and in no subtle terms urges everyone to buy the CD.

The crowd leap to their feet and Alfonso signs a few discs with the rest of the band. A teenage girl gazes at him in awe.

'*Ti posso dare un bacio?*' she says, asking permission to kiss my man, who drops his head in embarrassment, which she interprets as a *si*.

I watch the scene with amusement and pretend to give Alfonso a death stare when he looks my way.

Eventually he joins us, and drapes one arm around me and uses the other to lift Michele into the drummer's seat. We all giggle at the mixture of delight and concentration on the boy's face as he bashes the drums with as much might as his skinny frame can muster. I glance at Enzo, wanting to tell him how much it means to Alfonso that he came, but I know he would just brush it off. Instead I clap him on the shoulder with affection.

Now, more than ever, I realise that while I have struggled to fit in with the Procidans, the most important thing is that those who matter are around when it counts.

GENNAIO

RAVIOLI CON SPINACI E RICOTTA
(RAVIOLI WITH SPINACH AND RICOTTA)

Making fresh pasta can be exhausting, but the difference in taste is worth the effort. You can get away without using a pasta machine, but you should consider buying a pasta cutter (like a pizza cutter with a spiked blade, just smaller). Chef Alfonso says using a knife is inviting trouble. You can serve the ravioli with a simple tomato *sugo* (see March, just don't add the chilli), with a *ragu* (meat sauce) or with butter and sage (see below).

Serves 6

Filling:
400 grams spinach
200 grams ricotta
5 tablespoons parmesan cheese, grated
nutmeg, table salt and pepper (to taste)

Pasta:
400 grams plain flour
3 eggs
pinch table salt
50 grams butter
handful fresh sage leaves

Method

1. Prepare the filling first: boil the spinach, allow it to cool, and then squeeze it with your hands until every drop of water has drained out. Leave it in a pan to dry. When it is dried, chop, add the ricotta, parmesan and seasonings and mix thoroughly.

2. Place flour on the table or a large board and create a well in the middle, then crack the eggs into the well and add a pinch of salt. Using your fingertips, gently spread the flour into the middle, working from the outside inwards, and knead it for 15 minutes until it is smooth and elastic. (If the dough gets sticky at any point just dust with flour.) Tired? So is the dough. Cover it with clingwrap and let it rest for 20 minutes.

3. Roll out two sheets of thin dough, then on one of the sheets spoon teaspoon-sized portions of the filling, spacing them about 3–4 centimetres apart. When you have covered the first sheet, gently place the second sheet of pasta on top, then use your fingertips to press and flatten the pasta around the filling portions.

4. Use a pasta cutter to cut the ravioli squares around the filling, leaving a border of at least 2 centimetres. (If

you cut too close to the filling it will pop out of the pasta pillow during cooking!)

5. Cook the pasta for a few minutes; taste one parcel to see if it is *al dente*.

6. While the pasta is cooking, put the butter in a saucepan and melt it on a low flame together with the sage leaves. Drain the water and leave the pasta in the saucepan; dress pasta with the butter mix.

This dish seems fussy, but it's surprisingly simple in practice. Garnish with a fresh sage leaf or two and make a note to buy yourself a chef's hat!

FEBBRAIO

Home

Rain and wind batter the island and you wouldn't get me outdoors if you paid me. Toasty in a tracksuit, I am in the kitchen preparing lunch: a generous drizzle of good olive oil in a frying pan, some garlic to flavour it and a fistful of chopped cherry tomatoes with a little chilli to add some kick. I turn the flame off under another pan in which I have boiled some small green peppers with bicarbonate of soda, which takes out the bitter edge, and toss them in with the tomatoes. I stir until the tomatoes are a rich, mushy pulp, then toss some pasta into a pot of salted boiling water.

When the pasta is a degree short of *al dente,* I drain it and flip it into the saucepan, stirring until it is coated with sauce. As I place a fresh basil leaf on top I wish Alfonso were here to see my steaming masterpiece.

My cooking sessions with Elisa have increased my confidence in the kitchen. When Alfonso is around I am happy to let him hog the stove, but I now have the courage to experiment when he's away, my fear and loathing of the *cucina* having finally evaporated.

It's only just past noon, but I'm eating early so I have time to digest my meal before I go swimming. With the ocean dropping to freezing temperatures, I am keeping up my swimming routine by travelling twice a week to the local pool on Ischia with Gilda and her sister, Loredana.

At the pool, I switch into cruise control as my thoughts turn to Australia. In less than a week I will be winging my way home, and bringing Alfonso with me. My excitement is growing by the day. The monotony of laps eases my restlessness and by the time

Old men at the Chiaiolella port

I haul myself out of the water my body is in a state of exhausted relaxation.

With Alfonso in Naples teaching another computer course, I am happy to accept Gilda's invitation to dinner at Agave, the pizzeria in Chiaiolella where we celebrated New Year's Eve. Her friends Gina, a teacher at the school opposite our place, and Tania, my local accountant, are coming too.

In Agave's cosy dining room we each order a pizza and I listen to my friends gossip like ladies at a hair salon.

Gina reveals that she has a friend who is convinced her husband is cheating on her, because she has found certain suspicious receipts.

'One of them was from the pharmacy, so she went there and discovered the price matched that of a packet of condoms,' says Gina. Given we are on Procida, I have already learnt that, when gossiping, it is important to lower one's voice and invent pseudonyms for names.

'She wants to hire a private investigator,' Gina tells us. 'But she doesn't have the courage because she doesn't want her suspicions confirmed.'

'What she needs to do is to have an affair herself. Then her husband will explode with rage!' says Tania bluntly, making us all burst into laughter.

A working mother whose pizza-maker husband works nights at a local restaurant, Tania offloads some of her stress about juggling her office and home life.

'I'm like a bird in a cage, but when I escape, look out!' She winks, then tells us she has been with the same man for twenty-three years and is now aged thirty-eight.

I look at Tania with wonder as I calculate that she met her husband when she was fifteen. Which means . . .

'I know what you are thinking,' she says, one step ahead. 'Yes, I have only ever been with one man.'

'I don't believe it!' I exclaim, despite knowing that Tania is far from alone among women of her generation, only slightly older than me.

I stare at Gina and Gilda, laughing at my expression, and look at them with renewed interest. Their laughter reaches a chorus, and tears begin sliding down Gilda's face.

My suspicions are soon confirmed. Tania is not alone. The horror on my face causes renewed mirth and suddenly tears of laughter are running down my own cheeks too.

Composing myself, I try to explain that where I come from the custom is to sample the dating smorgasbord before deciding on your preferred dish.

At ten o'clock the mothers must return to their nests and I am happy to go back to my own, far from child-induced chaos. My biological clock continues to tick, but I can't help but think I need to know where home is before I bring another life into the world, God willing. Or am I just procrastinating because the concept of motherhood is still so frightening? I curl up with a book as the bleak weather continues to hammer the island.

Sunday dawns with a clear blue sky, just in time for *Operazione Primavera* (Spring Operation). The community working bee cleans certain zones of the island and now, after missing a few earlier occasions, I am ready to roll up my sleeves.

Dressed in old jeans and a jumper and sneakers, I arrive at the lookout above Corricella just after seven to find a small group of men already hard at work on the hill that slopes down to the port. I watch as they use large clippers to lop branches from the overgrown mass of oleander trees. The only woman present, I suddenly feel rather conspicuous. None of my other girlfriends has arrived yet; perhaps they'd had a late night at Bar Capriccio.

With some relief, I spy Enzo and Loreto, our doctor friend with whom we did the *vendemmia*, or grape harvest, and sing out hello.

I start working alongside the men, cutting branches up the hill. My legs feel heavier by the minute, but the fresh morning air and the cheer of the elderly men keeps me going, as does the sugary coffee and a slice of *crostata* that are served at nine o'clock by one of the men's tubby wives.

Graziella appears and we complete the work side by side. By the time we finish my legs are trembling from going up and down the hillside steps, and my jumper is stained with the milky sap that oozes from the branches. We lean on the railing overlooking the now neatly clipped hillside and enjoy the more expansive view of Corricella and Terra Murata.

Loreto gives me a pat on the back and introduces me to Guilio Esposito, the founder of *Operazione Primavera*, whom I met in passing during the *vendemmia*.

'So when's the next operation?' I ask him.

'I don't know, we never plan these things far in advance, but you will hear on the grapevine,' he says with a little smile.

Giulio tells me he was a reluctant sailor from his late teens until his early twenties, when he and his brother Gianni, also at sea, decided to return to their island home. A keen carpenter and ceramist, he opened a gift shop to sell his craftwork.

'The local sailors had money and they bought gifts for baptisms, communions and weddings,' he remembers.

Giulio founded Operation Spring in 1995, driven by his frustration with the local council which, he says, had all but abandoned the island.

'The illegal housing wasn't as bad as the general dirtiness of the place,' he laments. 'Whenever a *sagra* was held everything ended up in the sea. It was a black time for us.'

He spoke to two of his mates, Mimmo and Antonio, and they decided to tackle the filth head on. Armed with gloves and garbage bags, the men arrived at the petrol station at the port, where locals cleaning their cars or filling their tanks were tipping oil and other rubbish into the sea.

Using large fishing nets to scoop piles of rubbish out of the water, the group spent the day cleaning the area and, satisfied with their first effort, baptised their project *Operazione Primavera*, as it was spring at the time.

'How did the other residents react?' I ask.

'At first they were incredulous, but then there was a sense of shame, as if they were embarrassed not to have thought of doing something similar before,' says Giulio. 'Then there was diffidence, because the locals are like that. But soon they started to take part, and more people turned up to help as we spread the word.'

Giulio pauses and looks at me awkwardly.

'Maybe I shouldn't say it, but I am convinced that Procidans are a bit resentful of foreigners. They are happy living here and they don't want others to see how beautiful the island is,' he says, to my surprise.

'Are you suggesting they deliberately litter the island with rubbish to stop people from coming?' I ask, hardly believing my ears.

'Only some of them – and remember, they don't create mess in their own homes, just outdoors.'

'It just seems rather excessive – I mean, they are ruining the future for their kids!' I exclaim, my stomach turning as I remember the worst moments of the rubbish crisis.

The council's plans for the incinerator still haven't been confirmed, but happily the streets have returned to normal thanks to a new local garbage collection company and the improvement in the situation in Naples, where Prime Minister Berlusconi called in the army to help control rowdy community protests and succeeded in opening two new rubbish dumps. Meanwhile on Procida there are fresh rumours that the council is considering using a large chunk of land at the foot of the old jail as a space for composting and recycling rubbish.

According to Giulio, the Procidans' wariness of foreigners – and their desire to protect their territory – stems from the fact that in past centuries the island was constantly attacked and plundered.

'It's like a man who has a beautiful wife and doesn't want her to dress provocatively, because he knows very well that it could attract unwanted attention.'

'What makes you sure it's deliberate sabotage?' I ask, still surprised by his theory.

'Look, the Procidans don't want tourists. They never wanted them, because the island offered a good life and they had a lot to lose.'

When I suggest that this is not the case for restaurateurs and hoteliers, Giulio shakes his head.

'I was renting holiday houses, and working at the shop, but at the end of summer I didn't want to see any more tourists!' he says, making me laugh.

Describing it as a love–hate relationship with tourists Giulio has his own views on how the island should be promoted.

'Procida is such a rare place for its size and history, but I think tourists should just be able to buy a day ticket, letting them walk to the other side of the island and back, but not letting them stay. We already have ten thousand people on four square kilometres, and we can't build more restaurants and car parks. Otherwise it would be like Manhattan!'

Giulio predicts it will take at least another fifty years before people realise they must work together to bring positive changes to the island.

'It's not the council that needs to change, but the citizens – I mean, every population has the government it deserves, no? If they are arseholes, so are we!' he exclaims.

When I ask Giulio what he thinks of foreigners he offers me a warm smile.

'I don't mind friendly foreigners like you, who don't cause trouble and respect the environment around them.' He pauses. 'I've sailed all over the world, but I love Procida for its size – I mean, you could seize it with your hands! And I love the tranquillity. When I go to Naples, there is all that chaos, people will rob you, traffic . . . If your car breaks down it's a nightmare. If that happens on Procida, everyone arrives to help. And then there is the sea. What else could you want?'

When I tell him that Alfonso and I are about to travel to Australia, and we have to make a decision about where we want to call home, Giulio cuts me short. 'You either fall in love with Procida, or you have to leave. Eighty per cent of people leave.'

'I love Procida, but I don't know if there are enough opportunities here,' I reply, explaining that while I don't care if I am not rich, I do need more work stimulation.

'Here we say "Money is the last thing to worry about", but only rich people can say that!' says Giulio with a grin as his wife Gaetana calls him and he stands to leave. 'You can eventually grow tired of Procida, but be warned, if you think you can change it in even the smallest way, forget it! You have to accept it how it is. The only thing we need to do is make it more beautiful, just a little, for we Procidans.'

As our departure date draws near, I scan the Australian news sites to check the weather and a headline in the *Sydney Morning Herald* catches my eye. Based on a study by a researcher at the Australian National University's National Centre for Epidemiology, the story says that Australians who need others are the happiest of all, but a quarter of them feel they do not belong and are socially isolated. The path to happiness and wellbeing lies in simple things, like dining with your family and friends and socialising in general. It's not rocket science, but it's interesting nonetheless. For me, the words *isolation* and *belong* resonate. When we arrived on the island, I was sure I could handle anything it threw at us, solitude included. I grew up on a farm without any neighbours, I reasoned, and I had moved alone to foreign cities without a friend to call on, so I wouldn't have any problems.

As I read over the newspaper study I think of my current lifestyle. When Alfonso is in Naples, I have to force myself to be sociable. I am comfortable in my own company when I have things to do. Also, I am frustrated by the dialect I can't quite grasp, but I'm reluctant to ask everyone to speak Italian for my sake. It's no surprise to me that the ANU study found that immigrants from non-English-speaking backgrounds are among those who feel most isolated.

I turn off the computer and head off to an appointment I am very much looking forward to, and not just because I will be able to speak my own language. Since moving to the island, I have often heard the name of Myriam Narpeto, a former English teacher at Procida's nautical institute. Curious to talk to her about the school and her work in such a testosterone-saturated environment, I asked Enzo for her number and soon arranged to meet her.

Procida's Nautical Institute rises over
Marina di Sancio Cattolico

I am starting to think I am lost when Bottone pulls up on his motorbike, a smile and cigarette hanging from his mouth, the lenses of his Ray-Bans reflecting my own face. When I tell him where I am going he points to an apricot building with white borders, nearby.

'She taught me once,' he says before zipping off to the port.

I press on the only button next to the wooden door and a cheery voice instructs me in English to enter and walk up the flight of stairs.

I reach the top to be greeted by a petite, tanned woman in an elegant tailored suit.

As I extend my hand I notice that the front of her dark hair is streaked blonde on either side of her part, giving her a funky – if not Addams Family-inspired – look.

'I like your streaks,' I say as I shake her hand. In truth, I have already gleaned a little background information on the woman who immediately asks me to call her Myriam. A former pupil of Professoressa Narpeto told me that Myriam is known for her love of fashion. She once said that she dresses more and more flamboyantly when she is not at peace with the world. I wonder which is better: dressing up to the nines and putting on a brave face, or holing up at home like I do.

'Thank you, you are very kind,' says Myriam in clipped English with a British accent. 'When I got it done my daughter said I was mad!'

She ushers me into the living room, furnished with a set of brown velvet couches and antique wooden furniture, which she explains are family heirlooms.

Born on Procida, Myriam tells me that her mother was a dressmaker for her extended family, while her father spent long periods at sea. She points to some medals hanging on the wall; her father won them for bravery on the job.

'My father was a very generous captain – in fact, he died because of this,' she says, wringing her hands unconsciously. She explains that her father had just returned home from a year at sea when a sailor friend asked him to cover his shift so he could be present at the birth of his third child; he had missed his wife's two previous labours.

'It was a tanker, a type of ship my father had never liked, and when he asked my mother if he should do it she said no,' remembers Myriam. 'But after a restless night he decided to go. He left early in the morning, telling my mother not to wake my sister and me, and he went to Genova to board. Two days later, the ship was at Mestre, near Venice, when there was an explosion. He tried to save the crew, but he died.'

Forty-five years have passed, but I still offer my condolences to my host, who puts on a bright smile and explains how she grew up without her father.

After studying at a grammar school in Naples for five years, at the age of eighteen Myriam decided she wanted to do a language degree at the university. First, however, she convinced her mother to let her travel to England for six months to learn English at St Giles School, King's College, in Canterbury.

'I was the only Italian there, I knew no English, and I remember at breakfast on the first day everyone seemed to be saying "*Would you like* some jam?", "*Would you like* an omelette?". And I couldn't work out what this *Would you like* meant. I was so hungry, but I didn't know how to ask for anything!'

As I laugh, memories of my experiences in Rome come flooding back.

'I have a sunny nature, but in the beginning I suffered a lot. I was studying with students from all over the world, but I was so sad.'

When she completed her language degree, mastering not only English, but also German and French, she got some casual work as a language teacher on Ischia before she sat her teaching exams and had to nominate where she hoped to teach.

'My mother said, "Your father died for you, he worked so you could study. Why don't you teach at the nautical institute and stay on Procida, and make your father happy?" So I said okay, and soon I fell in love with the place,' says Myriam, breaking into a smile.

In 1971, then in her early twenties, Myriam began a career that would span just over three decades, learning everything about the various nautical subjects – from electrotechnics to engineering and navigation – in order to incorporate them into her English classes.

Febbraio

The fact she had been aboard many a boat with her father in her childhood helped, but her teaching strategy was also unique.

After two years teaching standard English, Myriam studied outside the classroom to learn the standard of technical English set in 1973 by the International Maritime Organisation (IMO), mandatory for sailors in charge of watch on ships weighing more than two hundred gross tonnes.

Like many similar institutions, the Procidan Nautical Institute did not offer the IMO language in its curriculum – until Myriam graduated in the subject.

'I thought it was wrong that so many of the kids were paying a lot of money privately to learn it, so I decided to teach it at the college,' she says, explaining that the IMO phonetic language contains simplified phrases to aid navigation. 'There are sailors of every nationality on board these boats, so it is imperative that a common language is used to avoid disasters.'

Pupils at the nautical college have to study for five years, but can go to sea after their first year. In their final year they must sit exams to become a captain or a pilot. Pilots, Myriam explains, guide ships into and out of the port, and are always well paid.

Only when Myriam finally pauses for breath can I ask her how important the institute, founded in 1874, is to Procida.

'It has played a central role, because Procida's wealth depended – and still depends – on the captains and sailors,' she says. 'Historically, there was at least one sailor in every family, and while there was a slowdown a few years ago, today there is a new interest in sailing because the contracts are short and the cruise boats can offer you a good life.'

I have read in the local newspaper that the first woman to receive a navigating diploma in Italy was a Procidan in 1953. She studied for her engineering qualification at the island's nautical institute.

Before Myriam arrived to teach there, only two or three women had studied at the college. But that soon changed.

'Other women began to enrol, and if I'm honest, I think my presence encouraged them,' says Myriam frankly.

Her face hardens when I ask if she had any difficulties with her male colleagues.

'If I have to tell the truth . . . yes, very much so,' she says quietly. 'There was a lot of envy, maybe because I was professionally fulfilled, because I had travelled and was educated, with friends all over the world. I felt full of things to give, but I wasn't conceited.'

She didn't win any more friends when her superiors asked her to pass one of her well-connected pupils when he hadn't done the required work and she refused.

Nepotism is still rife in Italy, with a good chunk of the working population being *raccomandata*, or recommended for a job, by someone with power.

'When it happened the first time I said, "No, I'm sorry, but what has this pupil done?", Miriam tells me, her voice rising with anger.

In one case, her refusal sparked a ten-year legal battle which she eventually won, despite not having proper legal representation.

Admiring her resilience, I ask Myriam if any of her pupils have lost their lives at sea.

'Oh yes, *so* many. I always go to the cemetery to visit them. It still makes me upset. I lost so many boys all over the world . . .'

I watch in dismay as tears slide down her face. I place my hand on hers as she composes herself.

'They were such wonderful men, and to earn a little more money, usually because they were from poorer families, they did the longest trips,' she says sadly.

Every year, she attends a special ceremony held on Procida to honour those lost at sea.

'I go for both my father and my students,' Myriam says solemnly, explaining that there is a procession at Marina Grande, then a wreath is thrown into the sea to honour those sailors whose bodies were never recovered.

'The ceremony destroys you. During that moment of silence you feel such emotion, so deep that it seems there's a cosmic hug between everyone present. I always wear sunglasses, because I get upset,' she says, a smile suddenly returning to her face. 'Today, my former students here on Procida are always asking me if they can call their newborns Myriam, while others called their sons Alessandro, like my father,' she adds with pride.

Just before she began teaching at the nautical institute, Myriam married a Neapolitan cardiologist, Giovanni, whom she met at Chiaia. When I ask if he was jealous of her close rapport with her students, Myriam nods.

'Very much so. At the start it was hard to make him understand, because his family was so rigid, so traditional. But with the help of my own mother he became more open.'

'So he understood that you were trustworthy?'

'I never did anything wrong,' says Myriam, laughing. 'Let me tell you, there were many times when boys did fall in love with me. I mean, I was well dressed, always wearing gloves and a hat. I was *different*.'

When I mention my own struggle to fit in, it's Myriam's turn to pat my hand.

'I totally understand, but I don't consider myself Procidan in the sense that I always show my feelings. I have even cried in class,' she says softly.

When I joke that I should either learn the dialect or simply toughen up she shakes her head. 'No. People must take you as you are.'

I smile, taking heart from her words while admitting that if I can't express myself properly or contribute in some way I simply clam up.

'No! You must listen to your instincts, and express yourself,' she insists in a teacher's tone. 'When I'm in church for example, and I don't feel like staying, I don't have any problems standing up and leaving, even if it's in the middle of mass. Even if everyone stares at me and people are indignant. Maybe they're envious, because they are probably thinking about how boring the sermon is, but then they sit there for an hour. I am not bad-mannered, though. I wait until the mass is over and then I go to confession and say, "Sorry, Father, but sometimes your sermons seem as if they were written a century ago!"'

Laughing out loud, I tell Myriam how I went to a party on Procida when Alfonso was away and, even though I was sitting with a bunch of my girlfriends, no one was particularly chatty and the loud music meant it was impossible to talk. I sat for two hours debating if it was rude to leave, before I finally made my excuses at midnight and walked home cursing myself for suffering in silence.

'You were well-mannered, but your face and body language would have indicated you were suffering,' Myriam points out. 'The best thing would have been to excuse yourself graciously. Because people are going to talk about you *anyway*!'

'So if you were in my shoes, would you stay on Procida or leave?' I ask.

'If you were my daughter, I would say go. See other things, travel, then return. I like Procida because I have finally found myself. I have an inner strength that I didn't have when I was younger like you.'

'I thought I was stronger –' I begin, almost apologetically.

'Procida is like a storm,' Myriam interrupts, 'and if it catches you unprepared you can collapse. You need to fortify yourself. I say go – not because Procida is bad for you, but because the more experiences you have, the more you learn how to face things. When you are serene you can come back.'

Myriam pauses momentarily as a door clicks shut below, but then continues, 'Procida can be cruel to foreigners who might be used to the anonymity of a big city. Because everyone knows everything about you. Last night I had pizza with some of my old pupils and when I mentioned I had an appointment with an Australian woman they all said, "Ah, yes, Penelope". I said, "How do you know her?" and they all said, "Who doesn't!" You see, I bet you don't know any of them!'

'I bet they are locals at Bar Capriccio,' I say, quietly amused.

A tall man with white hair and spectacles comes into the room and Myriam introduces me to her husband. I decide I should go now, so kiss her warmly on both cheeks and thank her for her time.

'See you soon – let me know when you feel like a coffee or a gelato,' she says, walking me down the three flights of stairs and kissing me.

The conversation of the past two hours keeps a smile on my face all the way home.

After months of anticipation, it almost doesn't seem real when finally the plane is bumping onto the tarmac in Perth.

As I walk into the airport terminal I catch sight of my sister Sal holding the latest addition to her tribe, seven-month-old Meg, whose toothy grin and thin tuft of blonde hair soon have us going gaga. I hug Sal and introduce her to Alfonso before I embrace Dad and Mum.

Back at Sal's house in Fremantle Alfonso meets the rest of the family – Sal's husband Craig and their two older kids and my sister Lisa, her husband David and their two young daughters. We walk out into the backyard where I stop suddenly and touch Alfonso's arm then point towards the back fence.

Stretched across it is a long strip of butcher's paper with the words, *Ciao, welcome home Penny and Alfonso.*

'The kids made it this morning,' says Sal. 'That wonky penis in the corner is meant to be Italy,' she laughs, hugging me again.

Our first week is spent with my parents and sisters' families on Rottnest Island, coincidentally my last holiday spot before I left for Italy six years earlier. For weeks before our departure, Alfonso had sworn he wouldn't swim in the ocean for fear of being taken by a shark, and the risk suddenly seems real when, on our first day at the beach, Mum spies a fin.

'*Cristo!*' shouts Alfonso, before he realises that everyone is running into, and not out of, the water.

'Wow, Pen, they've come in just for the foreigners,' says Mum, standing knee-deep in the water to get a better glimpse of the pair of dolphins frolicking nearby.

Alfonso's fear soon turns to pure joy of the teary kind.

'I can't believe they are so close,' he says in amazement, deciding it is safe enough to swim after all.

Each day brings new wonders for Alfonso – from locals who wander barefoot, unthinkable in Italy, to the quokkas, pelicans and spiders we see at close range during our bike rides around the island.

We say a very emotional goodbye to Sal, her husband and children before we catch a cab to the airport with the rest of my family. I am still sniffling on the plane when Lisa's three-year-old makes me laugh by twisting in her seat to tap Alfonso until he wakes. In a bizarre phenomenon, he always falls into a deep sleep just after takeoff and before the plane has levelled out, apparently due to the sudden change in air pressure.

Now wide awake, Alfonso and I help Lisa and her husband David keep their kids under control during the four-hour flight, which proves to be another curiosity for Alfonso.

'In the same time you could travel from Italy to the far north of Sweden,' he marvels.

From Sydney we drive with my parents to the outskirts of Orange, in western New South Wales, where they live on a big property far from the prying eyes of neighbours. Having grown up in an apartment complex, as is the norm in Italy, Alfonso is completely out of his element. We go for a long walk around the fence line and happen across a mob of kangaroos at dusk. Alfonso stands silently, his eyes as wide as a child's. For the next few days he is quick to suggest a walk in the paddocks, just so he can get a fleeting glimpse of the roos.

Our last days are spent in Sydney, where Alfonso judges Bondi Beach to be the most beautiful in the world. We do the coastal walk from Bondi to Bronte, eat mountains of Japanese and Thai food, take ferry trips around the harbour and dine out at a few old favourite haunts of mine.

After dinner on our last night, we stumble up the stairs to our attic room in Lisa's inner-city terrace.

With our bags already packed, we flop onto our bed and stare up at the sliver of moon visible through the skylight. My mind whirs with the emotion of a wonderful trip, and thoughts of the future. It's easy to fall in love with Australia again, and I think I am finally ready to return to my homeland. But how do I broach the subject with Alfonso? He seems smitten with the place, but if we move here he will have to abandon his band at a time when they have just released their second, well-reviewed album and could be on the brink of success. And the fact he is an only child complicates everything. I fall asleep wrapped in his arms before we are woken by the kids just after five.

There is a lump in my throat as Lisa takes us to the airport and I lose my composure completely the moment I have to say goodbye to my gorgeous little nieces, not to mention my big sis.

'Sorry, let's blame it on hormones, shall we?' I joke, wishing I could turn my tear-tap off.

Alfonso takes my hand as our plane sits on the tarmac before takeoff. Words and thoughts spill out in Italian and English as he tells me how much he loves my country, and how he now understands it is the best option in terms of work and lifestyle for both of us, not to mention a fantastic place to raise a family.

'Let's start getting organised and when our lease ends we can move to Australia. It will be another new adventure together,' he says, giving me a hug as my farewell tears turn to tears of happiness and excitement.

As the ferry enters the port of Procida we leave our luggage and walk out onto the deck to enjoy the view of Terra Murata. Just below it, the hot-pink La Vigna hotel stands out, as do the colourful houses that line the port below.

Exhausted from our travels, we take a taxi home. Inside our apartment I move instinctively to the lounge-room window to let in some fresh air. Beyond the lemon orchards the sea is calm apart from the ripple caused by a small fishing boat heading out to sea.

'I don't think we'll ever again have a view like this,' I say with a sigh.

Hilly walks on Procida are always rewarded with spectacular views

We throw our clothes in the washing machine and enjoy a two-hour nap before heading down to the port for an *aperitivo* at Bar Capriccio.

Behind the bar, Enzo has his head down, and we approach silently to surprise him. When he looks up his face breaks into a grin and he comes out to give us each a quick hug.

We pull up two barstools, order *due spritz* and tell Enzo about our trip.

I listen with pleasure as Alfonso recounts the highlights, from the dolphins on the first day to the coastal walk in Sydney. Every now and then a friend pops in for a drink and we are embraced and asked to tell them everything all over again.

'I really would like to go one day,' says Enzo as he slides another round of drinks onto the bar for Rosalba, the waitress, to carry outside.

Already feeling nostalgic for the tiny island and its community

'Well, you will have to come with us next time,' I say, looking at Alfonso with a smile. Instinctively, neither of us has revealed that we plan to move to my homeland permanently. We are simply happy to be back and want to enjoy the moment.

We take great pleasure in adapting to island life again. At our local greengrocer's Silverio and his family quietly welcome us back into the fold as we stock up on all manner of fresh produce. Next door, at the deli Antonio has lost none of his chirpy charm, slicing *prosciutto* for us and putting his gloved hand into the bucket of *mozzarella* to choose a piece the perfect size.

Struggling with our grocery bags on the short walk home, we almost lose our entire bundle when a car swerves at us. We laugh when we see our doctor friend Loreto behind the wheel, his favourite game being to pretend to run us over.

We are a few steps from home when we have to stop to let one of the island's buses inch pass. A hand suddenly appears from the driver's cabin and slaps the side of the bus, making us jump. We look up and see the cheeky face of Salvatore, a bus driver who is constantly pulling pranks on us at Bar Capriccio.

As I turn the key in our door I look at Alfonso with a mixture of happiness and sadness. I don't dare tell him that we can't expect to enjoy such a welcome wherever we settle in Australia.

The next morning I push open the familiar gate and skirt the vegetable patch to knock on Elisa and Michele's door.

'*Wei wei, bentornata!*' Elisa hugs me tightly, her large bosom practically crushing me. 'Your timing is impeccable. I'm just about to stuff some calamari Michele caught yesterday . . . Would you like to watch as you fill me in on your Australian trip?'

Without waiting for an answer she leads the way to the kitchen and spoons some coffee into the pot.

'*Vieni!*' she says, beckoning me to the sink, which contains a colander full of six large calamari.

Elisa smiles and nods as I recount parts of our trip, all the while cleaning the tubes of calamari in her hand and preparing the stuffing of egg, cheese and herbs.

In next to no time she puts the calamari in the oven and takes a seat beside me at the table.

Finally, I gather the courage to tell her of our plans to move to Australia.

'Pe, I am really happy for you,' she says. 'I know you miss your parents and sisters. It's time for you to return to your own family.'

As my eyes begin to mist with tears, I glance up to stop them falling, and catch sight of a framed collage of photos of Michele and Elisa's three children at various ages. In a smaller frame is a series of photos of Elisa and Michele's six grandchildren, mostly portraits showing dark, inquisitive eyes and shy smiles.

I think of the photos of my own nieces and nephews that we have plastered around our house, and feel a flush of excitement at the prospect of being close to my loved ones again.

'Will you visit us in Australia?' I ask Elisa, though I already know the answer.

'It's too long a trip for us, but you've made some good friends here on Procida. I'm sure you'll be back,' she says.

My voice cracks when I tell Elisa that Alfonso and I will remember our Procidan experience as the most special time of our lives.

'We'll try to come back once a year, if we can organise it,' I say optimistically as Elisa rises to retrieve the calamari from the oven.

'Take these home with you – I have four more batches in the fridge,' she says as Michele steps in the door. He has barely had time to embrace me before Elisa spills the beans about Australia.

'I think it's a wise move,' he says supportively before excusing himself; after four hours in his boat he is in need of a shower.

'We'll eat some of the calamari for lunch,' I promise Elisa as I head to the wooden gate.

As I open the latch I turn to see her standing on the doorstep, just like countless times before, waving at me with a huge smile.

I sidestep Vespas and brush off a dog attracted by the heavenly scent of the calamari as I walk home, a feeling of melancholy stealing over me at the thought of leaving Procida. But Elisa's words echo in my head: *It's time for you to return to your own family.*

She's right.

FEBBRAIO

CALAMARO IMBOTTITO
(STUFFED CALAMARI)

This recipe is easy if you let the fishmonger clean the calamari for you. Then all you have to do is stuff it and cook it. No excuses!

Serves 4

> 4 calamari tubes with some extra tentacles thrown in
> 2 eggs
> 2 slices white bread, crust removed
> 2 tablespoons *pecorino* cheese, grated
> 1 tablespoon soft cheese, diced
> handful parsley
> pinch salt
> pepper (to taste)
> 1 whole garlic clove, peeled
> extra virgin olive oil

Method

1. Wash the calamari, then set aside.

2. Crack the eggs into a bowl and add the hand-crumbled bread, *pecorino* cheese, soft cheese, parsley and salt and pepper. Mix well.

3. Spoon the mix into the tubes of calamari, filling each to the three-quarter mark and sealing with a toothpick. (Another option is to lightly fry the egg mix in an oiled frying pan for about a minute, to set all the ingredients together better, before stuffing the calamari. Taste-wise, there is no difference.) Be careful not to overfill the tubes.

4. Drizzle some olive oil into a pan and toss in the garlic before adding the calamari and tentacles. Keep the lid on, allowing them to steam.

5. After about 5 minutes, remove the calamari and place in a baking dish lined with oven paper. Bake in a medium-hot oven for about 20 minutes. (You can reduce the cooking time for smaller calamari.)

6. Serve piping hot.

There are endless ways to stuff calamari. Elisa raves about the simple method of stuffing them with garlic and parsley, while the best I have tasted was full of *provola* cheese and *radicchio*. It's up to you; just don't forget to keep an eye on your calamari in the frying pan, cooking them until golden. You don't want to make your *calamaro* too *gommoso* (rubbery)!

ACKNOWLEDGEMENTS

To Alfonso, for keeping me sane, loved up and superbly nourished. To my parents, Robert and Helen, and my sisters, Lisa and Sally, for your support, advice and encouragement, and to Maria Rosaria and Vincenzo Muras, for my second home in Italy.

My sincere gratitude to Deb Callaghan and to the enthusiastic Hachette team, in particular Bernadette Foley, Ali Lavau, Kate Ballard, Louisa Dear, Anna Waddington and Dianne Murdoch.

Special thanks also to Daniela Andreoli, Viviana Famulari, Charlotte Owen, Nic Parkhill, Rob Kelly, Penny Lion, Erin Keneally, Michelle Coffey, Rebecca Aduckiewicz, Ian Munns, Vivienne Stanton, Sascha Keen, Iain Shedden and Mandy Roberts for getting me over the finish line.

On Procida, my infinite gratitude to Vincenzo Scotto di Fasano and Gilda Gamba for your friendship and unfailing generosity from day one; to Elisa and Michele Scotto di Fasano, for leaving your front door open and accepting us as family, ditto the rest of the clan – Paola and Michele, Maria Pia and Stefano, Clara and Loredana Gamba and Giuseppe and Valentina.

Heartfelt thanks to the following islanders for their *amicizia* and assistance: Glorianna Costagliola d'Abele, Tania Costagliola d'Abele, Vittorio 'Bottone' Tarasco, 'Piti' Pasquale Ambrosino di Brutto Pilo, Carlo La Grotta, Ottavio Barone, Eliana Alto Mare, Michele and Candida Cardito, Erminia Scotto di Carlo e suo zio Nicola Scotto di Carlo, Nicola Carabellese, Maria Rosaria Ridda, Graziella Cerase, Gennaro and Antonio Scotto di Ciccariello, Maria Grazia Carabellese, Carlo Ambrosino, Claudia Esposito, Fabrizio Primario, Marina Altomare and Rosario Cervini, Loreto Scotto di Fasano, Enzo and Mara at La Vigna hotel, Gigi di Bernardo, Domenico 'Sorriso' Schiano di Coscea, Peppino Capobianchi and Saara Garcia, Clelia Ambrosino, Myriam Narpeto, Michele Staropoli and Gina Libissa, Marie-Claude Gouy and Giulio Badaluci, Giulio Esposito, Vanna Palledino, Marina Ambrosino, Luigi Nappa, Gabrielle Scotto, 'Evangelista', Elisabetta Montaldo and Piero Lucietto, Samantha Righi and Nico Granito, Vanna Palledino, Gabrielle Scotto and Ramon Scotto di Mase. To the Bar Capriccio girls – Nicoletta, Rosalba, Antonella and Luisa – for the cheeriest service on the island, the Capriccio regulars and *gli autisti pazzi*, Luigi and Salvatore, for the pranks and laughs.

Finally, thanks to Carlo Gambalonga and my former colleagues at ANSA*med*, Naples.

Chiedo scusa se ho dimenticato qualcuno!

SOURCES

BOOKS

Acitilio, Giovanna, Cariati, Antonella, Palladino, Vanna & Piedimonte, Anthony, *Procida, A Casket in the Sea,* Naples, Edizione Intra Moenia, 2003

Ambrosino, Clelia, *Il Panno di Lino*, Italy, Edizioni del Poggio, Poggio Imperiale, 2007

Ambrosino, Clelia, *Procida, Sapori Profumi Colori,* Naples, Edizione del Delfino, 2003

Associazione Vivara, *Vivara, L'isola della Luce*, Naples, Accademia Vivarium Novum, 2003

Cosenza, Giancarlo & Jodice, Mimmo, *Procida, un'architettura del Mediterraneo,* Naples, Clean Edizioni, 2007

de Feo, Vittorio & Knight, Fabrizio, *Procida, L'isola, il paese, l'architettura*, Naples, Electa Napoli, 1992

de Lamartine, Alphonse, *Graziella*, France, L Hachette and Co., 1858

Masucci, Maria & Vanacore, Mario, *La Cultura Popolare nell'isola di Procida*, Naples, Guida Editori, 1997

Morante, Elsa, *L'isola di Arturo,* Torino, Giulio Einaudi Editore, 1957/1995

Scuola Secondaria di primo grado 'Antonio Capraro', *I 'Misteri' di Procida*, Procida, 2005

FILMS

Il Postino (Italy, 1994), directed by Michael Radford in collaboration with Massimo Troisi

L'isola di Arturo (Italy, 1962), directed by Damiano Damiani

The Talented Mr Ripley (USA, 1999), directed by Anthony Minghella

Penelope Green was born in Sydney and worked as a print journalist around Australia for a decade before moving to Rome in 2002. Her first book, *When in Rome: Chasing la Dolce Vita*, recounts her experiences in the Eternal City. In 2005 she moved to Naples to work for ANSAmed, a Mediterranean news service. She found an apartment in the city's colourful Spanish Quarter and developed an addiction to the rich Neapolitan cuisine and coffee while writing her second memoir, *See Naples and Die: The Crimes and Passions of Italy's Darkest Jewel*. Penny and her Italian partner, Alfonso, have now moved to Australia. She contributes to publications including *Australian Gourmet Traveller*, *Madison*, *Australian House & Garden*, *Marie Claire* and *The West Australian's Weekend Magazine*.

www.penelopegreen.com.au

WHEN IN ROME

Chasing la dolce vita

We've all dreamed of an exotic life in a European city, but who actually goes? *When in Rome* shows what can happen when you are courageous (and perhaps crazy) enough to chase this dream.

With her thirtieth birthday on the horizon and her comfortable life in Sydney outside her front door, Penelope Green decided it was now or never. Undaunted by the fact she spoke no Italian, had no job, no friends and nowhere to live, and armed with only irresistible optimism and a fair dash of bravery, she was determined to carve out her own slice of *la dolce vita*.

SEE NAPLES AND DIE

The crimes and passions of Italy's darkest jewel

After three years living and working in Italy, Penelope Green needs a reason to stick around – true love or gainful employment.

When a job comes up in Naples – crime capital of Italy, home of pizza and the Camorra, and crouched precariously at the foot of a volcano – Penny launches herself into the unknown.

With her innate curiosity and eye for detail, she prises Naples open to show us the real city in all its splendour . . . and all its depravity. She uncovers a chaotic metropolis where crime and poverty blur with abundant natural beauty, and where the shadow of Mount Vesuvius is a daily reminder that life must be lived for the moment.

And when Penny meets a bass player in a local band, she thinks she might have found that other reason to stick around . . .